Machine Knitting

Designing with colour

Machine Knitting

Designing with colour

Alison Dupernex

The Crowood Press

First published in 2020 by
The Crowood Press Ltd
Ramsbury, Marlborough
Wiltshire SN8 2HR

www.crowood.com

British Library Cataloguing-in-Publication Data
A catalogue record for this book is available from the British Library.

ISBN 978 1 78500 685 2

Typeset by Peggy & Co. Design Inc.
Printed and bound in India by Parksons Graphics

CONTENTS

ACKNOWLEDGEMENTS

This book would not have been possible without The Crowood Press having faith in me to write this book in the first place.

I would not have been able to develop ideas and flourish as a business without Chris Birch, my fabulous knitter. She deciphers my hieroglyphs with good humour and skill. Huge thanks go to her.

I must thank my lovely models Amelia Sutcliffe, Hazel Green and Sharon McSwiney who brought the knitwear to life, and Henry Arden and Sussie Ahlberg for taking a number of the photographs for me that I have used in the book.

Thanks to Martyn Pugh who gave me access to his lecture notes regarding costings, which he delivers each year to undergraduate silversmiths and goldsmiths at Goldsmiths College, London.

A special mention must go to Anne Smith, the editor extraordinaire of *Machine Knitting Monthly*, who read through my draft chapters, offered support and advice, and corrected my ramblings.

And lastly, thanks go to my husband Simon, for proofreading the whole book and helping to write the chapter on the history of hand frame knitting.

I have thoroughly enjoyed all their company, and the journey was less daunting because of their help and good humour.

Thank you, thank you all!

ABBREVIATIONS

0	the punched hole in the punchcard, or the yarn in feeder 2
alt	alternate
approx	approximately
beg	beginning
C(s)	colour(s)
cm	centimetres
COL	carriage on left
cont	continue
COR	carriage on right
dec	decrease/decreasing
E	elongate by knitting each row twice
ff	fully fashioned
FI	Fair Isle
foll	following
g	grams
HP	holding position
inc	increase/increasing
k	knit
L	left
LH	left-hand
LHS	left-hand side
MC	main colour
MT	main tension
MT+1, 2, 3	main tension one, two or three sizes looser than main tension
MT–1, 2, 3	main tension one, two or three sizes tighter than main tension
MY	main yarn
N(s)	needles
NWP	non-working position
p	purl
patt(s)	pattern(s)
PP	punchcard pattern
PPE	punchcard pattern elongated
PPL	punchcard pattern locked
RC	row counter
rem	remaining
rep	repeat
R	right
RH	right-hand
RHS	right-hand side
s	slip
sl st	slip stitch
st st	stocking stitch
st(s)	stitch(es)
T	tuck stitch
TD	tension dial
tog	together
UWP	upper working position
WP	working position
WY	waste yarn
X	the non-punched square on the punchcard, or the yarn in feeder 1

INTRODUCTION

Knitting is an art you can take with you; it is portable, foldable and wraps around you, offering comfort and warmth. The great joy of the knitted fabric is that it is elastic and, due to its construction, more malleable than the warp and weft of a woven fabric.

This book is aimed at everyone who owns a knitting machine and also at those who don't but would like to know what is possible if they did. There are very few publications which address design and colour and push beyond the basics of how to work and use a knitting machine.

My aim in this book is to encourage you to design for yourself and take time over this, using good-quality yarn and planning out a project. There will be lots of ideas and variations on each project and loads of encouragement and ideas from you to unleash your design, your craftsmanship and your appreciation for the aesthetic. The skill of machine knitting is a world away from hand knitting, and yet it is a wonderful form of expression as the machine becomes an extension of your hand. There are machine knitting clubs worldwide with a loyal following. My hope is that this book with all my designs and patterns will ignite within you a spark, and that machine knitters who not only knit for pleasure but also those who make to sell will use the ideas and add creatively to them. I do assume that you know your machine well and are not an absolute novice, in other words that you are happy using either a standard gauge electronic or punchcard machine. You will already know how to memorize your card or mylar sheet, and at what row, as this is not covered in this book since there are already many excellent beginner's guides which cover the basics of machine knitting.

WHY KNIT?

We take elements such as a non-elastic thread and work with lengths of this by threading a loop through another loop to make a pliable, portable fabric which can take on the properties of a second skin. It will keep us dry, keep out the wind, yet provide shade in the sun. It is a flexible, pliable and lightweight fabric, which lends itself to various forms of decoration through choice of stitch, pattern, shape and colour. As a fabric, knitting is endlessly versatile and can be used for clothing, furnishings, cushions, rugs and curtains. As a piece of clothing it can protect, disguise and comfort. It can easily be changed, and a relatively small example can invigorate a tired outfit by, for example, adding a knitted scarf to an old favourite coat. A piece of knitting fashioned into a cardigan or coat can become an old faithful friend and constant companion for years.

The versatility of the knitting machine.

We live in a society which, sadly, treats fabrics of all origins as disposable when they have barely been worn. Mixes of threads and finishes mean that fabrics now have a longer life span, but we can make poor purchase choices as they are so cheap, and so we tire of them quickly, when we should perhaps invest more wisely and cherish them. As they are relatively inexpensive to buy, this adds to the perception that they have little value. The aim of this book is to encourage you to design and create an item which will stand the test of time. It will be appreciated, loved, and fulfil all the requirements perfectly of a piece of clothing or interior fabric so you will not want to lightly discard it and will be pleased to repair it if areas are worn and get threadbare. One item which is aesthetically pleasing and technically well-made is surely worth ten dreary, boring, cheaply produced items which will not satisfy any criteria in the long term, and may have an exploitative history.

Always have it in mind that you are designing something to last forever. Choose colours which will be adaptable to other wardrobe items. Include some basic wardrobe colours like navy, black, grey or beige.

In this book I use a myriad of colours and show you how to create a different style using the same stitch pattern and shape whilst changing the colours and also how to be inspired by the world around you and how to use this when designing. There are examples of colourways and stitches which you can adapt and use your own creativity to reimagine. Use this book as a catalyst to start to think about your own work in a different way, to take a risk and use unfamiliar colours or stitch patterns and to experiment freely. You can dip in and out of the book or read it from cover to cover but, above all, enjoy the sheer variety which you and your machine can create.

Slip and tuck stitch scarves in a landscape.

CHAPTER 1

A HISTORY OF HAND FRAME KNITTING

This chapter could easily be titled 'Standing on the Shoulders of Giants', as so many inventive people have been involved in bringing us to our present position. We start by looking at the history of craft hand knitting, and then move on to the invention and development of the hand frame knitting method by William Lee. We then look at the formation of the Worshipful Company of Framework Knitters, the further development and commercialization of the process, and the high-tech applications for knitted fabrics beyond garment manufacture.

THE INTRODUCTION OF HAND KNITTING TO BRITAIN

While the roots of knitting are unclear, we can be sure that it has been undertaken in many different parts of the world, over many centuries, producing items of great beauty as well as objects satisfying many different practical needs.

Prior to the invention of hand knitting, a precursor to knitting called 'nalbinding' was used to knot yarn. This is a labour-intensive technique where yarn is threaded through the eye of a sewing needle and then worked in the round through a series of loops. The oldest known nalbinding textile fragment was found in Israel in the Nehal Hemar cave, and dates to the seventh century BCE. Examples of socks using the nalbinding technique from the third to fifth century CE from Egypt can be found in the collection of the Victoria and Albert Museum, London.

Hand knitting is not as ancient a craft as many believe, with the oldest knitted items being found in Egypt and dated somewhere between the eleventh and fourteenth centuries CE, with a knitted sock fragment of this period being in the collection of the Victoria and Albert Museum.

Hand-knitted fabrics are created by interlocking a series of loops (stitches) which are then interlocked using a needle to hold the existing loop; a new loop is formed in front of the old loop and the latter is then brought over the new loop to form the fabric. Increasing or decreasing the number of stitches in a row widens or narrows the garment being created. Increasing the number of stitches in a row is achieved by moving outer loops sideways on a frame and creating extra loops, leaving a small eyelet hole in the fabric known as a fashioning mark. Decreasing the number of stitches in a row is achieved by reversing the increasing process and moving the loops inwards; the fashioning mark appears where two loops are compressed into one new loop. Garments shaped in this way are known as fully fashioned, as the knitted fabric is in the shape of the finished garment or garment piece.

Archaeological finds from cities in Europe show that knitting spread throughout Europe in the fourteenth century, and pictorial evidence supports this in the picture of the Holy Family painted by Ambrogio Lorenzetti c. 1345, where Mary can be seen knitting. Hand knitting also spread from the continent of Europe into Britain during the early fourteenth century, and the first British mass-produced knitted garments were probably cloth caps. English peasants had originally worn woven cloth caps, and this was gradually changed to wearing hand-knitted caps. The 'Monmouth Cap' is one of these, and according to Jennifer Carlson in her *Short History of the Monmouth Cap*, the industry of cap manufacture by hand knitters in and around Monmouth was well established by the fourteenth century, when records show 'Capper' as being a common surname in the town.

The manufacture of knitted caps was so important that the Cappers Act of 1571 specified that every person above the age of six years (except for 'Maids, Ladies, Gentlewomen, Noble Personages, and every Lord, Knight and Gentleman of 20 Marks Land') in England on Sundays and holidays should wear (except when travelling) 'a Cap of Wool knit, thicked and dressed in England, made within this Realm, and only dressed and finished by some of the Trade of Cappers, upon pain to forfeit for every Day of not wearing three Shillings four Pence'. Wives 'were constrained to wear white knit caps of woolen yarn, unless their husbands were of good value in the Queen's book or could prove themselves gentlemen by descent ...'. This Act was introduced as a form of protectionism for the English cappers against cheaper foreign imports, but was abandoned as unworkable some twenty years later.

Fine knitted silk stockings were introduced to England in the 1560s – Queen Elizabeth 1 was presented with a pair by Mrs Montague, the royal silkwoman. These were an item of extreme luxury, and were said to have taken two years to knit. The Queen was so delighted that she stated that she would only wear knitted silk stockings from then on. A quicker and cheaper method of production had to be found!

WILLIAM LEE AND THE INVENTION OF THE KNITTING OR STOCKING FRAME

William Lee, the inventor of the knitting or stocking frame, was born in 1563 in Calverton, Nottinghamshire, the eldest of nine siblings. His younger brother James was born in 1582, and was also closely connected to the development of the knitting frame. Their father, also William Lee, has been described as a gentleman and had a coat of arms and land amounting to 400 acres upon which he grazed sheep.

Depiction of William Lee.

William went to Cambridge University in 1579, first to Christ's College and then St John's College, graduating in 1582–83 with a BA degree. He went on to be ordained, and then became the curate of Calverton. In 1589, whilst in that post, he invented the knitting or stocking frame, which was designed to make woollen stockings on a flatbed; these pieces were later stitched together to complete the sock.

What the motivation was for his invention is unclear, but it is possible that he studied the movement of the fingers when observing hand knitting and sought to invent a machine that would mechanically make these movements more quickly, and this started his research in 1586. It took a few more years to make a working prototype, but by 1589 his stocking frame was working and he had taught his brother James and several other male relatives how to operate it.

William saw that one needle was needed for one loop or stitch and he experimented with twelve needles and a piece of wood. He initially made the needles by bending a length of wire with a 'beard' on the end. Over time he perfected sets of barb-shaped spring-back needles. His catalyst was when he realized he could place a loop at the back of the needle and a loop inside the beard; when the needle was pressed down, the back loop could be pulled forward and over the front loop. This was the start of hand frame knitting.

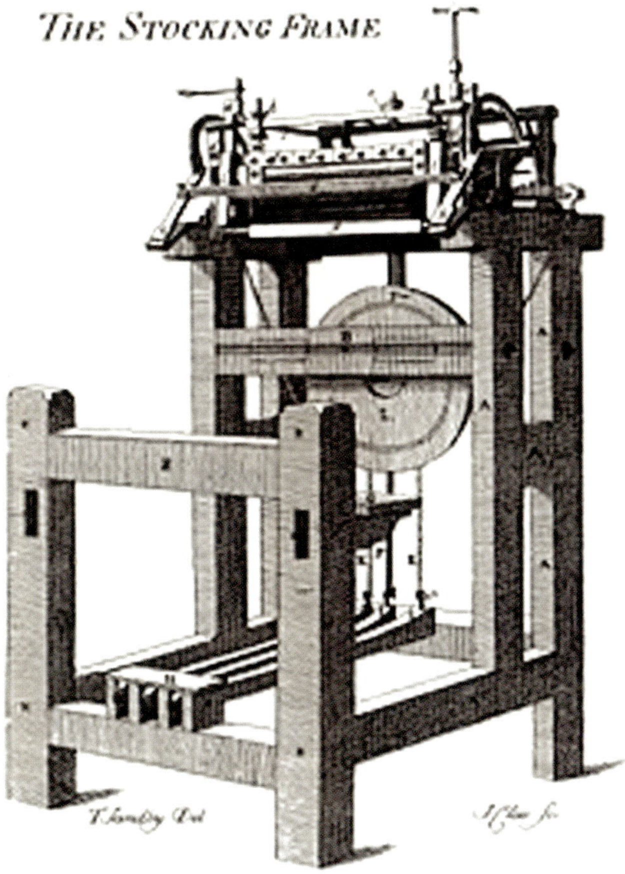

The stocking frame.

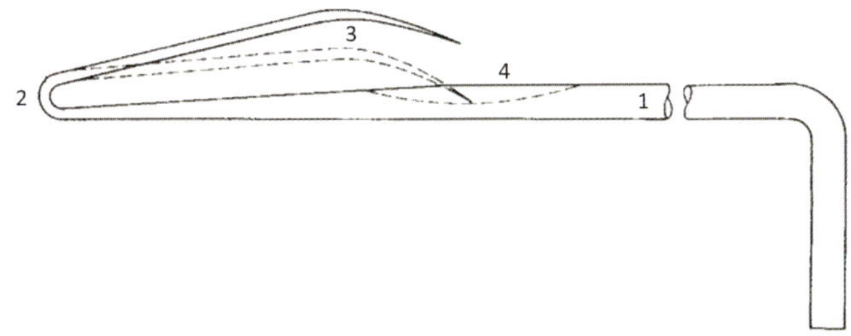

The bearded needle.

The original hook needles had to be modified and made longer and finer, as the stitches would not slide over the closed hook and would become caught up. He finally used a chisel to cut a slot into which he could press the point of the hook. A locksmith helped with this skilled process and the hook was hardened, thus the spring-back needle was invented. By 1589 the method of forming stitches was so perfect that most machines today still employ this technique. The main part of the frame was made of wrought iron fixed to a heavy wooden frame with integral seat and pedals. Several separate actions were required to make one stitch.

The bearded needle has a *stem* (1) around which the needle loop is formed, a *head* (2) where the hook is formed to draw the old loop through the new loop, a *beard* (3) which is used to separate the trapped new loop inside from the old loop as it slides off the needle beard, and an *eye or groove* (4) to enclose the tip of the beard when pressed shut to enclose the new loop.

William Lee relocates to London

In 1590 William and his brother James moved to London to further develop and expand his invention, leaving behind a group of relatives and friends to continue to work the frames. When his father died William's only inheritance was a ring, so he was desperate for funds to develop his invention. He hoped that Queen Elizabeth I would become a patron and ideally 'Letters of Patent' would be granted which would give him a monopoly but he realized that this might not be a popular idea as the invention could potentially put hundreds of hand knitters out of work.

The Queen did see a demonstration of the new machine when she was nearly sixty and expressed her excitement and curiosity. However, she refused to grant a patent, on the grounds that the frame only made thick woollen stockings and what was needed were fine silk stockings made by hand and to date these were usually imported from Europe. The Queen did encourage him to continue to develop his invention and when it was able to produce fine work in silk he might be awarded a monopoly.

William then found a patron in Lord Hunsdon, whose son learned to use a frame, and by 1599 he had developed an improved machine that increased the number of needles per inch from eight to twenty and produced a silk of finer texture. However, the Queen again denied him a patent because of her concern for the employment security of the kingdom's many hand knitters whose livelihood might be threatened by such mechanization. She said to Lee: 'Thou aimest high, Master Lee. Consider thou what the invention could do to my poor subjects. It would assuredly bring to them ruin by depriving them of employment, thus making them beggars'. Most likely the Queen's concern was a manifestation of the fear of the Hosiers' Guild that the invention would make the silks of its artisan members obsolete.

'The Art of Stocking Frame Work Knitting'.

Detail of the stained glass window depicting William Lee from Christ's College, Cambridge.

In 1600 William went into partnership with George Brooke: William was to provide the technology and Brooke the finance to produce the machine commercially. Brooke was to invest £500 in the project and the first £200 in profits were to go to Lee; all further profits would be shared between the two partners for a period of twenty-two years. Unfortunately, events conspired against William when in 1603 Brooke was arrested on a charge of treason and executed.

William Lee relocates to France

Queen Elizabeth 1 died in 1603 and William had to regularize his financial position to expand his business. He had grown increasingly frustrated with the English monarchy, firstly under Elizabeth I and then under James I, for failing to fully support his invention, fearing a backlash from the authorities for 'ruining' the livelihoods of knitters.

To be able to take advantage of the cheap labour available in London, he needed a monopoly so he applied for the Freedom of the City of London, which would mean that he could apply to become a member of a guild or livery company which would in turn grant him the exclusive monopoly of silk knitting. His intention was to join the Worshipful Company of Weavers as they appeared to have the nearest remit, and he was admitted as a 'foreign brother' of the Company in 1609 as a 'weaver of silk stockings by engine'. King James I then ruled that all monopolies would be abolished, making it difficult for William to capitalize on his invention, so he then set his sights on the opportunities available in France, which at that time was ruled by the Protestant Henri IV.

Lee had become friendly with the Huguenot family of de Caux who were refugees from France following the St Bartholomew's Day massacre of 1572. The family originated from Rouen in Normandy, an area well known for its textile industry, including hosiery.

Rouen was a thriving commercial port and had close connections with England. The Protestant French King Henri IV was very supportive of the industry and eventually granted Lee a patent on his invention, thus encouraging Lee to expand his business interests in France. Lee moved his frames and workmen to Rouen around 1609 with the help of Pierre and Solomon de

Caux. He was initially made most welcome and given funds to construct new machines. A contract dated 16 February 1612 between William and Pierre de Caux shows that William would supply eight knitting machines and six English workmen and would teach de Caux's workers how to build the machines.

All seemed to be going well; however, events overtook William with disastrous consequences. In 1610 King Henri IV was assassinated and his child son Louis XIII succeeded to the throne at the age of nine, with his staunchly Catholic mother Marie de Medici acting as Regent during his minority. Lee, an English Protestant, was now out of favour.

William moved from Rouen and around late 1614 he died in distress in Paris. A letter from a friend states that 'seized with grief he ended his life at Paris'. The Roman Catholic persecution of Protestants in France continued unabated, so many of the framework knitters moved back to England and joined groups which had been left in Nottingham and London.

National recognition was slow in coming for William but in 1882 a stained-glass window was erected in his memory in Christ's College, Cambridge.

Coat of arms of the Worshipful Company of Framework Knitters.

FORMATION OF THE WORSHIPFUL COMPANY OF FRAMEWORK KNITTERS

Around 1620 William Lee's brother James, having moved back to London, relocated to Nottingham and joined several other knitters. They had followed all the new developments and were not only knitting coarse worsted hose but also fine silk stockings. This confirmed the East Midlands as a key centre for the manufacturer of knitted items and there were now two bases of manufacture in England, Nottingham and London.

London had initially thrived with the making of fancy goods, hose and waistcoats. Silk was imported into the city and at the end of the seventeenth century the Huguenot silk workers, many of whom had originally settled in Canterbury, migrated to London and confirmed the establishment of what now amounted to an industry in Spitalfields where there were many other framework knitters.

Nottingham had the advantage that the sheep of Sherwood Forest were 'small in size but covered with fleece having the wool of the longest filaments and of a fineness equal to any in Europe'.

In 1621 the first Association of Frame Work Knitters was formed. By the 1650s hundreds of families worked in the industry. Other centres sprang up in Leicestershire and even some in Ireland. The manufacturers were keen to keep the industry in Britain, to maintain standards and to continue to develop the frames. Various centres on the continent tried to copy the English success but failed due to lack of skill. The English were exporting silk stockings and business was thriving. They argued that 'common or hand knitting', which was using woollen thread, was not harmed as they continued to make for the home market and therefore did not cause unemployment. The Association of Framework Knitters was anxious to keep standards high and drive out of business anyone who was not part of their organization and subject to their standards.

To this end, on 13 June 1657 The Worshipful Company of Framework Knitters was incorporated by charter by the Lord Protector, Oliver Cromwell. It was re-incorporated and its privileges extended by Letters Patent of King Charles II on 19 August 1663 with the style, 'The Master, Wardens, Assistants and Society of the Art or Mystery of Framework Knitters of the Cities of London and Westminster and the Kingdom of England and the Dominion of Wales'. The Company was incorporated by order of the Court of Aldermen as a Livery Company of the City of London on 9 June 1713, being sixty-fourth in order of precedence of the London Livery Companies.

Lee's stocking frame as illustrated in Charles Ray's *The Romance of the Nation*, 1935.

DEVELOPMENT OF THE FRAMEWORK KNITTING INDUSTRY

Before the Industrial Revolution, the textile industry in what we now call the UK was basically a cottage industry, with much of the work carried out by skilled women. It was the first industry to experience massive industrialization and technological change, and development of the textile industry reflects the huge social changes of the era, as well as the shift in power from rich landowners to those in control of industrial progress.

Sheila Mason, in her book *The Machine-Made Lace Industry in Nottinghamshire Derbyshire and Leicestershire*, gives an excellent description of the workings of an early knitting frame and reproduces a 1935 illustration:

> Lengths of wire with a hook at the end, needles, were fixed horizontally in a needle bar.
>
> Mounted vertically between each needle were specifically shaped steel plates called jack sinkers which formed loops in the thread lying under the hooked ends of the needles, the hooks were closed and the previous row of loops were drawn over the needles and the new loops to form a new course of knitting.
>
> The process was repeated until the required length of fabric was reached.
>
> The flat fabric hung down between the frame and the knitter.

When making stockings only one was knitted at a time and the fashioning or shaping of the leg required manual manipulation of the stitches in each row of knitting. On completion the flat shaped stocking would be removed from the machine and the selvedges seamed by hand. This shows that the basic principle of frame knitting has not changed very much today.

The original 1589 machine was cumbersome; it had eight needles to 2.5cm (1 inch), a knitting speed of up to 600 loops a minute, and it knitted thick coarse woollen yarn.

By 1599 this had been refined to twenty needles to 2.5cm (1 inch) and the manufacturing process was speeded up considerably to 1,500 loops per minute. Each machine had over 2,000 separate parts, all of which were made without calibrated machine tools.

In 1666 each machine required two workers and many separate movements were required to complete a row.

By 1727 stockings were now being made with a gore or a narrow clock (a name probably derived from the resemblance of the ankle design to the hands of a clock), which was a decorative but complicated heel shaping. The time it took to knit these was increased by one third, but the fit of the sock to the shape of the foot was substantially improved, making the sock more comfortable to wear. Sometimes the clocks were knitted in different colours from the main body of the stocking to add a contrast and to copy the look of the silk stockings of the wealthy which often had embroidery or fancy patterns at the ankles.

By 1730 a very fine cotton spun in India was being used to make the first pair of cotton stockings in England. These were made in Nottingham by Draper of Bellar-Gate using a fine 20-gauge silk machine.

In the 1740s the phrase 'as poor as a stockinger' was coined. Framework knitting was a cottage industry which included the whole family. The knitter toiled for seven shillings a week, his wife seamed the stockings and their children wound the thread from hanks. With a poor diet and little fresh air, such families were pale and emaciated.

In 1745 a new Act of byelaws was made for the Worshipful Company of Framework Knitters. They were very similar to those passed under Charles II. For the next eight years the Worshipful Company had to try and enforce their will on their knitters but the knitters were averse to paying the Worshipful Company dues and indifferent to the protection they were being offered. Many had taught their members of their family to use a frame and so in 1753 the Company was forced to abandon its role as policeman of the trade or be prepared to go to the law. The framework knitters took petitions to the House of Commons but after evidence was heard from both sides the Committee found against the Worshipful Company, which deprived them of further redress through the law. Gravenor Henson, in his 1830 book *The Civil, Political, and Mechanical History of the Framework-Knitters*, expresses his regret at the loss of protection which the Worshipful Company afforded the knitters, but he also acknowledged that the stability of such a system led to a natural aversion to innovation.

DEVELOPMENT OF MACHINE RIBBING AND EYELETS

The machines developed up to this point did not knit ribs (a rib stitch creates ribs or textured vertical stripes). The rib stitch consists of columns of knit stitches alternating with columns of purl stitches and the tuck rib led the knitters to try and emulate a hand-knitted rib.

The first attempts to produce machine-made ribbing were by 'latching up', and Wright of Ilkeston had made an attempt as early as 1730. Around 1750 a further development was made by Bowman, who made a tool which was capable of latching up two stitches at a time.

Bowman made several further attempts to improve the tool by increasing the number of needles set in it, but this proved impractical between the horizontal needles of the frame. His first attempt was one vertical to three horizontal needles, so giving a 3:1 rib. He was, however, unable to see his invention through some difficulties, and was advised by friends to show his samples so far to William Woollatt of Derby. Woollatt had a brother-in-law named Jedediah Strutt (also of Derby), who was a wheelwright, and he purchased the samples to develop further.

In 1758 Strutt produced the first fully machine-made ribbing – this would have been the first conversion from a single bed to a double bed frame. He continued to perfect this innovation and eventually broad and other patterned ribs could be worked, including coloured ones. In 1759 he patented the 'Strutts Derby Ribbing Machine' and started a great period of inspiration for development for the knitting frames. His improvements were granted two patents, No. 722 in 1758 and No. 734 in 1759.

The principles of the Derby Rib machine were soon applied to the eyelet hole mitts which had stitches previously transferred by hand. Samuel Betts was the first to combine the tuck presser with the rib machine to develop the 'tickler bar' which removed and transferred stitches to make eyelet holes. In this he was assisted by a man called Butterworth: Betts made the parts while Butterworth made them work in a practical sense, and they were granted a patent on their invention in 1764.

In 1766 the Tewkesbury Act was passed which regulated the quality of cotton stockings. It stipulated that eyelet holes should be knitted into the stocking which corresponded to the number of threads used in the yarn. The overall aim was to keep standards up and consistent, a difficult task as there were many small workshops.

A tuck presser, which allowed the machines to produce knitted lace, was then added to a plain frame, which could slide up and down and to work or not as required. Ticklers were fitted on the lead bar of the rib machine. At first, every fourth stitch could be removed and the machine racked over and the stitches in between could be removed. It took very little time for the ticklers and the tuck presser to be applied to every needle which, in turn, led to the introduction of knitted lace on a stocking frame. The patent for this refinement was granted to John Morris, a hosier from Nottingham, in 1763.

Around 1766, Arthur Else, a framework knitter based in Nottingham, assisted by a workman called Hammond, continued to improve the machine by developing a method of removing the stitches with a tickler of its own. They did this without the use of the rib machine. The eyelet work, though, was still inferior to that produced by hand in Spanish eyelet hole mitts, where the stitches were more delicately removed to give the impression of flowers and other motifs.

Having bought the patent for the Butterworth and Betts machine, Morris began to make yet more developments. He devised a method of working an eyelet into mitts knitted sideways and using two rows of ticklers. Robert Frost made the first mechanism which would select the needles to be worked on: he invented a carved roller which acted on 'slide ticklers': by pushing these forward any pattern could be achieved which had formerly been hand knitted. Around 1778 Broadhurst improved Frost's slide ticklers: he reversed the way the ticklers were selected and designed a cylinder with metal pins inserted and these raised the ticklers which were out of use. Clothing made in this way became popular; however, the process meant that many stitches were weakened and broke quickly, so this method of manufacture was abandoned.

HOSTILE REACTION TO THE TECHNOLOGICAL ADVANCEMENTS

Every development of the machine was met with hostility in some quarters, and in 1773 a frame which purported to manufacture twelve stockings at a time was destroyed by an angry mob of stocking knitters. The frame breakers were well organized and were said to be led by the mythical Ned Ludd whose headquarters was supposed to be in Sherwood Forest. The Luddites only targeted frames making cut-up stockings or hosiers who paid below the agreed rates. Their threatening and violent tactics worked for a while and a Bill prohibiting the manufacture of cut-ups was passed in the House of Commons in 1812 but rejected by the Lords.

In January 1812 some 50,000 knitters were facing starvation due to large amounts of inferior work being dumped on the market – standards were sloppy and the trade was in decline.

The poet Lord Byron, who was living at Newstead Abbey in Nottinghamshire, made his maiden speech in Parliament on 27 February 1812 regarding the desperate situation. He spoke with passion and understanding and argued for Government policies which would alleviate the atrocious work conditions against a Bill to make frame breaking a hanging offence. A copy of the speech can be seen at Newstead Abbey, and a flavour of this speech is outlined below:

> Considerable injury has been done to the proprietors of the improved frames. These machines were to them an advantage, inasmuch as they superseded the necessity of employing a number of workmen, who were left in consequence to starve. By the adoption of one species of Frame in particular, one man performed the work of many, and the superfluous labourers were thrown out of unemployment. Yet it is to be observed that the work thus executed was inferior in quality; not marketable at home, and merely hurried over with a view to exportation. It was called in the cant of the trade, by the name of 'Spider Work' …
>
> How will you carry the Bill into effect? Can you commit the whole country to their own prisons? Will you erect a gibbet in every field and hang up men like scarecrows? …
>
> But supposed it past; suppose one of these men, as I have seen them, – meagre with famine, sullen with despair, careless of life which your Lordships are perhaps about to value at something less than the price of a stocking frame – suppose this man surrounded by the children for whom he is unable to procure bread at the hazard of his existence, about to be torn for ever from a family which he lately supported in a peaceful industry, and which it is not his fault that he can no longer so support – suppose this man, and there are ten thousand such from whom you may select your victims, dragged into court to be tried for this new offence, by this new law; still, there are two things wanting to convict and condemn him; and these are, in my opinion, Twelve Butchers for a Jury, and a Jefferies for a Judge!

This extract certainly gives a flavour of the anger and resentment on both sides of the argument. Despite this eloquent speech, the Bill was passed, and frame-breaking was later commuted to life transportation but the knitters never forgot Byron's loyalty to them.

Many knitters also joined the Chartist meetings in the 1830s and 1840s but, as with the Luddites, they were imprisoned – nothing had really changed.

By 1831 with continual refinements by the frame makers, only one operative was needed but eleven separate movements were required to make each row. The machine was still only able to produce a stocking stitch: to obtain a ribbed fabric the work had to be removed by hand from the machine and the stitches reversed by hand, a time-consuming process.

In 1847 Matthew Townsend invented the tumbler or 'latch needle', and this was patented in 1849 (another claimant to having made this invention earlier in 1806 is Frenchman Pierre Jeandeau, but there is no evidence of its practical use). This replaced the 'bearded needle' invented by William Lee. The bearded needle required a presser bar and a staged process to pass courses of loops over the beard, but Townsend's invention used a shorter hook on the needle and a hinged latch, so simplifying the process and allowing the machines to operate without a presser bar. The latch needle was the forerunner of a new generation of machines but it was many years before this was realized.

The latch needle has a *hook* (1) which draws and retains the new loop, a *latch blade* (2) which pivots and locates the latch in the needle, a *latch spoon* (3) which bridges the gap between the hook and the stem and covers the hook when closed, and a *stem* (4) which carries the loop in the clearing or rest position.

Great technological strides continued to be made after the 1850s: a carrier for the thread was developed which made it unnecessary for the knitter to lay the thread across the needles; wider machines became more available; and stockings were cut from a larger piece of fabric and sewn together. Not all of these innovations were accepted by the knitters, particularly the 'cutting up' as this was seen as 'bad and deceitful' as they used fully fashioned shaping.

A depression hit the domestic knitting industry in the period 1830–50; however, another came to the fore, the machine lace industry. The initial impetus came from the framesmiths adapting the stocking frame to make lace.

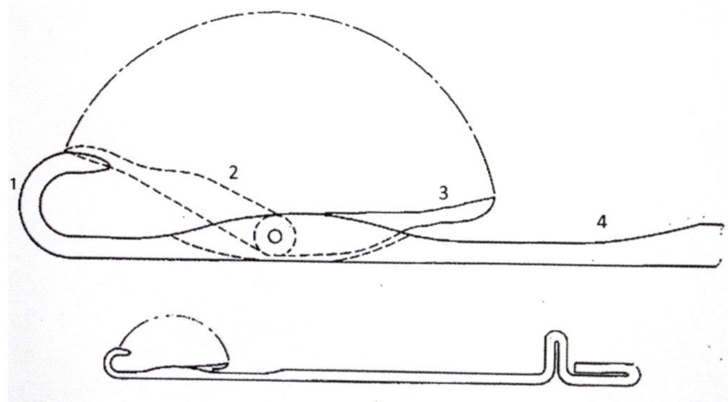

The latch needle.

KNITTED LACE MAKING

Although it had been known for a long time how to make eyelet holes, it was many years before anyone thought to extend the technique into making a knitted lace. An inventor called Hammond, who had helped Arthur Else, decided to look at the idea after studying the lace on his wife's cap. He used a machine with a tickler on every alternate needle, and then moved the stitch two stitches along the row. This action was then repeated with alternate stitches but moving in the opposite direction. This he called 'cross stitch' and it had the appearance of the wire ground found in Brussels lace. He further improved his design and manufactured a 'double cross stitch' which he called 'Valenciennes'. Sadly, he did not continue his experiments but returned to hand-knitted caps.

The period 1776–77 was a fertile one for experimentation. The aim was to make a lace with a hexagonal mesh, and several ways of achieving this were being looked at by various manufacturers. Eventually a regular mesh was formed by using a Derby Rib machine; however, this had to be stiffened with gum to keep its shape and when the fabric got wet the shape disintegrated. This was called point lace; no one is too sure who invented this but a man called Thomas Taylor obtained the patent for it. Taylor, not realizing its value, then sold on the rights and they ended up in the hands of two manufacturers called John and William Hayne. The Haynes realized its huge potential and perfected a way of stabilizing the lace fabric by creating a knot. This was a complex operation and took three times as long as before; however, it proved popular and later William Hayne further improved the method to make a smoother fabric.

As always, there were many squabbles and disputes regarding the ownership of lace-making patents, which meant that many worked in secrecy to perfect their methods. In 1780 Arthur Else obtained a patent for making 'ground lace', which was made with one strand of silk and one of cotton, the two being worked as one thread.

Machines for making net were increasingly made by machines which twisted stitches. These developments led to a completely new industry in the East Midlands – that of lace making – and by 1810 there were 435 warp lace frames in use, invented by Copestake and Brown and making Mechlin net.

Around this time Thomas Frost invented a machine to make figured point lace, using a piece of machinery which enlarged the lace stitches when required to produce an attractive knitted lace.

William Green was also working along the same lines and had invented a version of square lace which was used in the making of wig linings. Both methods were gradually superseded by point and warp nets which were cheaper to manufacture, so they were hardly used after 1812.

Another important figure emerged, that of William Dawson, who patented a machine in 1791 for making military sashes and discovered it could also be used for stay laces. He later invented 'Dawson's wheels' which had notches in them to perform the same function as performed by the Jacquard cards in a weaving loom. Dawson's wheels came into common use in 1807. In 1809 Kirkland of Beeston added wheels and manufactured a two-course silk net, and in 1811 Daycock and George Morrison made yet more alterations to produce silk blonde, a continuous soft bobbin lace in the natural creamy colour of the raw silk.

By 1815 there were over forty-five different types of knitting frame, all producing knitted or lace fabric, but they became a victim of their own success and had a denigrating effect on the viability of the industry.

Plain warp nets were later discarded and twist net introduced. New nets called mock twist, bullet hole and spotted warp were manufactured which, in 1822 led to warp tattings. In 1824 William Hardy devised a machine for spotting and figuring the mock twist fabric. Many rotary machines were built to produce lace in widths of 254–381cm (100–150 inches) to meet demand but by 1835 bobbin net began to be ornamented, and cotton warp tatting and warp silk blonde could not successfully compete.

Although knitted lace was being produced successfully on a commercial scale, the quality of the designs was sometimes questionable. William Felkin, who had been in partnership with William Vickers since 1832, at first as commission agents selling lace for smaller lace makers and later as manufacturers of knitted lace, describes the pattern books used at the beginning of lace making in the following uncomplimentary manner:

> There are rose trees with stems as straight as and bare as a hop-pole, flowers without a curved line in them, perfect triangles; masses of cloth work with hideous Hindoo or Chinese configurations, without the slightest approach to a flowering line in leaf or bud or stalk. In a word they prove the absence of all knowledge of the art and design in the machine lace trade of that time.

From this damning criticism of the prevailing standard of work came the suggestion of setting up a School of Design in Nottingham which would put them ahead of the competition – this duly happened in 1843.

MOVE FROM HOME-BASED TO FACTORY-BASED PRODUCTION

From the 1820s onwards there was a move from production based in the worker's home to factory-based production. This move was quite gradual, and in three stages. The initial stage was home-based production where the machines were rented by the workers and the yarn supplied by the hosiers, providing a flexibility in working hours but no guarantee of work and quite high fixed costs for the worker. This changed quite briskly to 'factory-style' production whereby a row of houses was built with communal workshops located on a floor above the row of cottages or in 'frameshops' which were able to accommodate the new wider machines, located at the rear of the properties

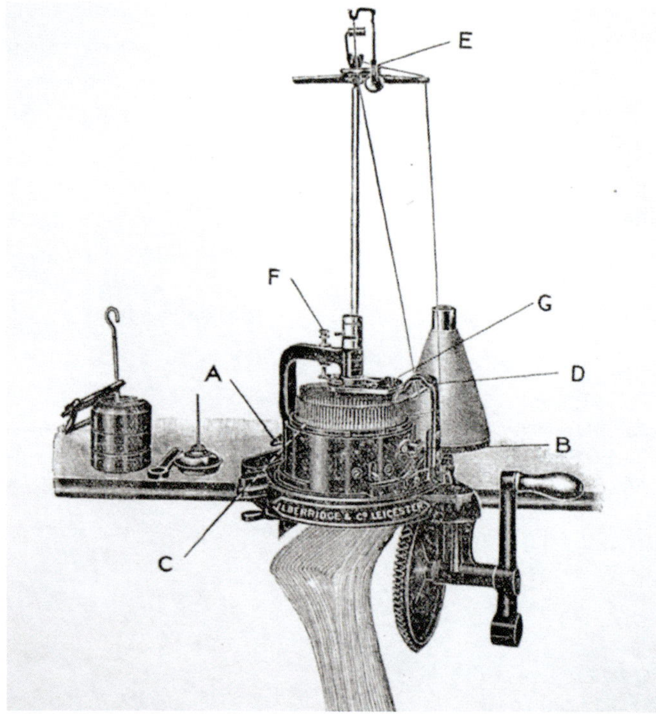

Griswold's sock machine.

(see the Wigston and Ruddington Framework Knitters museums for examples of these types of early factories). The final stage was full factory production, initially using steam-powered machines, where items could be produced more quickly and cheaply than those produced in the frameshops.

In the 1850s William Cotton of Loughborough, a warp knitting manufacturer, developed a steam-powered knitting machine and further developed this with patents granted in 1863 and 1864 for a rotary frame allowing garments to be fully fashioned – such machines being referred to as 'Cotton's Patent' machines.

The Cotton's Patent introduced a number of changes to the knitting process undertaken on a hand frame – the knitting bed was rotated through 90°, the fabric was drawn horizontally from the bed and a vertical needle bar and smaller sinkers were added. The original machine was fitted with four knitting beds, but this was later expanded to six and then eight beds.

The Cotton's Patent successfully transferred the hand and foot operations of the framework knitter to a machine that could be driven by rotary power from a steam engine, and with steam power harnessed by Cotton's machine large-scale factory production of fully fashioned knitted garments was now possible.

Drawings from Griswold's patent applications.

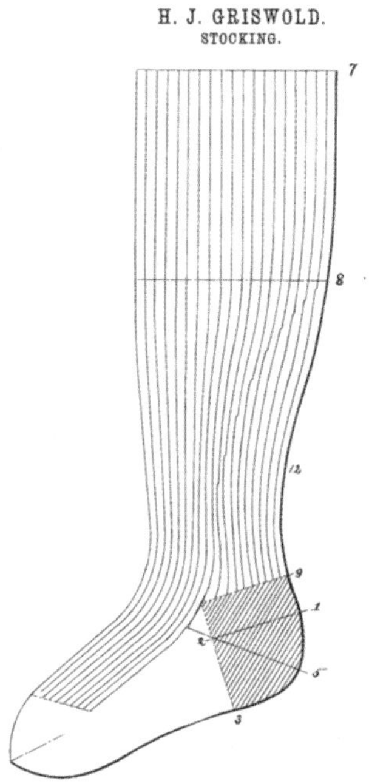

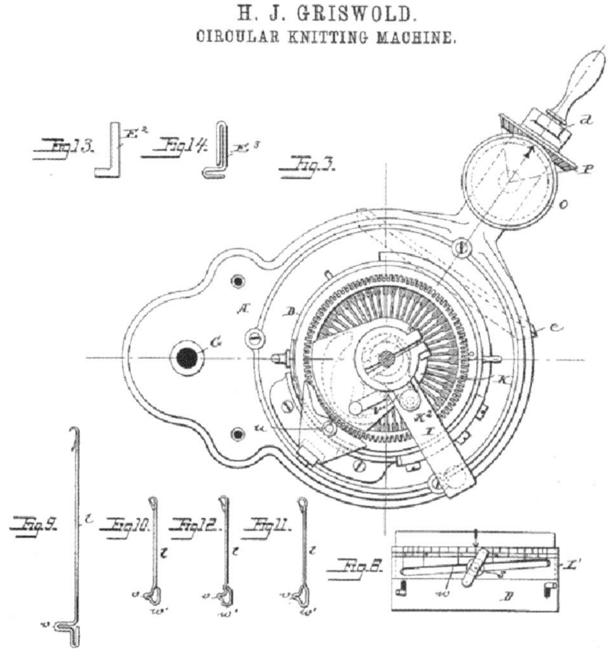

The capacity of the machines continued to grow and models were built with sufficient beds to produce in excess of twelve garments at once. Initially, Cotton's machines were supplied exclusively to Nottingham hosiery manufacturers Hine and Mundella, but after 1878 Cotton supplied his machinery to the open market and it remained a key machine in the industry for the next 100 years or so.

By 1878 William Cotton employed about 200 workers and over 100 machines were made a year. Factory production was beginning to take a strong hold on the industry, although there were still many frames in homes and frameshops.

Between 1862 and 1874 the number of factories doubled as the development of steam power lowered costs and stimulated firms to invest in new machinery and buildings to house these large machines, but the conditions the average factory worker had to endure were poor, especially those of the children. The growth in the number of people employed in the factories raised a general awareness of the conditions they suffered, and most employers began to understand that their workers would work more efficiently if well treated.

Trades unions were formed in the hosiery industry as early as the 1770s as a response to threats of cuts in wages and a recognition by the workers that their conditions of employment had to change, arguing for secure higher wages and shorter hours. With the consolidation of the workers into factories, there needed to be a way for the workers to collectively negotiate with the employers, so the Nottingham Circular Framework Knitters' Society was formed in 1857, followed by the United Rotary Power Framework Knitters' Society in 1865. The unionization of the workers and the number of unions continued to expand rapidly, until it was realized that the unions would have a more powerful negotiating position if they amalgamated. So, in 1888, the Midlands Counties Hosiery Federation was formed, representing workers across the Midlands region and in different sectors of the industry.

At this time, the British industrial model was falling behind that of the continent, where it was realized that it was vital to have an educated workforce, so that the workers could understand the technicalities of what they were doing and be able to improve methods, safety or competitiveness. Added to the lack of education, a largely hierarchical style of management was adopted by the owners, where the workers were treated as 'pairs of hands' and not usually encouraged to do other than to follow instructions.

In 1858, American William Clark Gist was granted a British patent on a circular machine with up to eight feeders, which meant that striped work of up to sixteen colours could now be made. Hine and Mundella bought the patent and further modified it to make it cheaper. Thomas Thompson saw Gist's machine, and used the latch needle to adapt the circular frame

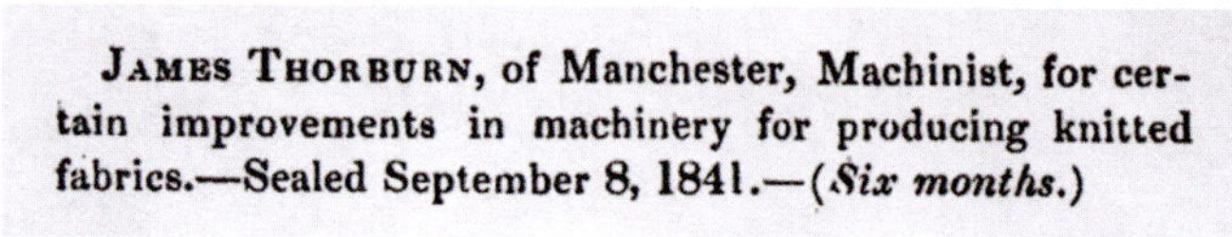
James Thorburn, of Manchester, Machinist, for certain improvements in machinery for producing knitted fabrics.—Sealed September 8, 1841.—(*Six months.*)

Outline of James Thorburn's 1841 UK patent.

to produce Derby Rib fabric. William White took out a patent in 1863 to make plain, striped and fashioned fabrics on the circular machine.

Increased demand led to increasing specialization to reduce costs and remain competitive, so different factories produced different items; a factory which specialized in ladies' seamless stockings used different machinery from one producing children's socks, although all came under the heading of hosiery.

The piecing together of garments and stockings had been done originally by hand, and then with a sewing machine, then the linking machine was developed by Campion of Nottingham around 1858; this linked a seam stitch by stitch with a type of chain stitch. Campion was granted a patent on his linker 'For the Improvement of Sewing Machines'.

1887 saw the development of the overlock machine and this had a huge effect on the fashion industry: it meant that raw edges were able to be neatened at the same time as they were sewn together. Thus many more items could now be cut out and sewn, rather than being fully fashioned, saving time spent shaping.

Many changes were happening in the industry. There were fewer framework knitters as cut work socks could now be made on Henry Josiah Griswold's sock machine of 1872. In 1874 the frame rent was abolished and the Education Acts of 1870 and 1876 prevented the use of child labour for winding and seaming.

The first automatic shaping of stockings was on the Shaw machine of 1879, using latch needles.

In 1878 Griswold added a second set of needles set horizontally in a disc at the top of circular knitting machine, so enabling rib knitting and the welting of socks. This invention was later improved and was granted patents in the UK in April 1886 and April 1888.

DEVELOPMENT OF THE DOMESTIC KNITTING MACHINE

In 1841 James Thorburn of Manchester invented a flatbed machine using bearded needles, but this was not a success as reports state that the yarn jammed.

William Felkin, in *The History of the Machine-Wrought Hosiery and Lace Manufactures*, states that the viable first domestic knitting frame was developed by Bakenheim and exhibited in Cologne during the 1860s; it had eighty-four needles and weighed about 6.8kg but no information is available as to how it worked.

In 1867 American pastor Isaac W. Lamb developed the first V-bed flat knitting machine suitable for use by home knitters, and was granted a US patent for his invention in the same year. The Lamb Knitting Machine Manufacturing Company was formed in 1867, and later built a hand-cranked sock knitter patented by Dr C. R. Tuttle in 1874 called the Tuttle Sock Machine, which the company still produces in a slightly modified form. The Lamb Company continues to this day in Chicopee, Massachusetts as the Lamb Knitting Machine Corporation, making both commercial and home-use knitting machines.

The Crane Knitter was invented by American Thomas Crane in 1867 and granted a patent in the US in 1869 with the following description:

> This invention relates in part to certain novel improvements on that class of knitting machinery wherein rectilinear reciprocating latch-needles are arranged in a row parallel to each other and operated by means of a cam which receives a rectilinear reciprocating motion over the needle-bed, and which causes the needles to advance and receive the yarn and then recede far enough to cast off the loops.

The machine was designed to be used in a domestic setting; it had 106 needles and a carriage which travelled back and forth along a bed. It was advertised in *Cassell's Household Guide* of 1870 as being capable of knitting a pair of socks in twenty-five minutes and being so easy to use that a child ten years old could learn to operate it in a short time. This was one of several sock knitting machines of that era, which included both flat and circular sock machines.

The Harrison Patent Knitting Machine Company was established in 1856 by William Harrison in Manchester. Harrison's were making powered knitting machines at the time of the 1862 International Exhibition held in London, and by 1878 an

Domestic Stocking Frame.—A small knitting frame, contributed by a mechanician named Bakenheim, to the Cologne Exhibition, is highly spoken of. With eighty-four needles, the machine is said not to weigh more than fourteen or fifteen pounds, and to be adaptable to any work-table. It is said to produce from ten thousand to thirty-five thousand points or meshes per hour, and to be worked with great facility. Whether it is a mere modification of the old stocking-frame, or of the circular knitting-machine, or an entirely new arrangement, is not stated.

Report of the Bakenheim invention in *The Journal of the Society for Arts*, January 1866.

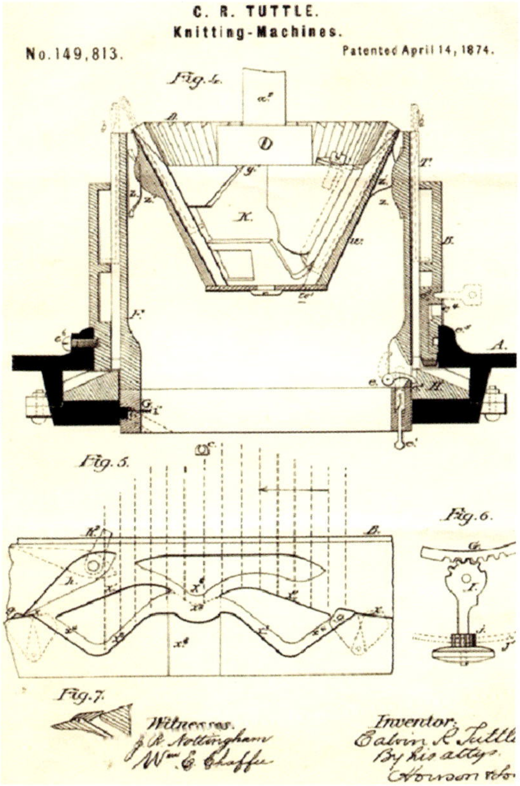

Early Lamb knitting machine (L); drawing from C. R. Tuttle's 1874 patent (R).

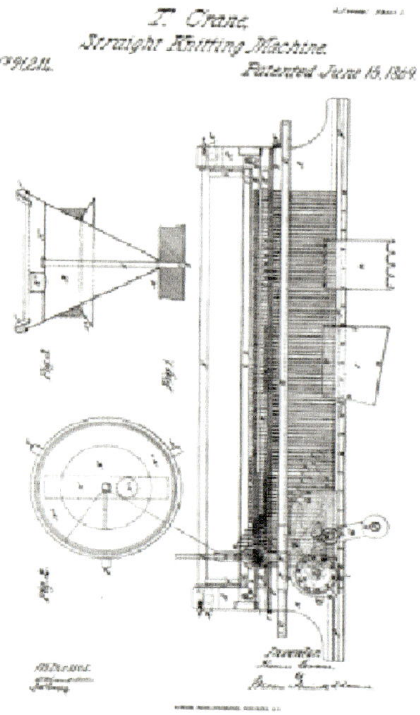

Early Crane Knitter (L); drawing from Thomas Crane's 1869 patent (R).

A Harrison advertisement from 1905.

image of the Lamb V machine was on their printed letterhead. By the early 1900s they were building both domestic hand and powered knitting machines.

The Harrison machine on the left could be powered by hand or by steam, had four cams in parallel and so was capable of making two rows of knitting with one turn of the crank. It was able to produce up to eighty courses of fully fashioned knitting per minute, and was suited to making soft vests, pants and cardigan jackets with a cotton back and a wool front. The machine on the right had 116 needles with seven needles to 2.5cm (1 inch) and was designed to make all sizes of stockings with single or double yarns, plain or ribbed, in wool, silk or cotton; it was capable of knitting sixteen pairs of fully fashioned ladies' stockings per day.

Harrison knitting machines were very well regarded and won a total of thirty-eight awards for pre-eminence of construction and capacity of work. The company was also the only British manufacturer of knitting machines to win ten gold medals for craftsmanship, including the prestigious Grand Prix Gold Medal at the 1908 Franco-British exhibition held in London, the first international exhibition co-organized and sponsored by two countries.

In 1881 Mr Grosser patented a Jacquard mechanism for knitting patterns which made a double bed fabric with a multi-coloured pattern included. This Jacquard card was adapted early on for the making of lace patterns but it seems that Grosser was the first to use it for colour work, so allowing the machine production of block-patterned knitted garments such as golf sweaters and other sporting knitwear. In 1892 James Foster introduced the first Fair Isle flatbed machine used for hosiery. In 1871, with the onset of increased industrialization, Japan sent representatives around the world collecting machinery of every kind, including knitting machinery.

THE TWENTIETH CENTURY

The end of the nineteenth century saw an upturn in both the British and the world economies but the outbreak of war in 1914 created both new challenges and opportunities for the

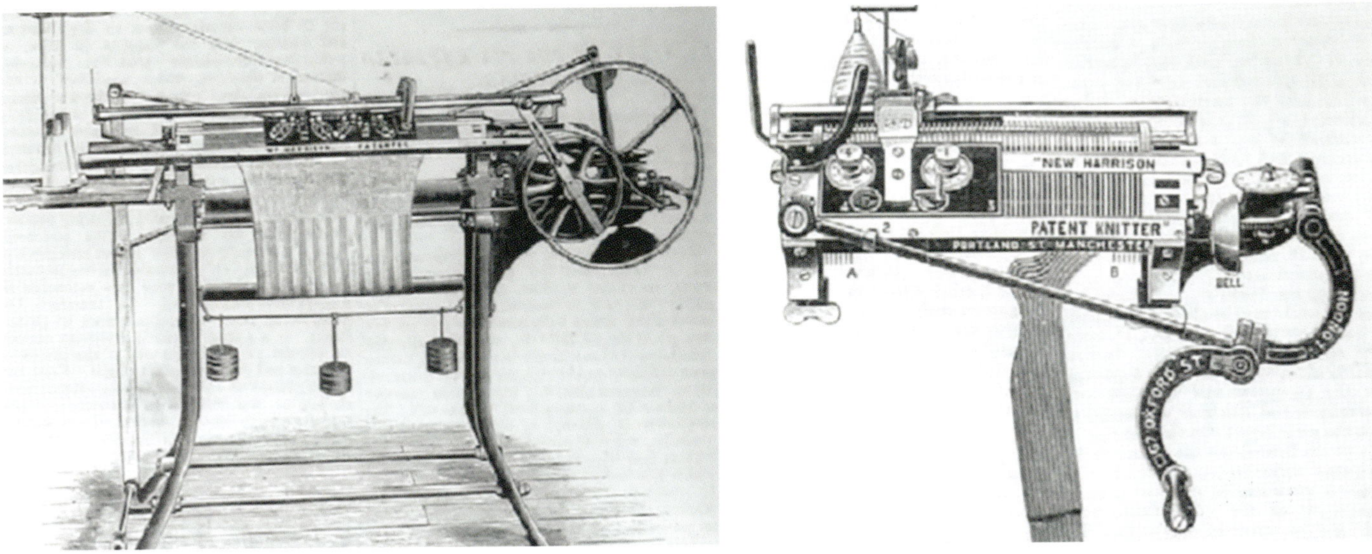

Examples of Harrison's knitting machines as illustrated in the *Textile Mercury*, July 1869.

Vintage Hagiwara knitting machine (L); Mrs Masako Hagiwara (R).

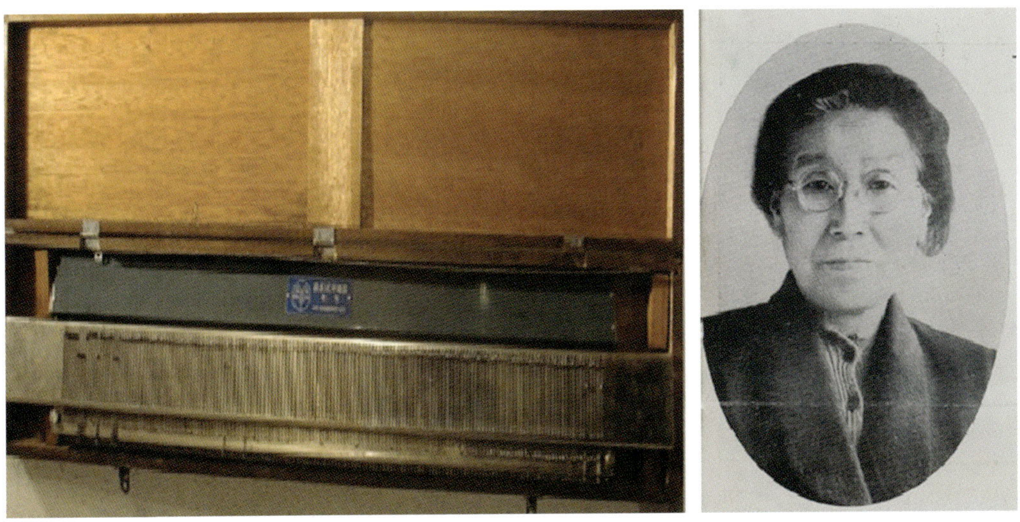

knitting industry: the challenge was that the previous worldwide economic growth stagnated as uncertainty spread across the world; the opportunity was the increased number of government contracts to supply garments for the troops involved in the conflict.

In the 1920s great strides were made to increase the versatility of the circular machine where the manufacture consisted of plain fabric which was then cut to shape. This process was speeded up by the development of electric cutters which could cut through several layers of fabric.

It is claimed that the first modern home-use knitting machine was built by Masako Hagiwara in Japan in 1924, and that this was a basic machine in which the yarn was laid across the needles by hand. Whether this date is true or not, Masa Hagiwara was granted a patent in the US in March 1959 for the invention of a 'Cam Device of Hand Knitting Machine'. It was not, however, until the late 1930s that a commercially successful modern-style domestic knitting machine designed for home use was produced.

DEVELOPMENT OF THE MODERN HOME KNITTING MACHINE

The first commercially viable home knitting machine was the PASSAP 120, which was launched in 1939 at the Swiss National

PASSAP knitting machine advertisement.

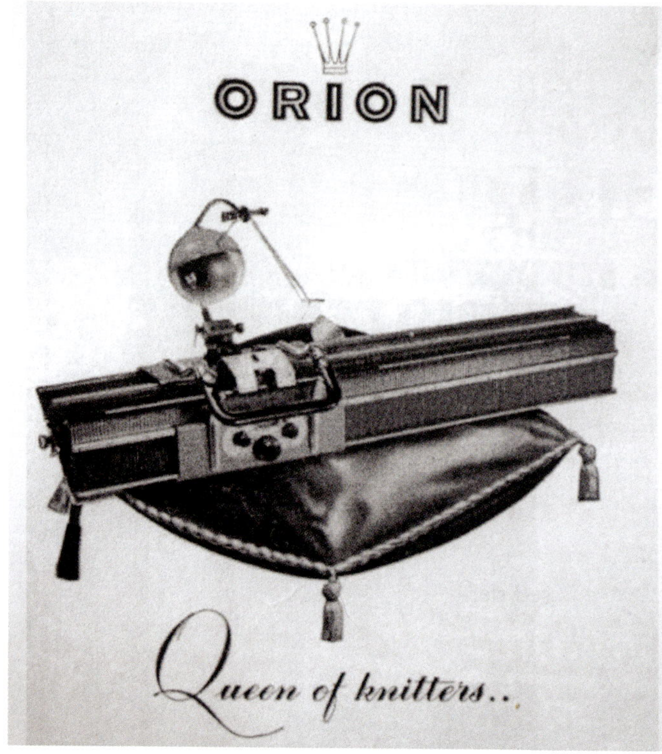

Orion knitting machine advertisement.

Exhibition. It was a modest single bed peg frame knitting machine with simple hooks, a wooden comb and a needle pitch of 5mm. To make stitches the knitting had to be pulled over the needle pins manually, and although it was about eight times quicker than hand knitting, owing to the outbreak of World War II it was only sold locally in Switzerland until the end of hostilities. From 1946 it was exported to Germany, France, Belgium and Luxembourg.

The original machine was superseded in 1954 by the PASSAP M 201, which used latch needles and had a carriage 201 needles wide and a 4mm needle pitch. With this machine the complete stitch was automatically formed, and the PASSAP pressure foot system introduced; a ribbing attachment was introduced a year later as an optional accessory. The PASSAP Automatic was launched in 1958 and was a single bed machine with an automatic yarn guide, and 1959 saw the introduction of PASSAP Duomatic, a double bed forty-stitch punchcard machine using a modular system with a wide range of accessories.

During the late 1950s a number of European firms such as Nitomat, Rapidex, Busch, Orion and Tumix joined with PASSAP to manufacture high-quality, precision single bed and double bed machines for use in the home. They had a manual selection for all stitch patterns with the exception of fisherman's rib, but were generally heavy and cumbersome machines which took up considerable space in the home.

The 1970s saw the introduction of the PASSAP Electronic 6000, opening pattern design to a freer form drawing-based approach, as opposed to the perceived limitations of the previous punchcard-based machines which required a more structured approach to pattern design. PASSAP was taken over by French company Superba in 1978, and stopped making knitting machines altogether in 1999.

Silver Reed (also known as Empisal, Studio, Knitmaster or Singer, depending on the market) started life as the Marukoshi Knitting Machines Ltd in 1952, producing the Model-1 knitting machine. In 1958 the firm of Girotex which produced a Swiss double bed machine amalgamated with Silver Reed. In 1967 the company name was changed to Silver Seiko Ltd, and was the first company to sell electronic home knitting machines, launching the Model 500 in 1977. It has produced Fine Gauge (3.6mm), Standard Gauge (4.5mm) and Mid Gauge (6.5mm) machines using both punchcard and electronic patterning.

Silver Reed is currently the main company producing domestic knitting machines and importing them into the UK.

The development of these machines meant that by the early 1970s home knitting by machine became a popular pastime for hobbyists, producing utilitarian garments such as school jumpers, basic fashion items such as jumpers and cardigans, and also some wildly colourful designs.

At this time there was also a revival of interest in handmade crafts and a general reaction against mass production, tending towards a more individualistic approach to fashion. Individual designers and sole traders such as Patricia Roberts, Kaffe Fassett, Carrie White, Susan Duckworth and Jamie and Jessie Seaton and large fashion houses such as Missoni and Chanel started producing high-fashion knitted garments using distinctive designs in a wide range of colours.

The designer knitwear produced in this era owed much of its uniqueness to the fact that the complex, multi-coloured and multi-textured designs used different yarns in many colours and could only be made by hand knitting or by hand framing. These designs were difficult for most companies to reproduce using the existing mass-production technology – the exception here being Missoni.

By the 1990s there were very few designers working as sole traders – times had changed, and in this trend-driven industry knitted garments fell out of style and were seen as unfashionable. Many of the wool-based yarns available to designers also required dry cleaning or hand washing when knitted into garments, and so were perceived as high-maintenance compared with man-made machine washable alternatives available on the high street.

Since the millennium, interest in designer knitting has had a resurgence, and the yarn manufacturers have responded by producing a wider variety of natural yarns that are colourful with a variety of mixes – all now machine washable. Becoming a knitwear designer is not just about creating a sketch on a piece of paper which suddenly becomes a finished garment. It also involves understanding the technology underpinning the manufacture of the garment, the way in which colours interact, an understanding of the characteristics of the different fibres used in the yarns, understanding how the garment will drape, how the garment will need to be cleaned, understanding and analysing the market you are aiming for, how much it will cost to make and how much it can sell for, sustainability, ethical issues, the challenges of running a business, and whether you can do all of these and still profitably enjoy the experience.

Colourful 1970s tank top pattern.

Many UK universities and colleges have responded by running degrees and other courses in textile design which enable the graduate to go into industry or work as a sole trader. It is once again an exciting and innovative time to be involved in this business so let us now look at where some surprising advances in knitting technology and application are taking place.

MODERN ADVANCES IN KNITTING TECHNOLOGY

The versatility of modern weft knitting technology has paved the way for sophisticated garment shaping to occur, providing inventive opportunities for designers. Garments produced on flatbed knitting machines can be classified into four shaping types: cut and sew; fully fashioned; integral knitted; and complete three-dimensional. The first two methods production methods are largely concerned with producing two-dimensional panels that require a supplementary sewing process in order to produce a three-dimensional garment.

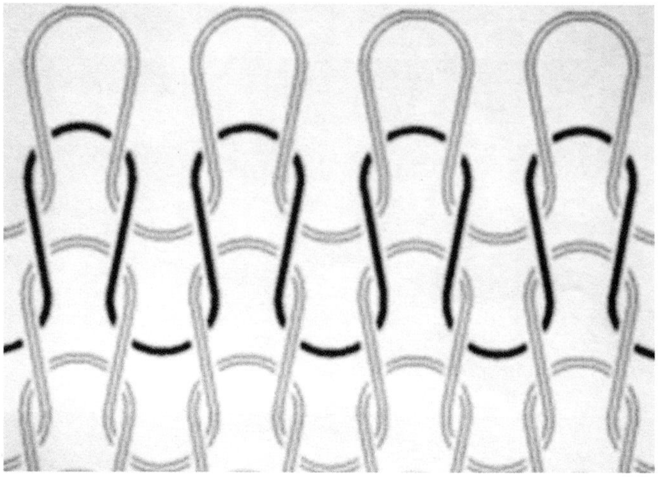

Weft knitting.

1. Cut and sew involves the production of continuous lengths of knitted fabric which are then laid flat, and shaped panels are then cut from templates. Once the panels have been cut to shape, they are joined together to create the finished garment.
2. Fully fashioned garments have shaped knitted panels which are then joined together to create the finished garment.
3. Integral knitting consists of two-dimensional panels with some three-dimensional sections, but not the whole garment. Examples of uses of this technique include knitting collars, lapels, stoles, pockets and buttonholes as part of the panel. Again, the panels are joined together to create the finished garment.
4. The complete three-dimensional shaping method produces a finished knitted garment, removing the need to join the individual panels together. When using circular knitting technology, it allows ready-to-wear three-dimensional tubular garments to be created without any seams, and is currently used to manufacture underwear, bodywear, outerwear, swimwear, home wear, sportswear and sanitary garments – all knitted directly from the yarn into a completed garment.

Knitting, besides being used for garments, is now being used extensively in specialist areas such as geotextiles, automotive textiles, sports textiles, agricultural textiles, the aerospace industry, electromagnetic shielding, filtration, protective textiles and medical textiles. Let's look at the last of these exciting developments in a bit more detail, the medical application.

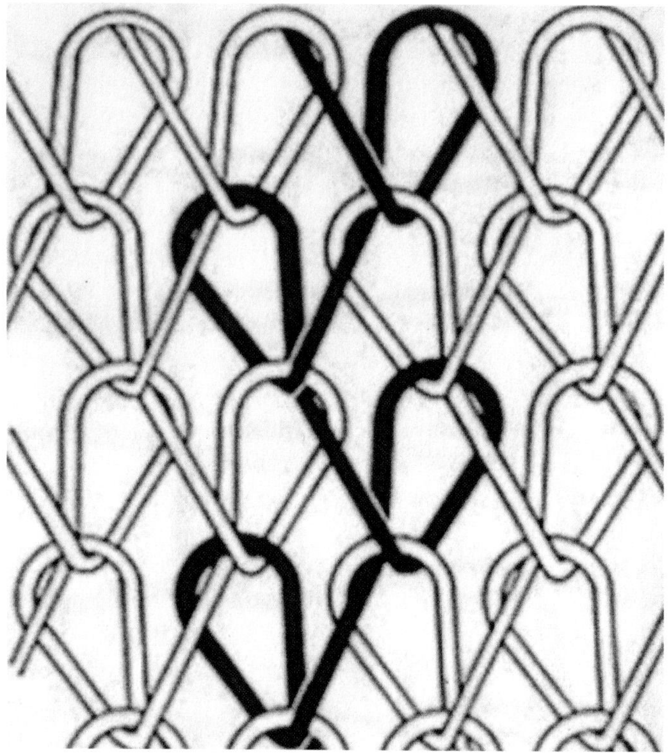

Warp knitting.

Medical applications of knitting

There are many kinds of medical textiles, including woven, non-woven, braided and knitted forms. Although knitted fabrics form a small part of the medical textiles field, they are used in many high-tech applications, having great breathability, permeability and moisture conductivity, and are constructed as either weft-knitted or warp-knitted fabrics.

Knitted fabrics are used medically for dressings, bandages, mattress covers, mattress padding and clothes for surgery, also for high-tech applications including artificial blood vessels, hernia patches, artificial ligaments, tendon scaffolds, cardiac support, expandable stents and artificial chest walls. Knitted textiles are chosen for application in this context due to their loose structure, great flexibility, high porosity, flexible structure and excellent forming technology and they are used with non-implantable, implantable and extra-corporeal textiles and healthcare and hygiene products.

Knitting technology is seen to be one of the key future developments of high-tech medical textiles research, especially within cell scaffolds in tissue engineering. For some cutting-edge examples of the development of this technology within the

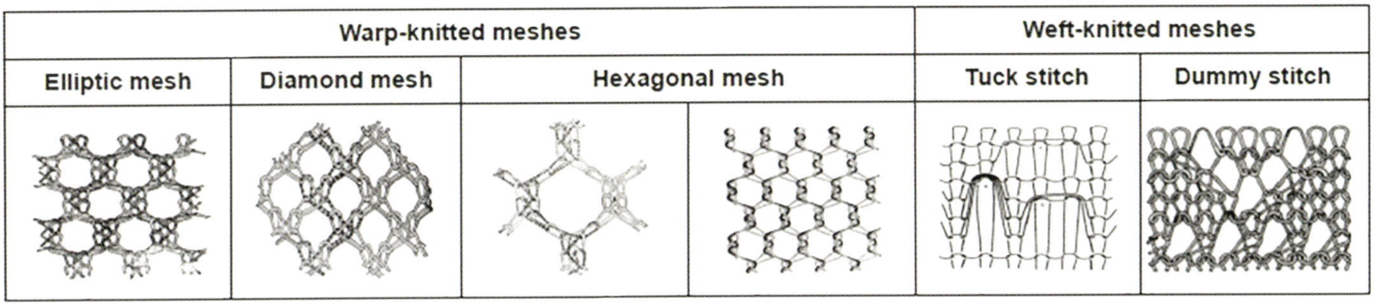

Examples of warp and weft knitted mesh structures.

medical field, have a look at the work of Professor Julian Ellis of Nottingham University.

CONCLUSION

In this chapter we have looked at the development of knitting from its origins as a hand craft through to the invention of the stocking frame by William Lee in 1589. We then considered the many and varied technological developments within the framework knitting industry and how this eventually led to a move from home-based to factory-based industrial production.

Along with these technological and organizational work-based changes we also considered how the employers in the industry looked to protect their monopoly and also maintain standards through the formation of the Worshipful Company of Framework Knitters in the 1650s, the hostile reaction to the technology by the Luddites in the 1770s and the Chartists in the 1830s, and to the rise of a more organized labour force through the formation of trades unions in the 1850s.

We then looked at the development of the modern domestic knitting machine and how it was used by designers and home knitters from the 1970s onwards to create both utilitarian and high-fashion garments, and how a recognition of the importance of this technology has led to the development of many excellent textile design degree courses, equipping students with the necessary skills to participate creatively in the industry as sole traders or within a large company.

Finally we looked at how knitting is used in a variety of high-tech industries, and had a more detailed look at some of the current medical applications of the technology.

This is an exciting time to be a knitwear designer, and I hope that this chapter has been of interest to you, that it has enhanced your understanding of how hand framed knitting has evolved since William Lee's invention, and how the technology has created opportunities for you to use with creativity and imagination.

If you are interested in further research into the history of hand frame knitting, I can highly recommend the Framework Knitters' Museum in Chapel Street, Ruddington, Nottinghamshire as an excellent place to start. The staff are exceptionally knowledgeable, very approachable and helpful, and are able to demonstrate the machines that they have on display.

Examples of the knitting machines at the Ruddington Museum.

CHAPTER 2

TECHNICALITIES, TECHNIQUES AND STITCHES

TOOLS FOR THE JOB

Small items

Transfer tools: everyone has a favourite, mine is the 3×1 and I use this almost all of the time. They are completely fit for purpose and enable you to carry out fully fashioned increases, decreases, cables and so on.

Latch tool: indispensable for casting/latching off, picking up dropped stitches.

Weights: these are vital to keep the knitted fabric slightly taut, so that it cannot bounce up and get tangled in the carriage. Some stitch patterns require more weighting than others. Tuck stitch in particular requires the side stitches to be kept pulled down. I use several smaller claw weights, instead of large ones.

Scissors: blunt-nosed sharp scissors are an essential tool.

Surgical spirit and oil: keep the machine clean and it will work better. Clean off any old oil with surgical spirit and lightly oil where necessary, not forgetting the underside of the carriage.

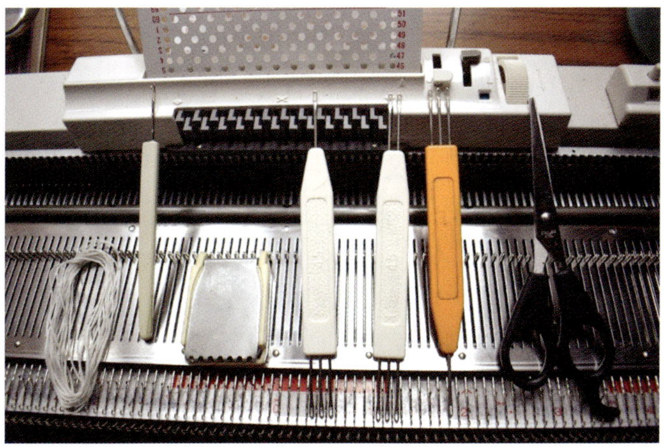

Tools for the job.

Hand-held vacuum cleaner: this is one of the most useful pieces of equipment. After every piece of knitting is completed, vacuum the machine. Gently clean along the needles and behind the carriage rail, thus preventing a build-up of fluff and keeping the tiny particles of wool down to a minimum. Once again, don't forget the underside of the carriage.

Tapestry needles: useful for picking up stitches and sewing up.

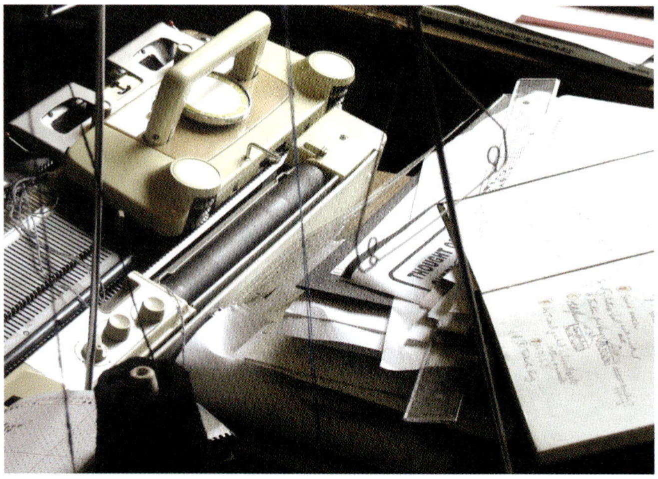

Punchcard knitting machine.

The linker at work.

The knitting machine

It is vital to get to know your own machine with its limitations and abilities; allow it to become an extension of your hand. Get to know what it is capable of and how this can be carried out – this will only be achieved by experimentation and following through ideas, which in turn will hone your technique.

Work through every aspect of your machine; in particular get to know the various stitches it can produce and how you can manipulate these. To this end, experiment with the patterning device which is the punchcard or mylar sheet and work out which stitches can be used with which pattern.

A word of caution – when mixing a fine yarn with a much thicker yarn, some machines work better with the thicker yarn in feeder 1, others vice versa. This is where you will get to know the vagaries of your machine. There are some elements which a Knitmaster/Silver Reed can do with ease and yet a Brother machine will struggle with, and vice versa.

The linker

The use of a linker is essential to piece work together neatly. These can be worked by hand, or by foot pedal for the electric version.

PLAYING WITH A CARD OR STITCH PATTERN

Depending on which machine you own and which pattern system you are using, you will know how many stitches wide the pattern repeat can be. All the patterns in this book will work over twenty-four stitches on a punchcard machine. Smaller repeats of two, three, four, six, eight, twelve or twenty-four will all work on this system.

Paper to card

A stitch is not square, so if you design on squared paper and punch a card from this the designed pattern will be squashed and stumpy. So always bear this in mind or use the proportional paper available on the Internet. As a general rule the vertical stitch size is less than the horizontal in a ratio of 4:5.

Start using proportional paper and draw a shape, one stitch to one little block. Colour in the grid and add repeats. If you offset the repeats this will aid flow and rhythm to the design, and this is on the whole more interesting than horizontal lines of pattern. Bear in mind that the design will be a mirror image; this will obviously be relevant if the design is not symmetrical, such as lettering, numbering and so on. Bold shapes are usually

Fretwork design from paper to punchcard to swatch.

Kelp Scarves.

better than lots of small intricate motifs. Small motifs will get lost in the overall pattern and may require copious amounts of colour changing and generally end up in colour chaos.

It is more useful and less wasteful to buy a roll of punchcard to cut to the length you need for a pattern, than to buy packs of cut card. Before you punch the card, check that the side repeats flow and are not disjointed; this is easily done by photocopying four times, cutting out the design and piecing it together. This method is a useful design technique and it is also worth bearing in mind that the squared paper is just a scale diagram and does not represent the actual size of the finished worked piece.

If you know what yarn is to be used and the appropriate tension used, try reducing or elongating on the photocopier to give you a better idea of what the finished larger piece will look like. Very often you only have to work out what one pattern repeat is, but you will normally have to punch out at least forty rows to allow the card to join up with the clips and rotate smoothly.

It is worth bearing in mind that you can elongate a pattern with either the elongate lever or with the lock card button. Certain machines will allow you to repeat each row. If this is required in a pattern it is marked up with E. Obviously if your machine does not have this option you will have to punch out the repeating row.

If you start off by marking the punchcard with a pencil, mistakes or last-minute alterations can easily be corrected. It does not matter whether you choose to punch out the positive or the negative of the overall design. It is recommended to punch out the one with the least stitches to save time. You can easily alter the yarns from feeder 1 to 2.

Make sure the holes are punched centrally as a little off centre can result in the wrong colour being picked up or a missed tuck or a slip stitch. If you are using a mylar sheet refer to the instruction manual and follow the instructions dealing with the transfer of the design. Always knit a test swatch and try out variations in colours and yarns.

Some patterns are geometric, such as the traditional Fair Isle patterns, so they repeat from the middle out and side to side. These are very versatile and elements can be cut out and changed from a band pattern to an all-over pattern by adding other elements. Several elements from one pattern can be included in one design.

To add interest, consider using tape to block out some stitches and vary the size of the design. Make some areas intense and busy, keeping others calmer and lighter. As a rule, I always try to keep the width of the pattern less than seven stitches, as this is the maximum for floats on the reverse of the knitting. Long floats are impractical and troublesome and will get caught up. To begin with this seems a huge limitation, but with practice it will become clear that smaller motifs can provide a myriad of limitless variations. If working on a double bed this float length limitation can be ignored.

Start off experimenting by punching out a card and make a basic sample with two colours. Then swap the foreground with the background; try also rolling the card back at random for several rows and changing colour. Lock the card for several rows, making sure that you make a careful and thorough note of everything done so you can refer back to it. You will not remember every detail, and sometimes it will be the combination of two or three changes which make a really interesting design. Normally when knitting, the card will move down every row – to elongate some machines have a lock card button; try locking for two or four rows at a time. Try adding plain rows in between, or stripes, or blocks of colour. The Kelp Scarf shows exactly what can be achieved by turning the card round and rolling it back at random.

Tuck, slip and stocking stitches and Fair Isle all mixed together.

Fair Isle knitted with wool produces a dense, firm fabric.

Tie labels onto the sample for quick reference. The easiest way to express all the practical elements is by writing down the RC (row counter), yarn feeder 1, yarn feeder 2 and pattern card selection. Your design notes should include the number of rows, yarn used, colour changes, pattern card changes and on which card row, and any other relevant information such as where to put the weights or tension. Keep all this information together with the swatch. Notice also that certain colours and colour combinations will react better than others, so try out another swatch bearing this in mind.

Try knitting a sampler scarf. Use two fine ends as one thread and mix your own colours to add variety. Experiment with different textures of yarn and combine several cards and several stitch patterns. Try mixing Fair Isle with a tuck stitch band.

Experiment with a different set of colours and the same patterning technique. It is surprising how changing the colours can produce a totally new style and look. Mix unusual colours together and try out other combinations. Mix together contrasting dark colours and work the same pattern with lighter softer tones to add highlights. Do not use all the same tone of colours as they will disappear into an uninteresting fabric. Adding flashes of black or white can invigorate a pattern.

Play with texture using the same pattern but changing the yarn and then felting in the washing machine. For example, use a thicker feltable yarn such as wool with a finer non-feltable yarn such as silk or cotton to add texture and interest to the fabric. Some wool will lightly felt and others require very little agitation to produce a very firm almost matted surface.

Knit small swatches, disregard for a moment how they might work in a larger piece, and play with the yarns, stitches and colour. All of these early experiments can be referred back to later and refreshed. They can be worked into a larger piece and with imagination be transformed into a furnishing fabric or an

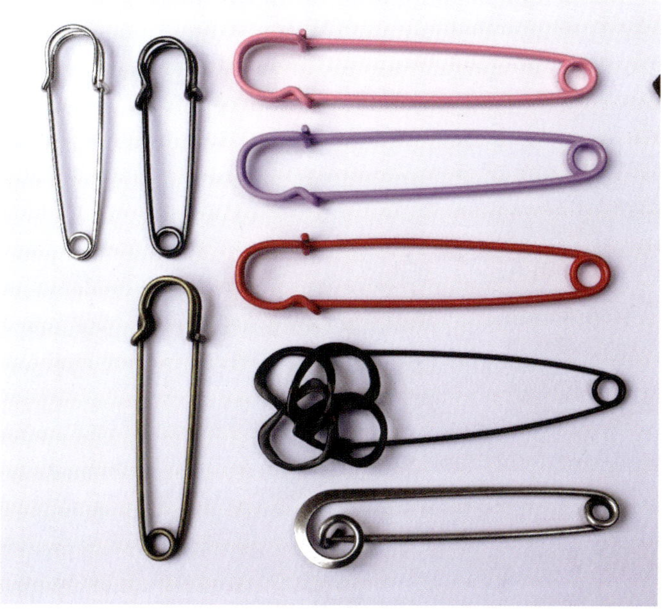

Variety of pins.

item of clothing. Sometimes your experiment in design can work straight away, but sometimes it can take a long time for you to envisage how your swatch design can be used – it can take not just days but years for the right moment to rework a design into something worthwhile, so don't always throw away swatches you cannot immediately use.

Always keep a notebook and pen handy to document not only what you are doing but also to write down any new ideas which you may have thought of as a by-product of what you are knitting at the time. Play, be inventive and have fun – but on the finished piece do not include too many new ideas as it will become muddled and lack definition – try to keep your design coherent and focused.

Although the single bed knitting machine produces patterns with two colours in a row (possibly three with slip stitch), this should not limit your design options as there are an infinite variety of colour combinations and stitch patterns that you can use. However, when using the Fair Isle technique, colours not being knitted in are carried across the back of the work as floats, and this will limit the stretch of the fabric produced and make it thicker. This is worth bearing in mind when designing using a Fair Isle style, as it will affect the choice of the thickness of yarn and drape of the finished item.

Variety of buttons.

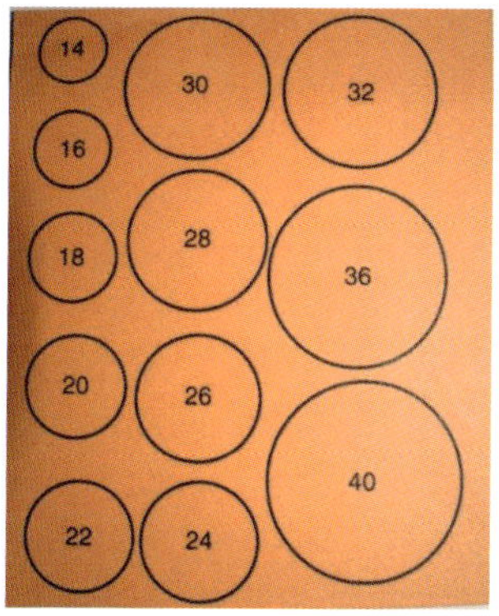

Ligne sizing.

Ligne	mm
14	9
16	10
18	11.5
20	13
22	14
24	15
26	16
28	18
30	19
32	20
36	23
40	25

HABERDASHERY

Pins: there are a variety of pins that are available as fastenings for jacket and coats.

Buttons: on the whole natural buttons are best – shell, wood or horn seem to work most sympathetically with natural fibres. Buttons are measured in ligne sizes. Buttons which are not round are measured at the widest diagonal point.

TENSION

Tension in all knitting is vital. The machine will pull and the weights distort the fabric being knitted. The yarn also may have an oil or dressing in it so washing the tension swatch prior to measuring is very important. When experimenting with various patterns and documenting, make sure this includes

Range of yarns spun by various manufacturers.

Shade cards from spinners and wholesalers.

notes regarding tension. All the tensions mentioned in this book are approximate as this is what I used; every machine is different so you will have to experiment.

Knit a swatch large enough so that a 10cm square can be measured with a generous border. If the knitted fabric is to be felted measure the swatch/test piece after felting. It can be an interesting exercise when felting to measure the swatch/test piece before and after felting. In your design book make a note of which yarns felt more than others, so you have a reference to return to for future design options. Bear in mind also that some colours in the same yarn range can knit up to a slightly different tension.

YARN

Renowned textile designer Anni Albers says: 'The material is full of suggestions. Take the material into the hand, learn by working with it, its resistance, its potency, weakness, charm and dullness. It is the source of unending stimulation and advises us in a most unexpected manner'.

On the whole I have not specified a yarn manufacturer as yarns and colours come and go with alarming rapidity and it is better to have the freedom to choose your own. In the patterns described later in the book I have included the colours which I have used as part of the design and materials process, but there are many different yarns available – use your imagination and experiment.

Industrial yarns

The yarn that you select will dictate a large part of the finished quality and character of your knitted fabric. Most yarns are denoted by their count number (or thickness), and the standard system in use today is the 'new metric' (nm). The 'nm' count number indicates the length in metres of one gram of yarn. So, for instance, one gram of 11nm yarn will be 11 metres long, and one gram of 1.6nm yarn (Aran weight) would be 1.60 metres long.

Under this system, two ends of 1.6nm yarn placed together would be equivalent to a single yarn of 0.8nm. When yarns in lengths are twisted together, they are denominated as 'ply', and 2-, 3- or 4-ply indicates how many lengths of yarn have been twisted together within each ply; the nm count number indicates the length per gram of yarn – the lower the nm count number, the thicker and heavier the yarn, and the less length of fabric that you can knit per gram.

When several ends of yarn are spun together this process twists the staples and filaments together into a spiral; the twist to the left is called an 'S' twist, and the twist to the right is called a 'Z' twist. The resultant spirals can then in turn be further twisted together to ply up into a thicker, stronger yarn.

Some yarn can be overspun and this will be obvious if you take a length, double it up and hold the ends, if they spiral around each other vigorously this will indicate overspinning. If this is knitted the resultant fabric will have a slant to the left or right; in a garment this is not appropriate. In a scarf it can produce an interesting slant to the ends or you can utilize it and mix it with other ends of yarn and create textured stitch patterns.

Industrial Counts

Yarn count	Approximate thickness
2/36s	Fine 1-ply
2/34s	Fine 1-ply
2/32s	1-ply
2/30s	Full 1-ply
2/28s	1-ply
2/24s	1.5-ply
2/20s	2-ply
2/16s	Full 2-ply
2/14s	3-ply
2/10s	Fine 4-ply
2/8s	Normal 4-ply

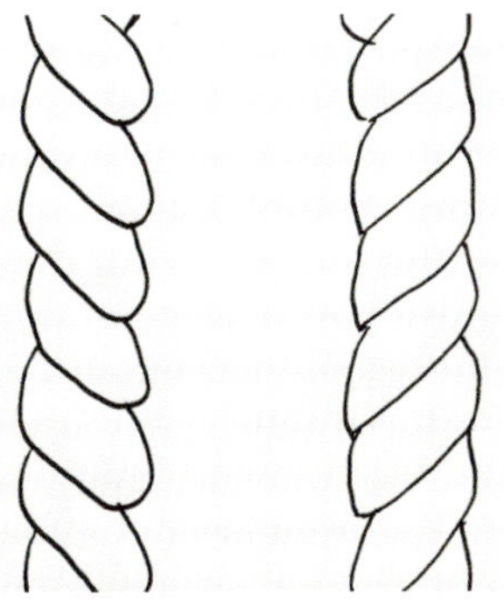
S twist and Z twist.

When using a particular yarn for the first time, work slowly to get the feel of it. Does it need coaxing through the machine? Does it pull unevenly? Is it evenly spun? How resilient is it? Once you have the feel for it you will naturally work faster and with more confidence. The yarn must suit the purpose and the stitch to be used. A thick bulky yarn will not fare well with an intricate tuck stitch and will create problems and catch up or drop side stitches, as a tuck stitch requires a fine smooth yarn.

Whatever you are working with, buy the best yarn you can afford as it will pay dividends. A really cheap yarn will produce a substandard garment which loses its shape and lustre – so choose carefully.

YARN FIBRES

Cotton

Cotton is ideal for people with sensitive skin. It does have a tendency to drop in length so allow the garment to hang to establish how much to adjust the finished length. When washed it absorbs water well and the weight has a tendency to pull the garment out of shape, so it will require spin drying. It is an ideal alternative if you have an infestation of moths and thus cannot use yarns such as wool or cashmere.

Wool

Wool has a unique structure in that the wool fibres are covered by miniscule scales. While one surface is water-resistant, the other is water-absorbent. The knitted structure is capable of absorbing 30% of its own weight of moisture before it will feel wet. This characteristic makes it extremely adaptable to wear in both warm and cool weather.

Some soft wool can pill and this is due to friction against the surface causing the short or broken fibres to rub together and these will eventually form little balls. Although this can look unsightly it will eventually stop and can be removed by use of a pilling comb or scissors.

Alpaca

Alpaca is hypoallergenic as it contains no lanolin. It is a natural fibre spun from combings of the alpaca and is a soft, strong and silky yarn which has the property of being warmer than wool.

Cashmere

Cashmere is a type of wool from the cashmere goat. It is eight times warmer than merino wool and is also lighter. The reason it is expensive is that the cashmere goat can only produce about 115g of fibre a year, making it a 'noble' fibre.

Silk

Silk is a natural protein fibre which is obtained from the cocoons of the silkworm. It is both soft and strong, possesses a natural sheen and drapes well. When blocked and pressed properly it holds its shape well. There are mainly two kinds of silk used commercially.

For mulberry silk the worms are commercially farmed and as silkworms spin within their cocoons they are then killed by boiling or piercing with a needle. The cocoon is boiled until it unravels into a silk thread. Because it has been bred for the

Cones of cashmere yarn.

Various shades of blue yarn showing choice of textures.

purpose it creates a smooth, soft and shiny surface which takes dye evenly.

Tussah silk is more animal-friendly as it is usually made from collected cocoons created by wild silkworms. These silkworms vacate and discard their cocoons, which are then boiled. The threads are much shorter and this limits the production of an even dye, so it can be patchy. This, however, is a characteristic of the yarn and adds to its charm.

Silk noil is made up of leftovers from the production of other silks so it can be textured and matt in appearance. It is generally less expensive than other silks.

Linen

Linen is made from the fibres of the flax plant and is a cool and comfortable fibre with a unique lustre. The fibres consist of almost pure cellulose, which enables the fabric to absorb and release moisture at a quicker rate than any other fibre. Linen thread is not easy to knit with, as it is a rigid fibre which resists wrapping itself around a needle easily. However, blended with another fibre such as wool, silk or polyester it becomes more malleable, and as such has become a very popular yarn to use.

Bamboo

Bamboo is obtained from the pulp of the bamboo plant and has become popular in recent years because it is eco-friendly and soft. The available yarns do vary considerably in quality and manufacture. Generally, they are fabricated into synthetic rayon made from cellulose extracted from bamboo.

Synthetic yarns

There are many synthetic yarns on the market, such as polyester, nylon and metallic threads. Also interesting to use are 'regenerated' fibres such as viscose rayon. These fibres are produced from cellulose, a natural substance which is then chemically reformed and spun to make rayon. These types of yarn can be pulled and pressed permanently out of shape; they can lose their elasticity and easily become baggy if not treated correctly.

It is a useful exercise to mix various threads together to make a unique yarn of your own and also to obtain the colour results which are you are looking for. Yarns of every kind can be mixed even of the same colour; each will have its own properties and the knitted fabric will reflect this.

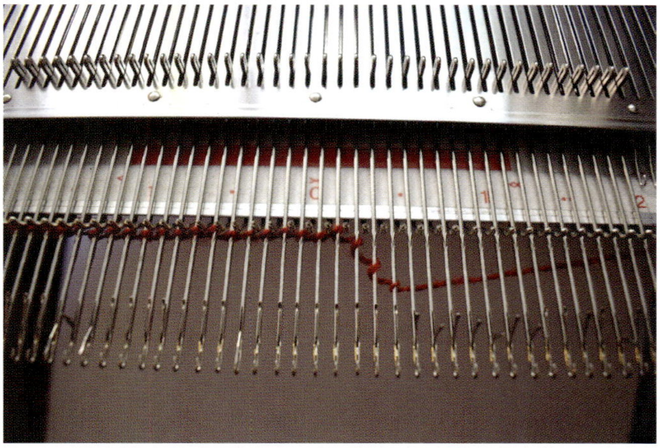

Wrap main yarn around needles in an anti-clockwise direction.

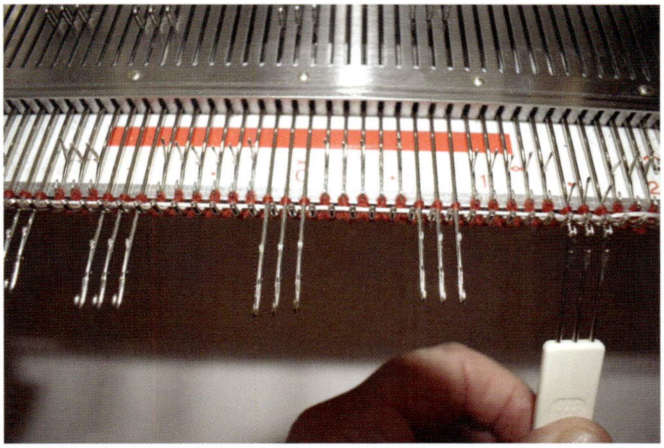

Place nylon cord between the sinker gate and needles.

CASTING ON

E wrap method

This method is used mainly for speed. (Before you start, check through the list of abbreviations.)

1. COR push all Ns to WP. MY wrap around each N from L to R in anti-clockwise direction.
2. K 1 row.
3. Place nylon cord between sinker gate and Ns, pull down firmly, using 3×1 tool bring every few Ns to WP. K 4–5 rows and remove nylon cord. Cont knitting.

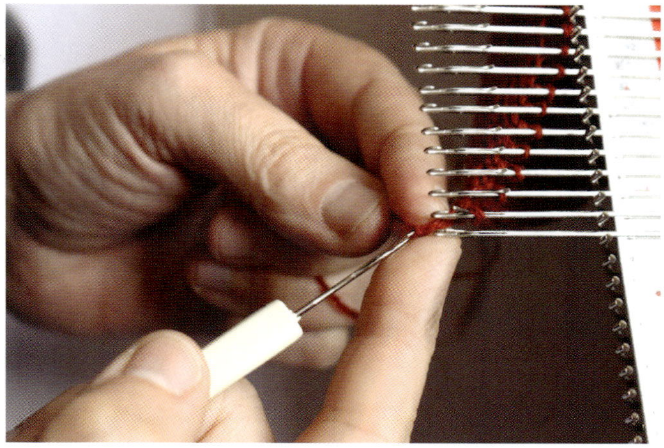

Using a latch tool, cast off the first stitch on the RHS.

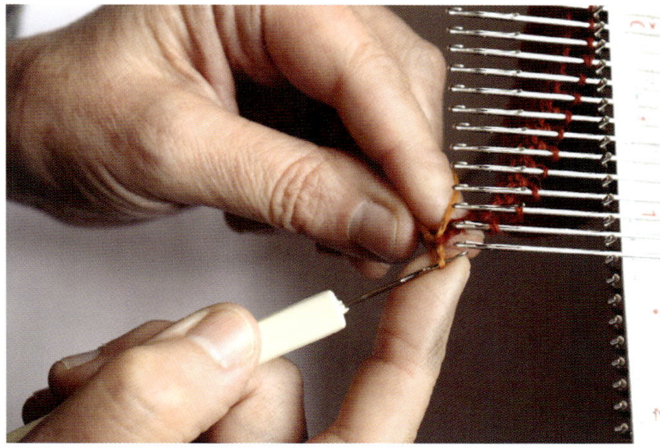

Using a separate length of yarn, draw a loop through the last cast-off stitch on the RHS (contrast colour used here to show up).

Adding an extra stitch for a loose edge

Sometimes it is necessary to have a very loose cast-off edge, in which case add an extra stitch between each of the cast-off stitches.

1. Use a length of yarn the same colour as the cast-off stitches (contrast is used in the picture to show up). Using the separate length of yarn, draw a loop through the last cast-off stitch on the RHS.

Cast off next stitch with latch tool and repeat by adding one extra stitch.

Continue to cast off one stitch and make one stitch until completed.

2. Cast off next stitch with latch tool and repeat by adding one extra stitch.
3. Continue to cast off one stitch and make one stitch until completed.

Yarn inspiration.

COLOUR AND STITCHES

There are four important aspects to consider when deciding which stitches work well with certain colours.

1. The use of colour in its own right – red, blue, green and so on. For example, in the indigo-dyed cardigan, the interest is predominantly in the colour and its mottled washed-out appearance.
2. Texture, either through the yarn choice itself or what you do with it. Is it thick, thin, slubby or smooth? For example, here the fine silk is knitted in stripes and juxtaposed with a soft smooth cashmere knitted and lightly felted into bobbles. Or the choice of stitch may be more important, such as tuck, slip, Fair Isle or lacy.
3. The quantity, proportion and balance of the colour used. Some colours are strong, or perhaps they are intense and only a flash or small amount is required. The Landscape Storm Jacket and Harbour Lights Scarf show that a little acid yellow lifts the green and ochres; however, only a few rows are needed in the overall design.
4. The surface spread – the overall effect of the colour and yarn combined and the choice of stitch. For example, look at the three coats all relying on mixing colours together, where the colours meet, flow into one another and create an overall spread with no real dominant hard stripe or shade. The first shows berry purple colours, the second flame reds and blues, and the final one the colours of a bluebell wood.

Indigo-dyed cardigan.

Fine silk knitted with cashmere and lightly felted to make soft bobbles.

As can be seen, different colours react differently when placed next to each other. Groupings of contrasting colours and shades of the same colours create different pulses across the knitted fabric, which in turn creates a vitality and energy. The 'pulses' can be enhanced by a myriad of small changes, such as density of fabric created by using chunky or fine yarn, a firm or loose tension, a smooth or textured yarn, a choice of warm or cool colours, the size and scale of the chosen motif or stitch pattern in relation to the size and scale of the finished cardigan or scarf, and so on. There is an infinite number of options to be considered; minor adjustments to any of the above can create dramatic changes in the look and feel of the completed fabric. All of above are facilitated by using the mind, eye and hand working in unison, plus feelings, emotions and experiences that make a catalyst to create a piece of fabric with energy and life, across a textured and decorative surface.

Landscape Storm Jacket and Harbour Lights Gold Scarf.

Landscape Coats in Berry, Flame Reds and Blues, and Bluebell Wood.

Felted Donegal Jacket: soft subtle colouring and lightly felted.

TO FELT OR NOT TO FELT

The texture or surface created when a colour is knitted adds to the overall character of the fabric. The surface of an egg, your skin, a polished wood tabletop or the bark of a tree are enhanced by the underlying texture as well as the colour. Look to make similar choices regarding the surface of your knitting – would it enhance the finished piece to lightly felt it? – this can dramatically change the character.

Felting is also known as milling, and this can be achieved by placing the finished woollen article in a washing machine. A 30° wash will remove any oil or dressing in the yarn but will probably not felt the fabric, although it may feel much softer. A 40° wash will lightly felt most yarn; some lambswool is particularly susceptible to machine washing and will produce an extremely dense fabric. It is vital to experiment with a small swatch; this will enhance your knowledge of the yarns you are using and how different colours and stitches react to your particular washing machine settings.

The knitted fabric must be partly or totally made of wool for felting to take place. The texture of the felted fabric is altered to a closer knit and it will bulk up and become denser – although this does not mean coarse – and in some cases the yarn will fluff up and become much softer in feel after felting. This finish affects the perceived colour and will also give the fabric pattern a less distinct shape, becoming hazier and more ethereal. How pronounced you want this to be is a choice you need to make for the finished piece of work, depending upon the look and style required.

The perceived colour also changes in different types of lighting and this can influence mood and emotions. The more you study colour, the more you understand that you are on a journey and there is no end point, no destination – you will be continually building on and expressing what you have experienced/learned before, automatically refining, elaborating, distilling; you embrace the complexity of patterns, where you can use them and with what colours and then you pare it down to a bare minimum of colour change and simple pattern. Pairing loud raucous colours with quiet, softer colours will build up a rhythm which will rise and fall across your work.

Always remember that when any knitted fabric is worn the wearer enters into a sensual environment of touch, feel and colour. It can inspire contemplation, joy, comfort, warmth. Instantly the wearer is interacting with the piece of craft. The fabric is there to be touched and this sensation can be soft, knobbly, diaphanous, chunky or smooth; the choice you have is endless.

Wall of Colour Cardigans, back view.

Slip stitch stripes.

Slip stitch Wave Scarves.

WHICH STITCH TO USE

Slip stitch

The basic principle of this stitch is that the yarn does not knit the non-selected needle but floats across the fabric on the purl side. This ultimately has the effect of making the worked fabric narrower and shorter, so extra rows will have to be worked for a required length. It is an endlessly versatile decorative stitch. It can be delicate and understated or, used in a different fashion, can be bold and textured.

A subtle slip stitch pattern would be:
X0X0X0X0X0X0X0X0X0X0X0X0

In the scarves shown here, the main interest is in the stripes; the subtle slip stitch pattern makes a firm dense fabric. However, it can be made more interesting by slipping for six rows and then knitting two stocking stitch rows. This is known as tea cosy stitch but it can be used for edgings and in between colour changes for a decorative effect, using the knit side as the right side.

Using a thicker weight yarn for the two slipped rows between colour changes will create a subtle textured pattern; in this case the purl side is the right side.

With the correct fine yarn it is possible to slip stitch for eighteen rows and change colour every few rows. Be aware that this effect will pull up the length of the knitting, making it wider, but the resulting texture and pattern will be exciting.

The 0 hole of the punchcard is the slipped stitch and with this in mind it is possible to design some wonderful textured stitch patterns using the cards which are supplied with the knitting machine or punching your own. Colours can overlap other colours and intricate designs can emerge.

Donegal Jacket in slip stitch.

Tuck, stocking and slip stitch in multi-coloured stripes.

Sculpted Jacket and Scarf.

Selection of tuck stitch scarves.

Tuck and slip stitch colour combinations

Slip stitch can be used in combination with other stitches such as Fair Isle and tuck stitch and with colour changing to make for interesting and innovative fabrics. The same pattern can be used for each stitch pattern and depending on which stitch is used first a different texture will appear.

Tuck stitch

In many ways tuck stitch and slip stitch are quite similar, and in some instances when experimenting with a decorative, surface or textured pattern the results can work better by using the other stitch. For example, it can prove troublesome to try to tuck stitch over more than ten rows, but easier to if you use a slip stitch. The tuck stitch can give a delicate lacy look to scarves and jackets, and draw the threads together to make a more circular pattern.

When using tuck stitch, the non-selected stitch is held in the hook of the needle, so there is a limit to how many threads can be held, depending on the weight of the yarn and rows knitted before the work becomes snarled, and stitches are dropped either side of the non-selected needles.

The tuck stitch will produce an interesting decorative fabric but it will shorten the finished fabric, so more rows will be

Fair Isle Harris Tweed scarves.

required for a given length to be knitted and it will widen the work so slightly fewer stitches are required.

Fair Isle

This is possibly the most used stitch produced by the knitting machine. The idea of knitting two colours in a row in seconds is very appealing. The variations from the traditional Shetland stitch patterns are endless, creating geometric or flowing organic patterns, and Fair Isle is the stitch to use.

True Fair Isle came originally from Spain and only uses certain patterns which are based on the Armada Cross. However, the term 'Fair Isle' has become generic and now describes a particular pattern and technique. Fair Isle knitting can change colour from stitch to stitch, but only two colours are used in a row. Most traditional Fair Isle patterns today are made up of small patterns repeated across the work using the basic stocking stitch.

Designing for Fair Isle is relatively easy as each stitch can be a square in your design, and with the aid of colouring pencils and squared paper wonderful intricate designs can emerge. The only concern is the floats across the back of the work; always be aware that floats over more than seven stitches are too long and are likely to get caught up.

Thread lace

This is not a true lace stitch but a punch lace which uses a fine yarn together with a thicker yarn to make a lace effect. This, however, can be enhanced by cutting threads and using a shrinkable thread mixed with a shrink-resistant thread.

Traditional vintage Fair Isle pullover.

Lace-effect stitches create Balloon Moon scarves in Cream, Blue and Bright colourways.

CHAPTER 3

THE DESIGN PROCESS

It is whatever we do which makes us. Through doing it, seeing it and making it we learn to test ourselves and, in that process, come to know ourselves better.
Antony Gormley

THE PHILOSOPHY OF DESIGNING

The six stages for designing creative knitwear are basically:

1. Finding the initial source and inspiration.
2. Drawing an idea of shape and stitch on punchcard paper.
3. Punching out the card and knitting a sample swatch.
4. Evaluating and changing anything which needs changing.
5. Knitting the piece.
6. Finishing, felting and pressing.

This is, however, a very simplistic view, and while these are the stages that I go through, there is much more of a journey to be made before a design can be completed. Consideration must be given within each of the above stages to the desired aesthetic quality, the best practice technique, the effort involved and the overall cost.

A fundamental starting point is to understand that the basis of a good knitted fabric is the interaction of different fibres and their elasticity when knitted together with skill and imagination to fulfil the criteria of good design. How will the textile piece be made? Question if that is the best method and look to see if there is a better way to achieve your design goal. What about the aesthetic quality or styling, and the shape? What colours will be used? What is the overall appearance of the stitches? And so on. Both the method used and the aesthetic requirements need to be in balance to create a successful piece of work.

They need to be regarded as a whole to ensure that the design will work on every level; in other words the piece needs to perform its function and be aesthetically pleasing – it must work as a whole.

There are numerous examples of products which 'work' and are technically excellently made but lack beauty. They are textiles which have been made to a high standard and are perfect for the job they are doing but lack any artistry and therefore are boring to look at. Contrariwise, there are textiles which contain innovative ideas, colours and stitches but are badly made or badly styled, and this overshadows the decorative artistry. So, both criteria have to work in unison to make a well-designed and functional textile.

To achieve this the maker has to balance their mind, heart and hand and make sure that all these particular elements are working in unison and worked into the knitted textile.

Your mind must ask logical questions such as: What colours should I use? What am I making? What stitch pattern should I use? What are the likely problems that I may encounter? How will I solve them? And what are the practical aspects of the work?

Your heart triggers emotions and feelings and can be used to address the aesthetic aspect of your work. Why use a certain

Variety of scarves.

colour? Can I experiment and take a risk? Is it successful? How tactile is my project – smooth and soft, or bobbly and crunchy – and which will work best for my design? Is it beautiful?

Your hand is how can you obtain the results required, the execution of the project; in other words, technique. Your hands are the tools for the job, and what wonderful tools! It is crucial to aim to make an item which is practical and fit for its purpose and yet be decorative to meet your aesthetic criteria. Very often a poorly designed item addresses only one or neither of these criteria. The aim is to build on a firm foundation and to fully satisfy both criteria.

BE CREATIVE AND TAKE A RISK

In 1968, designer-maker and Professor of Furniture Design at the Royal College of Art, David Pye wrote a book called *The Nature and Art of Workmanship*, where he explained the distinction between mass production – the workmanship of certainty – and that of the artist-craftsperson – the workmanship of risk. He explains that when you know the exact results of what is going to be made this can be barren land and ultimately demotivating. Feeding yarn or fabric into a large machine which churns out the same results time after time is not particularly creative. It is an end result in itself. If, however, you are working and a complete change of direction presents itself and the design develops in an unforeseen direction then this is taking a risk, and the results can be uncertain. This can be an exhilarating and creative way to work, and may well ultimately feed the desire to hone skills and build on your knowledge and technique. The design process may suggest brighter colours or a change in stitch pattern, weight of yarn or rows between a pattern to allow a pattern to breathe rather than disappear. Decisions need to be made – for example, is it possible to mix two yarns together to make the 'right' change?

It may be that over the years of trial and error your technical skills are perfected, but there is always room for creative development, and this will only come about through experimentation and risk by trying out new ideas using your knitting machine. Risky surprises are enlightening and fun to work with, and also a learning experience.

David Pye further states: 'workmanship is the exercise of care plus judgement plus dexterity and this will only be honed through example and practice'.

Although, in many ways, the basic technique of knitting has remained unchanged, advances have been made with machines – patterning devices can be attached and shapes dictated; however, it is surely better to build on a firm foundation and know and understand how a stitch and stitch patterns are constructed and build on this knowledge so when you use the more advanced machines you can understand better how they work. For example, during the design process ask yourself how many rows can be tucked with a certain quality of yarn before it becomes impossible to work. Is the yarn strong enough to stretch and fashion a certain cable? If not, is there another yarn that will complete the task, or will it require mixing two yarns together to add strength?

Always be open to inventing new working methods and techniques. There is nothing wrong with constantly questioning: What do I do next? Constantly re-evaluate the techniques and colours you have used and the aesthetics and usability of items you have made to enhance your overall skills as a designer-maker.

Yarns and risk

We should also be open to learn from the materials we use; holding the yarn in our hands is not only a tactile experience, it is possible to test its strength, quality and lustre. Ask yourself how this particular yarn can be used to best advantage.

It is an interesting thought that in years gone by the craftsperson was involved in making the yarn being used, so a knowledge of its properties – from shearing, to combing, carding, spinning through to knitting – was learnt. The maker had a 'feel' for the materials, knew the weight, count and malleability and this informed the choice of techniques to use. While it is obviously not necessary to go to these lengths today, it is essential to get to know the materials you are using and have a respect for them.

While spinners of yarns have progressed by mixing cashmeres, wools and polyamides with silks to add strength and durability, and chemical finishes have created wonderful machine washable yarns which are shrink-resistant, the dyers have been creating hundreds of shades of soft subtle colours and vibrant fluorescent smooth, textured, dip-dyed, random yarns. A basic single bed twenty-four stitch pattern repeat machine (or electronic machine) can keep pace with all these innovations if the knitter is prepared to experiment and also to be innovative. Yes, the machine can knit a thousand rows using only two colours in a Fair Isle pattern in half an hour but to work this way is energy-sapping and very monotonous. Use the mechanism of the machine with versatility. Work with an open mind and when careful and meticulous planning of a project throws up a surprise due to either materials used or technique or a combination of both, make use of it in an imaginative way.

We live in a world that requires immediacy and to an extent the use of a knitting machine endorses this, but this is not taking full advantage of it as a tool. We must get to know the materials and the equipment we are using.

Knitting machine at work.

If we cooperate with the materials, we will not demand that it produce something which it clearly is not capable of. The catalyst is the material, in our case, the yarn, and to impose an idea which worked well with a previous project idea will mean that we are not entirely open to new and innovative ideas, merely reproducing a previous piece of work but in a different material.

KNOWING THE MACHINE

We can also learn from the machine – how it will react with a particular yarn? Will it make a loose open fabric or a tight dense fabric? The results of this process will encourage and inform what items can be made and you will get to know your machine and its idiosyncrasies – every machine has them! The finished piece will inevitably have your own characteristics stamped on it as a piece of work by you, almost your signature, but allowing the materials and the machine into the design process will keep the ideas flowing and you and the work fresh and innovative.

The aesthetic and technique elements need to work in unison with the head, heart and finally the hand. There are instances in the past where machine knitting has had a bad press as being trite and producing boring and uninteresting work but this is not inherent in the machine itself, rather a feature of the skill and knowledge of the operator, together with any cost and time constraints present when completing the garment.

There must be a relationship between the working yarn and the work process. It is the choice of yarn and stitch which provides texture and interest and is fundamental to whatever

Examples of risky colours combined to good effect.

we are producing. Through excellent work practices we can make the craft into an art. For example, cashmere and other woollen threads are soft and pliable but this outcome can be changed by mixing them together and perhaps by knitting with a low tension or using a close stitch pattern and lightly felting; thus a soft but densely constructed fabric can be produced. Experimentation should be constant; allow time for your imagination and constructiveness and inventiveness to blossom – this is a positive and absorbing way to work and live.

The materials we use are of paramount importance; they are the foundation on which we build and how we use them satisfies not only a practical need but also a spiritual one. Using a machine should not divorce us from appreciating and allowing the materials we use full rein to experiment and be inventive. It is an exhilarating process to work and design within these limitations of the yarn and machine and will result in a greater understanding of ourselves; therefore our self-confidence will grow and the excitement and pure pleasure of creating will make the soul sing! This is a tangible antidote to the extraordinary and, at times, chaotic world in which we live.

Constant questioning, experimentation and development will lead into other areas such as dyeing, felting, sculpture and so on. The limitations of the materials and machine are, in fact, liberating. Rather than firing off in all directions, becoming bewildered and achieving very little, the limitations and boundaries set act as an anchor and with this to hold onto we are not overwhelmed, but focused and able to build on ideas and experimentation.

LEARNING FROM THE PAST

It seems that in our race to speed up the process of making we have lost or simply not given ourselves time to develop or extend our skills. It is interesting to note that with only basic tools and materials the artisan of past times was capable of producing the most intricate and exquisite work, which we are sometimes no longer capable of making. The Victoria and Albert Museum has, in its collection, a piece of hand knitting portraying various animals and stitch changes which is so finely knitted that we are no longer able to produce work of this quality today. It is not just a time issue; we no longer seem to have the patience or desire to hone our skills to that of the level of the past masters in antiquity.

It is always good practice to constantly refer back to designs and ideas in your archive as it will help to put your current work into perspective; it will also indicate if your thought processes have plateaued, progressed or regressed – the results of this reflection can spark new areas to explore and develop. Sometimes a fertile seam of exploration can be ignited by a fairly small catalyst such as the availability of a new yarn or colour. Sometimes it can be a thread which has been around for a long time but has come back into fashion, or we have learned to use it innovatively with new stitch techniques.

Consider how a design will look from a distance – some will have greater impact from afar yet the closer you get this impact will disappear and the elements which first attracted you dissolve. Conversely some designs which are intricate with lots of colour changes can appear interesting and colourful but the further away you view, the overall impression is a study of chaos or a lack of focus in the design. It is a useful exercise to pin samples up on a board and critically study the design over a few days – view them with fresh eyes constantly, and envisage what a larger piece will look like. Sometimes an unexpected pattern emerges, perhaps at odds with your original idea of harmony, or has it disappeared into busy chaos?

Designs often emerge out of the gloom, through a process of experimentation. Do not let the fact that you may be using an expensive yarn such as cashmere inhibit its use. You will need to obtain a true assessment of its capabilities and using a cheaper, rough yarn will not be an indication as to how well a theory put into practice will work.

Consider designing a risky jacket as five separate pieces – right and left sleeve, right and left front and back. Treat each piece as a separate design and colourway. You will only really know if it works well and in colour proportion when all the pieces are put together. This is an exciting and invigorating way to work and a catalyst for so many more ideas – each piece could represent different aspects of a walk in the woods, or different seasons walking the same path, or simply five different boats turned over and showing their weathered, barnacled, scraped hulls. Mix colours together – use no flat colours.

Sometimes a colour may be used which was not intended due to lack of concentration, or a mistake, or inadequate lighting, and this intervention can, sometimes, be built upon rather than unpicking the work. It is often worth taking a risk, as this can push the design into a better direction than the one intended when we started out.

St Ives Sand Scarf.

THE PRACTICE OF DESIGNING

You need to constantly look around at other crafts and study what other makers are working on. Some are using traditional designs and updating them using colour – try looking in particular at hand knitting and the use of colour and pattern. Decide what it is that appeals to you in this work and look in detail at the work of other designers such as Kaffe Fassett, Brandon Mabley, Missoni and Ralph Lauren, to name just a few. Look them up on the Internet and very often one search will lead onto another; many designers are very open and welcoming about explaining their sources. Look at their inspiration – will that help you in a different way, does it lead you into an area which you had not thought of? If you are studying a particular genre look up the name or associated names on a search engine and it will suggest various other names. Search all of these: some will be blind alleys but others an explosion of ideas, and all will be broadening your knowledge. Any word suggestions when reading through an article should be followed up and the results can be surprising. Write down all your ideas, some of which you may never work on but they may lead onto a better idea or allow you to recognize design combinations that you do not find aesthetically pleasing and so can put to one side.

Artists and their lives and work are an endless depth to plumb. While reading a number of biographies about Van Gogh, each highlighting a different aspect of his paintings, I noticed a small corner of snow on a ploughed field and the colours he had used, which I had never before seen in this combination: lilac, grey, black, aqua, cream, white, beige. I had been working on sand ripples on a beach at St Ives, and had already completed two colourways I was happy with, but the combination of these colours used by Van Gogh in this picture lit a fire in my brain – I later looked at David Hockney's paintings of fields and his completely mesmerizing colour palette. A pattern may be inspired from one design and the colour palette used from another; always keep an open mind.

Sometimes this process can take a while in gestation, so be patient, work on several variations of one idea and one swatch design will always lead onto another.

There are many books which are invaluable design resources. *The Grammar of Ornament* by Owen Jones is one such that I am constantly returning to. Keep a notebook and sketch out rough ideas; always annotate your sketches and this will remind you, sometimes years later, what the catalyst was. Make a note of your thoughts and ideas regarding colour and yarns, creating an archive by constantly seeking out and looking in depth at

Inspired by David Hockney's coloured fields, a marled yarn is used in three colourways: blue, bright and pale.

One of my bookshelves.

My scrapbook and notes of cuttings.

certain colour and yarn combinations. Try to understand what it is in particular that draws you to certain colours and their combinations. Translate what you are seeing into your own yarns – for example, a seascape may be sky blue, pearl white and also slate grey.

Keep a scrapbook of cuttings, sketches, threads of yarn, etc., and write by the side of each your initial thoughts and ideas. Sort out images for patterns and textures, sketch and make notes, take photographs and group them together; for example, abstract patterns and shapes from nature such as leaves or bark. What about architectural texture from bricks and manhole covers, distressed doorways or the hull of a boat? Always be analytical – why do certain colours work, what is it about that shape? – to build up an archive of sources of design ideas. There are always limitations to be thought through, such as over-long floats at the back of the work, so work on some infill designs, but take care not to lose the initial pattern in a mist of dots, and explore the balance between background and foreground.

Always take the opportunity to look and study knitwear designs from across the world, particularly traditional stitch patterns. Historically, knitting used a limited palette of colours as there was simply not the variety of dyes available, so effort went into devising clever complex colour combinations which had an elaborate effect, but on closer inspection you can see that only two colours were knitted in a row. Look in particular at traditional Fair Isle yoked sweaters from the Shetland Islands and, for a complete contrast, Scandinavian jackets with their distinctive two-colour patterns. Both are hugely successful timeless designs and a great deal can be learnt from them.

Abstract expressionism

This is the style of abstract art developed in America by people such as Jackson Pollock, Mark Rothko, Barnett Newman and Willem de Kooning in the 1940s and 1950s, and gives the impression of improvised spontaneity whilst also having the effect of being emotional or expressive, underpinned by the idea that art should come from the unconscious mind, so creating simple compositions with large areas of colour intended to produce a contemplative or meditational response. Barnett Newman summed up this movement as follows: 'Instead of making cathedrals out of Christ, man, or "life", we are making it out of ourselves, out of our own feelings'. The philosophy behind abstract expressionism lends itself to designing with colour – the starting point can be from nature, figurative or purely from the mind using the basic elements of a shape and paring them down even further. For example, fine vertical lines may provide a structure on which colour and texture are built up.

Look at how artists use colour and shape. What is it that you like about certain combinations of colour? Look at nature – the sea, the sky, the rocks – we are surrounded by sources. Look at other designers, but don't copy and try not to replicate what they have done as this is not a creative way to work. Of course, an element of their design can be a stimulation or starting point to your design process, and you will grow by developing your own design from that initial inspiration. Merely to make what another person has made is fine for someone who is starting out and learning a technique by copying, but can prove creatively stunting for a more experienced designer-maker. If you are inspired by elements from different sources, then your own creative energy will take over and lead you on to other experiments and ideas and gradually you will build up knowledge and confidence. This will lead on a practical level to a creative and inspirational design archive which you can always refer back to at a later date.

If it is not possible to obtain a specific shade, create your own by working with a few fine different coloured threads to develop your own beautiful subtle-coloured marled yarns. Try oranges and brown together, or lime green with a darker teal green. Some shades are more dominant, so you may need one thread of a dark blue to two of a paler blue – try out different balances of colour. Always keep rigorous notes to refer back to, as you will not remember at a later date what combinations you made to create what effect.

Morvah Oak's fine vertical lines.

If you want a defined pattern, use a smooth-textured yarn, and if a softer edge to the pattern is required, use a hairier yarn. Experiment with silk, cotton and wool – each will have its own lustre and texture and this will all add interest to a piece of work.

Knit up a reasonably sized sample piece, and see how the colour, texture and shapes react together. View the piece in a mirror or take a photograph, and this will show up any flaws or imbalances which need to be rectified. For example, a dominant dark shape can be toned down or an indistinct shape sharpened up by adding a few more carefully placed stitches or colour changes. The swatch or sample piece should be about 100 stitches wide and 100 rows long. I always like to try out a variation of other colourways, normally a minimum of three – a dark, a light and a bright colourful one. As you design and place colours together, be prepared to change these as you knit them together if you feel they are not working proportionally together.

Creating colour swatches

For a dark swatch: create a symphony with threads, such as a simple Fair Isle pattern with browns but adding a coral/chilli shade to highlight and react with the browns, bringing out their

Dark colours montage.

Venice Dark scarf.

Pale colours montage.

Landscape Cardigan with Bridget's carpet inspiration.

Bright colours montage.

Bright and colourful knitting.

colour. Try adding dark purple, as that will always change the colour of brown and intensify it.

For a light swatch: think of pebbles in greys, creams, beige and moss or a sandy beach. Add all the light colours together in your stash. Warm up cool colours with a splash of pink – this works well with greys and pale blues.

For a bright swatch: mix together all the brightest colours – clash blousy pink with emerald green, acid yellow with violet. If you find this difficult, look at the colour circle and it will help.

CONCLUSION

Allow the tools you are using to teach you a particular skill which in turn can push you in a different direction. For example, if the linker is on a loose setting the linking stitches will show through as a bar joining both fabrics together. This can show the integrity of a piece of work, like the hammered surface of a silver bowl; it is proud of how it is made and can stand out even more if a different contrasting colour is used, but there is no room for sloppy workmanship here – if the linking stitches show then they must be evenly picked up and neatly linked together.

A really well-designed garment will need very little change – during the years it will transcend the trends and fashion; tinkering with it will devalue its original intensity and delight.

Linked pieces with stitches showing for decoration.

CHAPTER 4

DESIGNING WITH STRIPES

PAINTING WITH THREAD

Stripes are one of the simplest design motifs to create and use in your designs as all you need to do is draw straight lines and fill the spaces between with a contrasting colour or texture – after all, a stripe is just a band that is a different colour or texture from the surrounding surface. Stripes have been used as a natural design motif by textile designers for millennia, and like any other basic design, it is possible to raise stripes to a fine art.

One way to do this is through sheer complexity – by multiplying, slanting and varying the thickness of the stripes (and scattering some other elements amongst them) it is possible to create designs of tremendous complexity and visual interest. Each band must have a clear identity so when you step back the different colours or textures will start to interact, and as you move further away a field of closely modulated harmonies will open up.

The stripe format is not new or original but it can still look contemporary and exciting. It has been a catalyst for artists and designers such as Bridget Riley, Gene Davis, Kaffe Fassett, Paul Klee, Dan Flavin, Gerhard Richter, Franz Kline, Jasper Johns, Anne Wilson, Daniel Buren, Sherrie Levine and Piet Mondrian, and they have used it in a myriad of ways, so attempting to define which particular influence is foremost is a complex task.

It is possible to have lots of fun experimenting with complicated arrangements of stripes and their width. Broad bands of Fair Isle, tuck stitch or slip stitch can sit next to plain pinstripes. Borders of contrasting colours can be added and placed next to an intricate pattern which produces a flickering effect within the overall pattern. Contrasting a solid block of colour with pinstripes, such as a large dark block juxtaposed with a variety of pinstriped bands, can magnify a dramatic colour choice, and in turn lighten gentler luminous shades.

Treat the knitted work as an artist would a picture and use ratios as a guide, two fifths to three fifths. The Moroccan Jacket design, for example, uses seemingly random small stripes for two fifths and pulsating repeated stripes in related colours for three fifths.

Consider the addition of colour to your work almost like a composer of musical notes except you are composing with threads. Complex knitted stripes can be compared to a piece of music, the stripe being the note, and the colours and groupings of colours the rhythm. I find this analogy helps when designing and it can often give form to an abstract idea. Be open to the design 'twitter', which relates not only to social media and birds in the trees, but also to the pulsating sounds, some sharp, high and low notes. Although you may have decided and made a firm decision as to colour choice, be open-minded and prepared to improvise and make changes. Go against an obvious choice or one you feel safe with; try a substitute and use a complementary shade to stimulate a surprise and tension.

Stripes of every kind.

Having looked at and studied many artists, such as Jasper Johns and his targets and flags, Paul Klee and his blocks of colour and, of course, Bridget Riley and her stripe paintings, each has played a part in inspiring my colour selection.

There are exhaustive possibilities – hard edge, brightly coloured, uniform in width, thin or wide stripes – these can morph into a mesmerizing design of depth and complexity.

Juxtaposed primary colours create an optical vibrancy when viewed from a short distance. Stripes can be clustered into groups of two, three or a dozen or more, and when seen they take on an appearance of bands of colour within other bands of colour, so a layering-up of colours creates a dynamic surface decoration.

The Wall of Colour collection was designed following experimentation with a few ideas and colours and getting a sequence going from, for example, red and green two-row stripes and changing this halfway through the sequence to a four-row stripe in a different shade of green and blue to add interest and surprise. Try combining wider stripes with pinstripes – break it up with a simple uniform stripe by adding clusters of thin stripes at either end of the sequence. Interrupt the rhythm and flow. Open up spaces by including white and/or black, as this will allow the other colours to breathe and give them space.

Do not underestimate the simple line of a stripe; by making minimal changes to width and colour an intricate, complex, rich and luxurious design can be produced. The colour becomes the means for defining how wide or narrow the stripes are, the interval between each, and the choice of colours to use. Experimentation with the interval between the stripes can lead to interesting spatial results.

Stripes can be softened by adding a second or third coloured thread and offsetting colour changes, or kept to a hard edge depending on what is most appropriate for the design.

Colour choice is important and the grouping of certain shades can make for calm intervals in an otherwise frantic pattern, and vice versa, and a rhythmic almost musical effect can also be caused by the introduction of irregular colours and shades of yarn.

Keep evaluating your work and progress and be clear about where you are heading but don't have entrenched ideas as to what your finished result will look like – be flexible and always reflect on the aesthetics of your design as it emerges and be open to improvements. Doggedly ploughing on with one idea can result in an uninteresting piece of work which can ultimately sap your inspiration and motivation, and your enjoyment in the design process can easily evaporate.

Any colour achieves a variable identity when placed next to another colour; for example, black will look much darker when placed next to white or a pastel shade, rather than red. This knowledge is useful when setting up a stripe rhythm so think about making a symphony of colour and linear rhythm.

The landscape is made up of lines and stripes piled one on top of the other. For example, look at a seascape – the horizon line touching the sea, and the sea touching the land. Some of the lines will be heavier, weightier, pressing down on the block of colours below, while others are lighter and airier with a soft colour in between. Imagine these landlines made up with yarn. Ask yourself: What colour do I see in the sky grey, cream or blue? What shades of yarn do I possess that are similar? How can I distinguish between the sea and the sky? Would I need to mix colours together to create the correct shade?

The machine knits in horizontal rows so already you have stripe capacity and this can be made into a block of colour or a thin more directional coloured line. These lines can travel up, down or across, or diagonally left or right. There is a huge difference between horizontal and vertical stripes and how they are perceived. Vertical stripes have an energy while horizontal stripes are more tranquil. But when horizontal and vertical stripes are placed together a tension is created and other stripes can be seen emerging; for example, as seen in a plaid or tartan design. Wide stripes morph into blocks and become less directional than narrower stripes, which appear more nervous and create more energy. When colour is added, the pattern to these stripes creates an infinite variety of ideas to discover and develop.

Striped cardigans and scarves.

Altering the depth of the stripes and including black and white not only sharpens up the other colours but creates a real sense of movement. Adding a diagonal stripe disrupts the flow and a tension is set up with the juxtaposing horizontal and vertical stripes. If the whole design uses diagonal stripes it stimulates movement and appears to travel up, across and over the edge of the work.

On a practical note regarding the grouping of colourful stripes, the eye is kept busy travelling from one section to another and, when deployed in an item of clothing when worn, the movement of the stripes can disguise areas which the wearer would rather remain undetected. Stripes are amazingly versatile and can easily be adapted from a small sample piece of work to a larger scale.

Working in a series of garments can also be beneficial by re-presenting the same design elements but using a different scale and palette.

Squeeze Scarves in Lilac, Red and Green.

SQUEEZE SCARVES

The bright primary colours are inspired by the work of the St Ives artist Terry Frost. The shape at the ends of the scarf depicts the prow and stern of a boat, and the colours in between are all squeezed together. The colours create a movement and bounce back and forth creating a motion, like boats in St Ives harbour on a blustery day.

I have not specified a yarn because this a great scarf for using up odds and ends. The prow and stern shape at the ends are knitted in a wool and the colours between are knitted in various similar weights of cotton and silk and anything else lying around in the colour I wanted.

Method

Using yarn chosen for prow of boat, E wrap cast on 20 sts and k 1 row.
Inc 1 st at each end of every row until 70 sts.
Work stripe pattern running through all Cs, for 6 rows, 8 rows, 10 rows, and rep this row sequence until about 500 rows have been completed.
Using colour you have chosen for stern, reverse shaping as for prow and cast off loosely.

Materials
Finished weight 100g.

Lilac colourway
Cs: green, black, purple, pale blue, yellow, iris, royal blue, dark green, lilac.

Blue colourway
Cs: cornflower, lilac, red, bright blue, apricot, orange, bluebell blue, purple, red, black.

Green colourway
Cs: yellow, turquoise, orange, bright green, ochre, pale green, red.

Measurements
Width 24cm, length 164cm.

Tension
MT 7• 30 sts – 30 rows = 10cm.

Machine
Standard gauge electronic or punchcard.

BAUHAUS SCARVES

The Bauhaus Scarves were made after looking through an archive of *Crafts* magazine written in the 1980s which featured an article describing the woven wall hangings of Anni Albers, and to accompany the article were lots of fascinating colourful images of her work. Anni Albers joined the Bauhaus in 1922 and was one of the leading innovators of twentieth-century modernist abstraction. Committed to uniting the ancient craft of weaving with the language of modern art, her designs used blocks of colour and simple stripes with only a few colours, leading to designs overflowing with movement.

Inspired by this article I originally designed a large blanket throw which consisted of several knitted stripes which were sewn together to make a bed cover. However, I got rather carried away and knitted too many pieces, so a long piece of knitting was going spare, which I realized would make an excellent scarf design. It was this piece that became the first of many scarves using this pattern.

Using only five colours the scarf is made up of 100-row blocks, some plain and some striped. The finished scarf is then machine washed and lightly felted. This is a versatile pattern which can be used in many colour combinations.

Method

Using three random colours tog, E wrap 100 sts. Set RC000.
100 rows, k 10-row stripes using A and B.
100 rows, A.
100 rows, k 10-row stripes using C and D.
100 rows, k 10-row stripes using C and E.
100 rows, C.
100 rows, E.
100 rows, k 10-row stripes using D and A.
100 rows, D.
Using three random colours k 1 row.
K 1 row with 1 colour MT 10 and latch off.
Sew in ends and machine wash on 40°, 800 spin speed, to lightly felt.

Stripes and blocks of colour using Donegal wool make up the Bauhaus Scarves.

Materials

Knoll Yarns Soft Donegal wool is used here: choose five colours which you like and call them A, B, C, D and E. Note that C is the dominant colour.

The quantities for each colour are A 80g; B 40g; C 110g; D 70g; E 60g.

Bright colourway

Cs: A Firefly 5569 (orange), B Brosna 5522 (pink), C O'Byrne 5550 (lime green), D Healy 5551 (lilac), E Gara 5534 (yellow).

Soft grey misty landscape colourway

Cs: A Silver Mist 5580, B Melvin 5523 (khaki), C Vichy 5572 (green-blue), D Swilly 5507 (cream), E Eske 5529 (grey).

Green colourway

Cs: A Ballycastle 5502 (dark green), B Neagh 5506 (forest green), C O'Byrne 5550 (lime green), D Kirwan 5545 (bright green), E Beltra 5528 (green-blue).

Measurements

Width 29cm, length 206cm.

Tension

MT 8• 33 sts – 42 rows = 10cm after felting.

Machine

Standard gauge electronic or punchcard.

Striped Bauhaus Throw using Donegal wool.

BAUHAUS THROW OR SHAWL

Strip knitting creates some interesting results. This throw is comprised of 12 strips each 22 stitches wide and 9 blocks of 60 rows, using 8 colours in all. The template can be adapted to using bright colours, blues, greys and creams and is as versatile as the Bauhaus Scarf pattern. Each colourway will result in a throw of a totally different character.

I have tried to describe the colours used so you can choose another yarn manufacturer; this has proved difficult in some cases as the colours are very subtle with slight changes. The inspiration was a seascape, so this should help!

Materials

Finished weight 600g.

Knoll Soft Donegal wool.

Cs: A Sheelin 5520 (black), B Swilly 5507 (cream), C Duffy 5537 (pale khaki), D Silver Mist 5580 (grey), E Malone 5548 (pale blue), F Eske 5529 (grey), G Finn 5515 (blue), H Greese 5509 (mid-grey).

Measurements

Width 96cm, length 148cm.

Tension

MT 8• 28 sts – 35 rows = 10cm.

Machine

Standard gauge electronic or punchcard.

Stripe chart

RC	1	2	3	4	5	6	7	8	9	10	11	12
540	C	F/B	F/C	G	D/B	C	A/C	A/C	F/E	B	A/B	A/H
480	A/B	A	F	E/H	E	E/H	E	A/C	F	A/F	A	D
420	E/B	B	G	B/H	C	A/G	A/C	A	D/G	A/G	B	A/D
360	D	A	A/B	H	F/E	A	E	C	F	A	D/C	D
300	G	A/B	A/B	B	F/G	B	F/E	F/B	F/G	H	D/C	D/C
240	F/G	D	D	A/B	A	F/C	F	D	A	D/C	F	F
180	E/C	G	F/G	F/G	D/C	A/C	B	A/C	C	A/B	A/B	B
120	A	F/G	F	E	E	E	A/B	A	D/C	C	A	A/C
60	A/B	C	D/C	D/C	A/B	E/F	H	E/F	F/B	F/G	F/G	G

Striped Bauhaus Throw, detail of crochet edging.

Method

For strip 1, E wrap cast on 22 sts using A and k 10 rows.

Change to B, k 10 rows rep stripes to RC60, k 60 rows A and cont to follow chart until all stripes have been worked.

Note: when working striped blocks, wrap colour not being used around end N every 5 rows to prevent loops and pulling up at edge.

Label each strip with its number.

Making up

Sew strips tog, taking care to match stripes across perfectly.

Crochet an edging around the completed throw if required.

Bauhaus Throw/Blanket.

Wall of Colour Jackets.

Striped felted Donegal Wall of Colour Jackets.

WALL OF COLOUR JACKETS

The jackets are saturated with colour; the stripes, bands, pinstripes and lines are used as a catalyst to create a rhythm. The stripe is the vehicle, the conduit, to develop varying combinations of colours, and these change their character depending on which other colour they are set against, and thus the rhythm of the work changes.

The jackets were knitted as a series. The aim was to experiment with colour and have fun with placement and fine lines. Most of them do not have blocks of colour to break up the fine stripes, the only exception being the Moroccan Jacket, which has large blocks of black and navy colours.

The jacket is knitted from front edge to front edge, in the round. The sleeve is a dropped shoulder. The shape is very simple as it is the colours and how they react with each other which is the important issue, and shaping would cut into this and disrupt the coloured stripes. The front is wrapped over and fastened with a pin.

Both the sleeves are knitted with different stripe combinations to add to the chaos of colour!

Always wrap the cut-off threads around the end needle twice; this will give a neater finish and they can be cut off before the finished garment is placed in the washing machine. The resulting felting will then secure them.

Pick various colours which you think will work well together, but be prepared to discount some and add others not originally chosen. Use lots of colours, all the same quality and weight but from several manufacturers, as they will all felt differently and add to the interest. The finished weight was 400g so that will give an idea how much of each colour you will need.

Measurements
These are approximate as it does depend which yarns felt densely and which have a looser feel.
Medium size: approx chest 94cm, armhole 20cm, sleeve length 45cm.
Large size: approx chest 120cm, armhole 25cm, sleeve length 52cm.
In the method below, the large size is the second set of figures, and where there is just one figure then it is the same for both sizes.

Tension
MT 8• 26 sts – 54 rows = 10cm after felting. You will need to check the felted piece carefully.

Machine
Standard gauge electronic or punchcard.

Method

Basic pattern

E wrap cast on 155 sts and k in st st for 80 rows, changing C every 2 rows. RC80.

Shape collar

Cast off 20 sts at R edge.
K 84 (120) rows RC164 (200).

Shape armhole

Cast off 60 sts (70 sts) at R.
Cast on again over the 60 (70) Ns.
K 216 (290) rows RC380(490).

Shape second armhole

Cast off 60 sts (70 sts) at R edge.
Cast on again 60 sts (70 sts).
K 84 (120) rows RC464(610).

Shape collar

Cast on 20 sts at R edge. 155 sts. K 80 rows RC544 (690) and cast off.

Sleeves

Push 60 sts (74 sts) to WP.
Using 3 strands of yarn, E wrap from L to R and R to L.
Using 1 thread yarn, change C every 2 rows; all the while shape sides by inc evenly to 130 sts (150 sts) over 180 (206) rows.
Cast off.

Making up

Join shoulder seams. Join centre back seam of collar and sew collar into position. Set in sleeves and join side seam.

Machine wash at 40°, 800 spin speed. Pull firmly into shape after garment is removed from machine and still damp and malleable. When dry give a firm steam press.

The Wall of Colour Jackets can be made with Knoll Soft Donegal wool for a thicker, outdoor look. Use the same large pattern as above but check the tension when felted. An ideal tension should be 29 sts – 44 rows = 10cm. Adjust the pattern accordingly.

Popsicle Jacket.

Popsicle Jacket

The Popsicle Jacket shows pulses of two shades of green in blocks, with a counterbalance of a pink and lilac block of fine stripes. All the colours in between are bright and clear blue set against yellow, next to brown. Three or four shades of red with a dark blue create quieter areas before bursting forth into primary red and yellow stripes. The image I wanted to create was brash and like a funfair atmosphere.

Firecracker Jacket.

Sky Flight Jacket.

Firecracker Jacket

Imagine a firecracker and the noise and the crack as it explodes – what colours does this bring to mind? Place all the red colours together and add other clashing colours like yellow, apricot, lime green – it is a case where 'anything goes'. Keep returning to the red so that a rhythm is set up and add areas of small blocks of stripes in dark navy and purple, as this will create a contrast. The addition of black and white will always sharpen up the other colours. Break up pulses of red with lime green or yellow. Some of the sections of colour stripes can be repeated with a different set of stripes, and the result will be quite different.

Sky Flight Jacket

Stripes using yellow and pale blue are repeated once and followed by navy and lilac stripes to make the blocks for the Sky Flight Jacket. The stripes are repeated more or less throughout with flashes of lime green added for two rows to ignite a dull pink and khaki which is placed on the right front to juxtapose with the brighter, livelier left front. The joy of all these jackets is that there are no right and wrong colours; some work better together than others, but so much is going on that in the overall result it will normally work well.

Moroccan Jacket

Imagine looking at the awnings on a Moroccan market and the smell of the spices which are evocative of the colours of cinnamon, paprika, cayenne and curry. Earthy stripes, some of four rows are livened up with flashes of bright pink, and large blocks of black and navy make this jacket quicker to work than the other examples. The two sleeves differ, with a small set of stripes repeated from the main part of the jacket and the rest knitted with navy or black.

Yellow Signal Jacket

The inspiration for the colours in this jacket came from looking out over the sea and beyond the harbour and through the mist to the lighthouse flashing its yellow signal. The main stripe colours are shades of blue, green and grey with navy to add contrast and then a large stripe of three shades of yellow to indicate the flashing light. The ochre, apricot and acid yellow colours also help to keep up the rhythm of the colours rather than having a solid block of one colour only.

Moroccan Jacket.

Yellow Signal Jacket.

Yellow Signal Jacket, detail.

Yellow Signal Jacket, detail of cuff braiding.

	Medium	Large
A	70cm	75cm
B	56cm	62cm
C	15cm	15cm
D	21cm	25cm
E	25.5cm	31.5cm
F	16cm	17cm

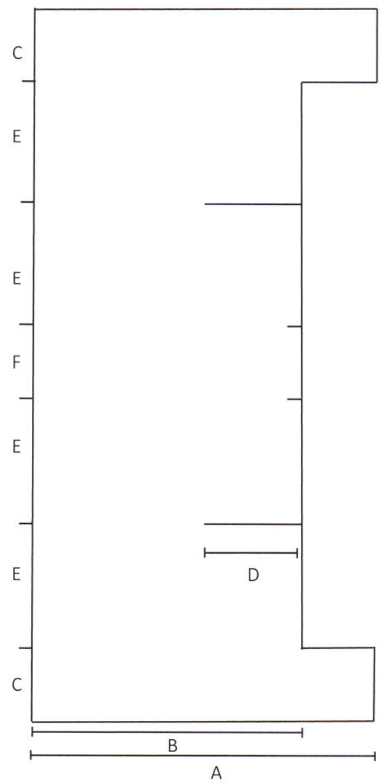

	Medium	Large
G	20cm	21.5cm
H	45cm	52cm
I	38cm	42cm

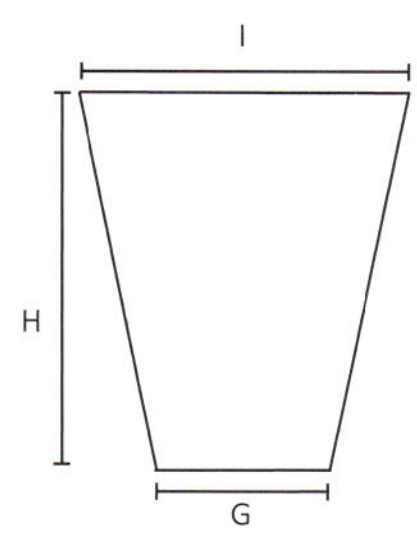

Wall of Colour Jacket schematic.

Donegal Cushions in wool.

Donegal Cushions in wool.

Donegal Cushions, detail of coloured stripes.

DONEGAL WOOL FELTED CUSHIONS

Donegal wool is a wonderful yarn to use as its characteristic is to have small flecks or 'nepps' of other colours embedded within it, and so it adds a richness to any piece of knitting. All the cushions were made using Knoll Soft Donegal in varying shades. Rather than list the ones I have used, the accompanying photographs of the cushions will give an idea of the striping and colour repeats.

The stripes, some of which are two rows and others four, set up a rhythm across the surface. Some colour combinations are repeated several times to create a large area of calm, while other bright colours purposefully clash to create a busy vigorous surface.

Decide what your inspiration is, and draw stripes on a sheet of paper to follow. Alternatively have a design concept in mind and pick up the colours as you go along – this can be a very free way to work; however, you must have a clear idea of what colours you will need to balance others.

The cushions are sewn up and a zip added, and then they are lightly felted in the washing machine at 40°, 800 spin speed. The wool softens up considerably and the colours settle together.

Materials

Various shades of Knoll Soft Donegal or other wool.
Large cushion: 400g wool.
62cm × 42cm feather cushion pad, zip if required.
Small cushion: 200g wool.
36cm × 36cm feather cushion pad, zip if required.

Measurements

Large cushion: 62cm × 42cm.
Small cushion: 36cm × 36cm.

Tension

MT 8 26 sts – 40 rows = 10 cm after felting.

Machine

Standard gauge electronic or punchcard.

More gloriously striped cushions.

Inspiration for the Landscape Coats.

Method

Note: large cushion instructions are in brackets.

Cast on 98 sts (110 sts) using WY, k 1 row with nylon cord and change to MC and start to change C according to your inspiration.

Wrap thread ends around last N to keep edge neat; these can be cut off when work is finished.

Work 140 (265) rows for front and same for back, 280 (530) rows in total.

Pick up cast-on edge, k 1 row MT 10 and latch off.

Sew both rem sides tog, and add a zip if required.

Machine wash at 40°, 800 spin speed.

If you stripe on both sides rather than having one side plain, you can colour the stripes in a different way for a different style.

LANDSCAPE COATS

All the following coats are knitted with two or sometimes three threads together. The joy of this process is that you can build a picture and landscape image. Using many photographs of the landscape and distilling exactly what it is that inspires and delights you is an invigorating way to work.

The basic pattern has little shaping as it is the colours that express all the movement, and drape is required to allow this process to flow. The coat is fastened with a pin at the front.

Bluebell Wood Coat.

Bluebell Wood Coat, detail of colours.

Bluebell Wood Coat

Bluebell Wood uses various deep colours such as dark green, navy blue, black, purple, maroon and a denim blue. The colours depict a dark damp wood and nestled in amongst the trees and undergrowth are bluebells like sapphires lifting the darkness. The balance of colours is mainly dark with a little denim as this colour seems to express the balance I was looking for.

Fire on the Hill Coat

The contrast of bright red, pink and sky blue with navy and turquoise is eye-catching. I chose the colours and then gave the coat a name. The proportions are about half reds and half blues so the overall stripe looks broad but with lots of other colours within it.

Harbour Lights Coat

The boats in the bay at St Ives on a moonlit night were the inspiration for this coat. The reflection in the water of the boats and the neon lights from the café and restaurants around the harbour meant that many colours which were not obvious shades worked well together. Colours used for this were brown, blue, navy, amethyst, bright orange, purple, maroon, olive green, ochre and slate grey. It all makes an unusual combination.

Fire on the Hill Coat.

Fire on the Hill Coat, detail.

Harbour Lights Coat.

Harbour Lights Coat, detail.

Pale Blue Coat.

Nocturne Coat.

Pale Blue Coat

Sea mist and all the pale blues, creams and greys on the yarn shelf made up this coat, with soft and subtle cream, blue, pale green, grey and lilac.

Nocturne Coat

Broad stripes of purple and blue are the overall effect, but the broad stripes are made up of several twelve-row narrower stripes. Colours like teal, navy, iris, turquoise, denim blue and purple are used. A dark night and reflections on the sea were the inspiration.

Pebbles Coat.

Pebbles Coat, detail.

Pebbles Coat

Looking at some photographs I had taken of pebbles, I wanted to use a limited colour palette but not have a washed-out dreary coat, so with the inclusion of black and white the contrast made the other shades of grey sharper and appear to have more character. Four shades of grey were used together with black and white.

Walk Along the Shore Coat.

Walk Along the Shore Coat, detail.

WALK ALONG THE SHORE COAT

This is exactly what the title suggests – take a walk along the shore and note down all the colours that you can see – starting with beige, pink, lilac, green, white, through various shades of blue from grey to bright and so on. Indulge in this lovely exercise for both the body and the creative process, and then go back to the machine and knit up what you have just seen and experienced. The artist Terry Frost once set himself the task to ride around on a bicycle and observe how many shades of yellow he could see in the countryside – the result was in excess of seventy-two.

Decide which colours you are going to use and gather them together. A tip is to put all the thicker colours in one row and all the thin colours in another: this not only separates them but makes it easier to keep track of where you are. Feed them up

Materials
Finished weight 600g.
Choose a thicker yarn and a fine yarn to mix together; for example, 2/16s and 2/28s. A variety of shades is needed to create a garment and colour story. Have an even number of fine yarns and an odd number of thicker yarns as the colours are less likely to repeat together.

Measurements
The sizing is flexible. This sample garment: around chest 128cm, length to shoulder 74cm, sleeve length 43cm.

Tension
MT 8 22 sts – 48 rows = 10cm after machine washing on a wool setting.

Machine
Standard gauge electronic or punchcard.

from the floor, letting the threads run through your fingers to give a tension. Wind the cut ends of threads around the last right-hand needle and cut them off later.

Method

Main part
E wrap cast on 180 sts using a fine and a thick yarn. RC000.
K st st for 12 rows.
COR change fine yarn to another fine C and k further 12 rows.
Change thicker yarn to another thicker C and k 12 rows.
Cont to change Cs every 12 rows, those at R side of machine bed alternating from thick to thin.
Change Cs every 12 rows, 8 times RC96.

Shape collar
Using Cs, cast off 20 sts at R edge. 160 sts remain.
K 108 rows. RC204.

Shape armhole
Cast off 60 sts at R edge, cast on again 60 sts.
K 264 rows. RC468.

Shape second armhole
Cast off 60 sts, cast on 60 sts.
K 108 rows. RC576.

Shape collar
Cast on 20 sts on R edge, k 96 rows, RC672. Cast off loosely.

Sleeves
E wrap cast on 60 sts. Cont to change C as set, inc each end of every 4th row until 126 sts.
Cont to knit without shaping until RC672. Cast off loosely.

Making up
Join shoulders and collar to back. Join centre back seam of collar. Set sleeves in armholes and join sleeve seams.

A	94cm
B	78cm
C	22cm
D	22cm
E	30cm
F	15cm

G	19cm
H	43cm
I	42cm

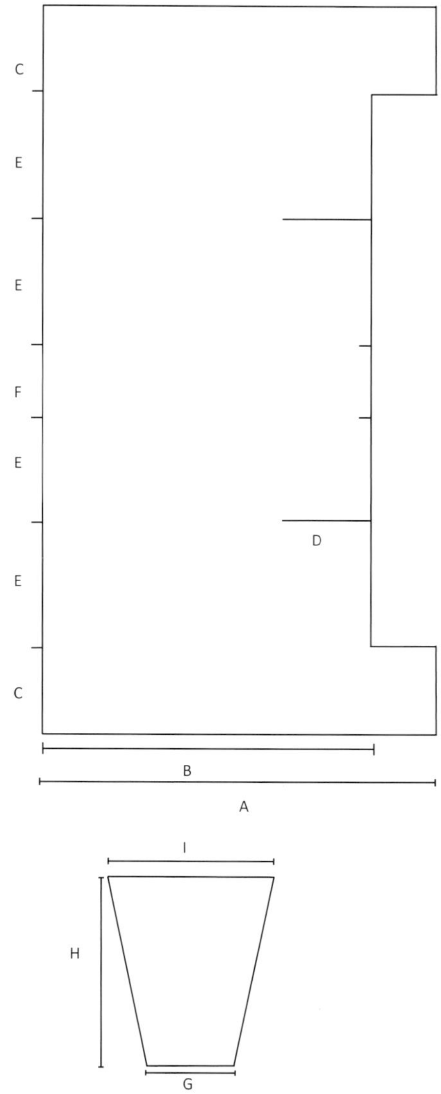

Landscape Coat schematic.

Three shorter Landscape Jackets.

LANDSCAPE JACKETS

A shorter and smaller version of the coat pattern is used for these but all the colour information is the same as previously described.

The first jacket uses greens, yellows and browns in various shades, mixed with a little navy blue. The second, Nocturne, uses the same colours as the coat; however, the interest when knitting these jackets is that each one turns out slightly different as the colours swing to the front of the work and back. The third, pale jacket mixes camel, white, pale pink, vanilla, pale green, ochre and denim blue, all the colours found in a summer flower border. For the final jacket of the four, the clashing yellow and bright emerald green was like a rough sea. Adding other colours to complement, such as bright purple, olive green, turquoise, navy and denim blue, creates an unusual mix of colours.

Method

Follow the Wall of Colour basic pattern instructions, but change colours as described in the Landscape Coat method.

Storm Jacket.

Materials
Finished weight 450g.
As above for Landscape Coat.

Measurements
The sizing is flexible. Finished jacket measurements: around chest 102cm, length to shoulder 54cm, sleeve length 50cm.

Tension
MT 8• 22st × 48 rows = 10cm after machine washing on a wool setting.

Machine
Standard gauge punchcard and electronic.

Hebridean Jackets in Donegal wool and silk.

Large Collar Coat.

Hebridean Jackets

Knoll Soft Donegal wool is mixed with a lightweight silk or wool to make these jackets so they have a more rugged look than the other coats and jackets and work well as an overcoat. The Landscape Coat pattern can be used, but make the length shorter.

The green and brown colours used were Soft Donegal wool in the following colours: O'Byrne 5550, Clare 5530, Gara 5534, O'Farrell 5549, Graney 5525 and Caragh 5513, mixed with a fine wool in bright green, ochre, denim, orange and olive green.

LARGE COLLAR COAT

The coat has a large collar which can either hang loose or be pinned to wrap over.

Materials

Finished coat weight 550g.

The example was knitted using shades of beige, pale green, charcoal and three different shades of grey. The previous coat instructions regarding colour and mixing remain the same.

Measurements

The sizing is flexible. This sample garment: around chest 92cm, length to shoulder 93cm, sleeve length 43cm.

Tension

MT 8• 21 sts × 40 rows = 10 cm after machine washing on a wool setting.

Machine

Standard gauge punchcard and electronic.

Method

E wrap cast on 164 sts using a fine and a thick yarn. RC000 k st st for 10 rows.

COR change fine yarn to another fine C and k further 10 rows.

Change thicker yarn to another thicker C and k 10 rows.

Cont to change Cs every 10 rows, those at R side of machine bed alternating from thick to thin.

Mark for shoulder when RC100, using contrasting thread. Cont to RC180.

Shape armhole

Cast off 60 sts, cast on 60 sts.

K until RC250 and mark with contrasting thread. K to RC290 and mark with thread.

K to RC360.

Shape armhole

Cast off 60 sts. Cast on 60 sts.

K to RC430 and mark with contrasting thread.

K RC540. Cast off loosely.

Sleeves

E wrap cast on 62 sts. Inc each end of every 4th row until 120 sts.

Cont without shaping to row 140 and cast off.

A	93cm
B	31cm
C	30cm
D	19cm
E	17cm
F	30cm
G	43cm
H	56cm
I	90cm
J	14cm

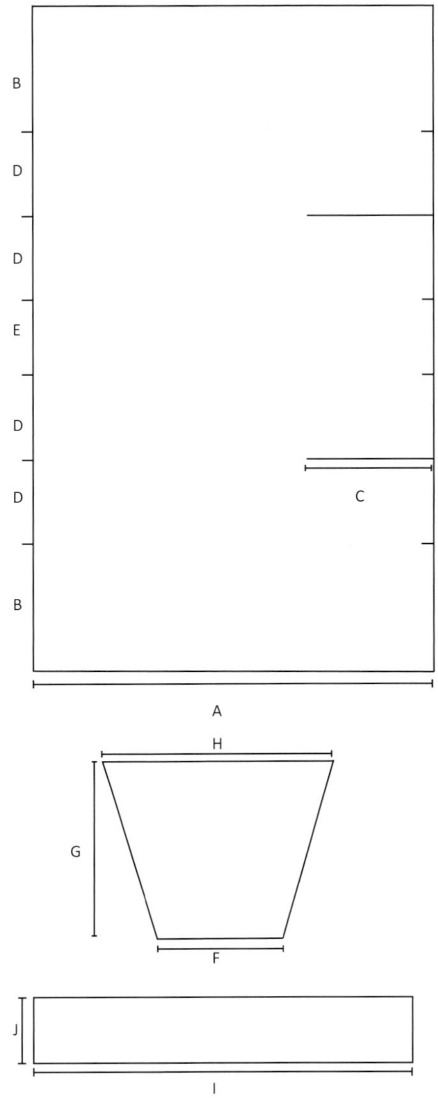

Large Collar Coat schematic.

Collar

Join shoulder seams by matching marking threads.

With wrong side facing, pick up 64 sts from L front edge to shoulder. Pick up 28 sts across back of neck and 64 sts to edge of R front.

K 60 rows.

K I row MT10 and latch off very loosely.

Making up

Set sleeves into armhole and sew down side seam.

Floral Wave Coats in Pale, Purple, Red and Blue.

Floral Wave Coat, Pale colourway.

Inspiration for Pale Floral Wave Coat.

FLORAL WAVE COATS

These garments mix tuck, slip, stocking and Fair Isle stitches.

Fine and thicker yarns of varying colours can create interesting surface texture, and when a complementary stitch pattern is worked into the design it is lifted from the mundane. The coats shown have been worked with a variety of fine yarns such as 2/34s, 2/32s and thicker yarns ranging from 2/28s to 2/8s. Using a rhythm of four rows for each stitch pattern and an alternate hole punched card, a great variety of striped waves can be created.

The surface pattern changes depending which comes first – the slip or tuck stitch. Add in stocking stitch and in one example a Fair Isle stitch pattern and it all becomes very exciting. It is worth remembering that slip stitch narrows the fabric and tuck stitch elongates it. Fair Isle and stocking stitch will also pull the fabric in, so you have a readymade hem with gentle waves and this will be emphasized depending on which yarn is used, thin or thick.

Use an odd number of colours so that the stitch patterns will alternate as you work through the colours.

Place all the colours in a row and work through them, feeding some up through your fingers from the floor.

Pale Floral Wave Coat

This is made in a variety of soft colours in green, cream, pink, blue and brown, and a few stronger colours like teal and denim to create an accent.

Floral Wave Coat, Purple colourway.

Inspiration for Purple Floral Wave Coat.

Purple Floral Wave Coat

This coat involves a variety of colours in black, charcoal, green and blue, and some mid-range colours such as purple and paler blue.

Floral Wave Coat, Red colourway.

Inspiration for Red Floral Wave Coat.

Red Floral Wave Coat

A variety of colours in this coat includes red, purple, ochre, olive green, charcoal, maroon and black.

Floral Wave Coat, Blue colourway.

Inspiration for Blue Floral Wave Coat.

Blue Floral Wave Coat

This coat is predominantly in shades of blue (bright blue, klein blue) but with strong dashes of related colours: purple, teal, pale green and lime green and turquoise.

Method

Note: the wrong side is used as the right side.

Wrap all ends twice around last N on RHS as this will secure edge.

MC E wrap cast on 185 sts and k 2 rows. COR.

Start to patt and follow sequence for which coat is being made. RC000.

K 128 rows.

Materials

Finished weight 550g.

Measurements

The sizing is flexible. Finished measurements: around chest 114cm, length to shoulder 74cm, sleeve length 39cm.

Tension

MT 7• 22 sts – 48 rows = 10 cm after washing.

Machine

Standard gauge electronic or punchcard.

Punchcard stitch pattern

X0X0X0X0X0X0X0

0X0X0X0X0X0X0X

For the Pale, Red and Blue Coats the pattern sequence is 4 rows each of tuck, slip, stocking stitch, tuck, slip repeated.

For the Purple Coat the sequence is 4 rows each of tuck, slip, stocking stitch, Fair Isle, tuck, slip repeated.

Collar shaping

Cast off 20st on RHS.

K 144 rows RC272.

Shape armhole

Cast off 60 sts, cast on 60 sts.

K 323 rows RC595.

Shape second armhole

Cast off 60 sts, cast on 60 sts.

K 144 rows RC739.

Cast on 20 sts on RHS. K 128 rows RC867.

Cast off using 1 added stitch between, for a loose cast-off. (Check back to Chapter 2 under the heading 'Adding an extra stitch for a loose edge'.)

Sleeves

MC E wrap cast on 60 sts. Inc 1 st each end of every 6th row until 114 sts.

K 180 rows. Cast off.

Pale Floral Wave Coat, comparison of right and wrong sides.

Blue Floral Wave Coat: the LH sample was felted and the RH one washed on a 30° wool wash.

A	93cm
B	74cm
C	22cm
D	24cm
E	33cm
F	16cm

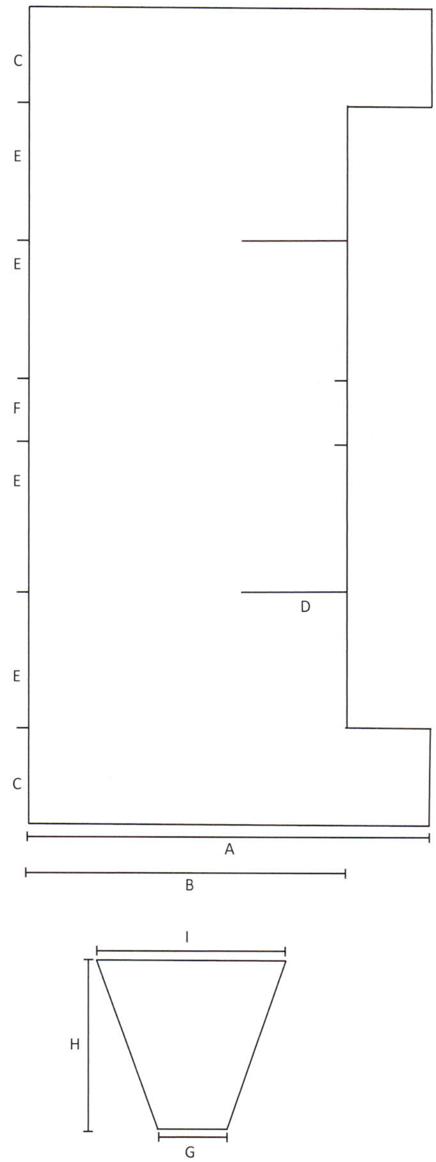

G	22cm
H	39cm
I	45cm

Floral Wave Coat schematic.

Making up

Remember that the wrong side is used as the outside of the garment.

Join shoulder seams. Join centre back seam of collar and sew collar along back of neck. Set in sleeves and sew down side seams. Cut off ends.

Machine wash on wool wash setting.

The original thought was to lightly felt the coats. However, when a sample swatch was tested and washed at 40° the waves of colour became indistinct and the clarity of the colours and stitch pattern was lost, so this idea was abandoned.

Consider if you prefer the less textured knit side, in which case you will need to take this into account when sewing up.

Riley Coat, using dark colours with flashes of bright turquoise and red.

RILEY COAT

The Riley Coat is so called as the stripes and colours are inspired by the striped pictures painted by Bridget Riley. The unstructured style lends itself to a variety of colourways, from dark, soft and subdued to bright and breezy. The versatility of the large collar means that the garment can be turned upside down and the striped collar then becomes a deep bottom border.

The basic method can be used to make a striped collar and sleeves with a plain body, or large 40-row stripes with a slip stitch detail between each large stripe. The length can be altered to make a jacket or coat and the sizing is large, oversize to fit a variety of shapes. The sleeve style is loose with a dropped shoulder.

Materials
MC: any fine 2/20s 2-ply.
Cs: small amounts in as many shades as you want.

Measurements
This sample garment: around chest 177.5cm, length to shoulder 57cm, sleeve seam 37.5cm.

Tension
Approx 28 sts – 36 rows = 10cm over st st MT 7•
The knit side of the garment is the right side.

Machine
Standard gauge electronic or punchcard.

Stitch pattern
XOXOXOXOXO

Method

Main part
E wrap cast on MC 190 sts. K 10 rows. Using any C, k 6 rows sl st*.
Using next C, k 10 rows in st st.
Using next C, k 6 rows in sl st*.
Rep * to * 7 more times.
Using next C, k 10 rows. RC154. Cont in st st.

Shape collar
Using MC, cast off 30 sts at R edge. 160 sts rem. RC000 k 120 rows.

Shape armhole
Cast off 60 sts at R edge, leaving empty Ns in WP.
Cast on over these Ns. Set RC at 000. K 120 rows, place marker at R edge.
K 80 rows, place marker at R edge.
K 120 rows. RC320.

Shape armhole
Cast off 60 sts at R edge, leaving empty Ns in WP. Cast on over 60 Ns. RC000. K 120 rows.

Shape collar
Cast on 30 sts at R edge. 190 sts.
Using any C, k 10 rows st st*.
Rep * to * 8 more times. RC154. Cast off.

Riley Coat, using lighter seaside shades and worn upside-down to show striped border.

Sleeves

E wrap using MC cast on 70 sts at centre of machine. RC000.

Shape sides by inc 1st at each end of the 6th row and then every foll 6th row and, at the same time, k 6 rows.

Using any C, k 6 rows in sl st*. Using C, k 6 rows in st st. Using next C, k 6 rows sl st*.

Rep * to * 3 more times. 90 sts. RC60.

Cont in st st. Using next C, cont to inc on every 6th row from previous inc until 100 sts, RC90.

Cont to inc and at same time, using C, k 6 rows in sl st.

Using next C, k 6 rows st st.

Using next C, k 6 rows sl st. 106 sts. RC108.

Cont in st st, using next C. Cont to inc on every 6th row from previous inc until 120 sts. K 18 rows. RC168.

Using C, k 6 rows in sl st. Using MT+2, k 1 row and cast off using latch tool.

Making up

Join shoulder seams to markers. Join centre back seam of collar and sew collar into position. Join sleeve seams. Set in sleeves.

If you require large stripes after the collar stripes work three 40 rows st st, k 6 rows sl st stripes for each front and eight 40 rows st st, k 6 row sl st stripes for the back.

To make a shorter jacket cast on 170 sts but keep all other shaping the same.

If you use the same style pattern but without the slip stitch pattern and a different configuration of stripes, a very different garment emerges. It is the contrast between a fine 2- or 3-ply wool and a fine cotton or silk stripe which defines this light and easy-to-wear coat.

A	67.75cm
B	57cm
C	30cm
D	22cm
E	33.5cm
F	22cm

G	25cm
H	38cm
I	43cm

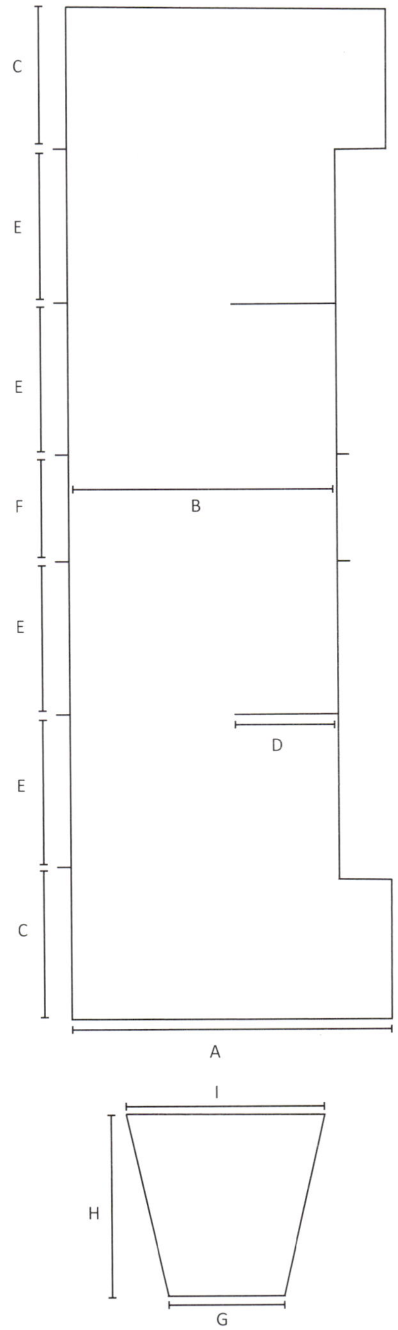

Riley Coat schematic.

Seastripe Coat, Araby colourway.

Materials
Finished weight 230g.
MC: any suitable 2/3-ply wool yarn in various Cs.
Cs: cotton or silk yarn, small amounts in as many Cs as you like.

Measurements
The sizing is flexible. This sample garment: around chest 120cm, length to shoulder 97cm, sleeve seam 37cm.

Tension
28 sts – 36 rows = 10cm measured over st st MT 8.

Machine
Standard gauge electronic or punchcard.

SEASTRIPE COAT

Method

The stripe pattern consists of MC 14 rows. In C1, k 10 rows. Rep 4 times, changing C1 to C2, then to C3 and C4. Rep C changes every 4 striped rows.

Main part
E wrap cast on 200 sts. Work stripe patt for 86 rows.

Shape collar
Cast off 20 sts at R edge. K 82 rows.

Shape armhole
Cast off 60 sts at R edge, leaving empty Ns in WP. Cast on over these Ns.
K 86 rows. Place marker at R edge.
K 48 rows. Place marker at R edge.
K 82 rows.

Shape armhole
Rep as before for armhole.

Shape collar
Cast on 20 sts at R edge. K 82 rows, cast off.

Sleeves
E wrap cast on using three different coloured ends of wool yarn, wrap yarn back again from R to L. Braid cast on.

Using one end, cont in stripe patt, at same time inc 1 st at each end of next row and every foll 4th row until 120st. K 34 rows. Cast off.

Making up
Join shoulder seams to markers. Join centre back of collar and sew collar into position. Join sleeve seams. Set in sleeves.

Machine wash on 30° wool cycle and this will lightly felt the wool stripes to add texture.

Using the same style pattern but using small stripes and a range of alpaca, cashmere and wool, yet another variation can be added.

Blue Seastripe Coat teamed with a large Sapphire Fragments Scarf.

Smaller pin stripes.

Pin stripes detail showing the contrast between fine and thicker yarns.

Three colourways of the Oversize Coat.

OVERSIZE COAT

The idea of using a basic pattern and making a large luxurious coat was too much to resist. This is a warm coat which fits many sizes due to the generous collar and drop shoulder sleeve. The stripes are blocks of colour with a small slip stitch detail between.

The first colourway is based on an oyster shell, using pale pinks, cream, beige and grey. The second recalls the colours of a pheasant, shades of brown and denim blue lifted with bright red stripes. Finally, the Country Blue version uses every shade of blue, from bright to dark, and incorporates some marled yarns with grey and peacock blue combined.

Materials
Finished weight 700g.
Use a variety of colours to suit the theme you are inspired by.

Measurements
The sizing is flexible. Finished size: around chest 142cm, length to shoulder 75cm, sleeve length 40cm.

Tension
MT 8 29 sts – 42 rows = 10cm.

Machine
Standard gauge electronic or punchcard.

Stitch pattern
XOXOXOXO

Method

E wrap C1 cast on 200 sts*. K 12 rows.
With C2, k 2 rows sl st*. Rep * to * 7 more times, changing C each time.

Collar shaping
Cast off 30 sts at beg of row.
2 rows sl st, 40 rows k. Rep ** to ** twice more.

Armhole shaping
Cast off 60 sts, cast on 60 sts.
Rep ** to ** 8 times.

Armhole shaping
Cast off 60 sts, cast on 60 sts.
Rep ** to ** 3 times.

Collar shaping
Cast on 30 sts for collar and rep * to * 8 times, then cast off loosely.

Sleeves
E wrap cast on 35 sts and *k 6 rows, sl st 2 rows*.
Rep * to * 4 more times, at same time inc 1 st at each end of next 3 rows and every foll 3 rows until 130 sts.
K 40 rows, sl st 2 rows, k 6 rows, sl st 2 rows, k 80 rows.
Sl st 2 rows, k 2 rows and cast off.

Making up
As previous coat.

A	88cm
B	75cm
C	21.5cm
D	29cm
E	26cm
F	21cm

G	24cm
H	40cm
I	42cm

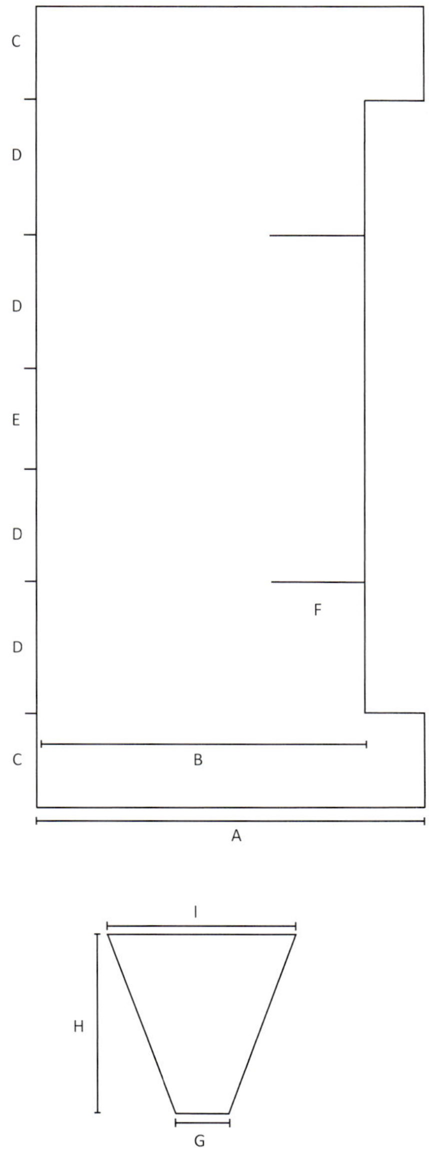

Oversize Coat schematic.

Gold Wave Cardigan with a plain block at the top.

WAVE CARDIGAN AND SCARF

The basic Wave Cardigan lends itself to any yarn, from fine silk to a 4-ply Donegal wool. The boxy drop shoulder and unstructured shape can be easily adapted to be made longer and wider. The top panel can be left plain or the stripes continued. To make the cardigan longer add another 30-row stripe before the armhole shaping. The sleeve can be lengthened by adding a 30-row stripe. Add an extra 10 stitches on each front and 20 stitches for the back to make a large size. All other shaping remains the same.

Materials
Finished weight 240g.
Cs: 2/32s yarn used double in a variety of six Cs: C1, C2, C3, C4, C5, C6.
6 buttons.

Measurements
The sizing is flexible. Around chest 96cm, length back neck to bottom edge 55cm, sleeve length 37cm.

Tension
Approx MT 7• 27 sts – 38 rows = 10cm.

Machine
Standard gauge electronic or punchcard.

Punchcard stitch pattern
0X0X0X0X0X0X0X
The reverse side is the right side of the work.
The slip stitch pattern is worked over 4 rows throughout.

Method

Back

E wrap cast on 140 sts using C1.

C1 6 rows k, C2 4 rows sl st, C3 6 rows k, C4 4 rows sl st, C2 6 rows k, C5 4 rows sl st, C4 6 rows knit, C6 4 rows sl st, C5 10 rows k, C3 4 rows sl st, C6 30 rows k, C4 4 rows sl st, C3 30 rows k, C1 4 rows sl st, C4 30 rows k, C3 4 rows sl st.

At the same time, inc 1 st each end of every 15 rows, 5 times.

Shape armhole

Dec ff 1 st each end of next 10 rows.

Cont with C sequence: C1 k 30 rows, C2 4 rows sl st, C3 k 30 rows, C4 4 rows sl st, C2 k 26 rows.

Shape shoulder

Place into HP 15 sts at each end of every row 4 times and 20 sts once. C5 4 rows sl st, 1 row k, and place onto WY.

Blue Wave Cardigan.

Autumn Wave Cardigan.

Right front

Cast on 70 sts using C1 and rep as for back up to armhole shaping.

Dec 1 st ff at armhole edge every alt row 5 times.

At same time dec on front edge 1 st ff every 4th row until 20 sts remain. Cont working in patt until shoulder shaping.

COR place 15 sts into HP at beg of next row and alt row. K 1 row. Place 20 sts into HP. K all stitches into WP and place shoulder sts from back onto front shoulder sts. K I row MT+2 and latch off.

Rep for L front.

Sleeves

Pick up 140 sts from armhole shaping on front and back pieces. C2 k 1 row, 4 rows sl st.

Dec 1 st at each end of every 3rd row until 60 sts remain. C3 k 30 rows, C4 4 rows sl st, C2 k 30 rows, C5 4 rows sl st, C4 k 30 rows, C6 4 rows sl st, C5 k 10 rows, C3 4 rows sl t, C6 k 6 rows, C2 4 rows sl st, C3 k 6 rows, C1 4 rows sl st, C2 k 6 rows, C3 4 rows sl st, C1 k 6 rows and latch off.

Button band

With reverse side (right side) facing, pick up 40 sts across back of neck and 130 sts down R front.

C3 k 1 row, 4 rows sl st, C5 k 4 rows.

Place buttonholes to line up with first bottom sl st and 3rd, 5th, 6th, 7th and 8th by transferring one st to adjacent N and leaving empty N in WP. K 4 rows, k 1 row MT+2 and latch off.

Rep for other band.

Making up

Sew down side seams and sleeve seams. Join band on shoulder. Sew on buttons.

Gold Wave Cardigan, detail.

A	54cm
B	27cm
C	31cm
D	55cm
E	23cm
F	53.5cm
G	56cm

H	42cm
I	24cm
J	37.5cm

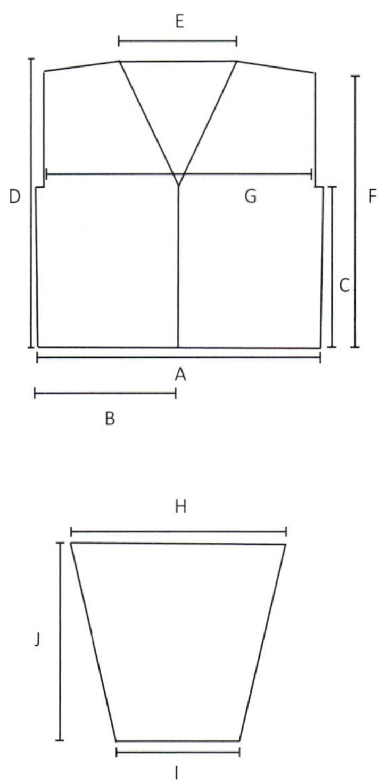

Wave Cardigan schematic.

Blue Wave Scarf.

Wave Scarf

The scarf uses a single thread of the yarn and the stitch pattern above. Repeat the 30-row stripe 14 times and then the bottom border sequence.

Seascape Cardigan, variation.

Seascape Cardigan, detail.

SEASCAPE CARDIGAN

The basic Wave Cardigan pattern can be adapted to make a plain cardigan. The changing of the colours is random within a seascape colour palette; however, at certain rows the same colour coincides to help to keep to the seascape theme. The two fronts, sleeves and back are all different and this cardigan is especially good for practising colour balance. Too much of a strong dark colour such as navy will unbalance the whole garment.

CHAPTER 5

COLOUR

SHAWL WRAP COAT

A light, fine 1-ply 2/32s weight yarn is used to make this coat; rather than stripes throughout, the wrap is knitted in blocks of colour with striped accent on the sleeves. The front collar drapes and wraps around the body, up and over the shoulder making this design an ideal cover-up for evenings out. The detail is on the sleeves and the changes of colour for the collar. The sizing is large as it will drape and swathe around the body.

Materials
Finished weight 700g.
MCs: MC1 navy, MC2 maroon, MC3 purple.
Cs: C1 ochre, C2 orange, C3 red, C4 grey, C5 mustard, C6 black, C7 grey.
The knit side is the right side of the work.

Measurements
The sizing is flexible. Around chest 160 cm, length to shoulder 86cm, sleeve length 29cm.

Tension
MT 7• 29 sts – 42 rows = 10cm.

Machine
Standard gauge electronic or punchcard.

Punchcard stitch pattern
0X0X0X0X0X0X0X

Method

Back

E wrap cast on MC1 160 sts, *k 6 rows. C1 sl st 6 rows, MC1 k 4 rows, C2 sl st 6 rows, MC1 k 2 rows, C3 sl st 6 rows*.
RC000 MC1 cont in st st 280 rows, at same time inc 1st each end of every 20th row, 5 times, 170 sts remain.

Shape armholes

Dec 1 st ff at beg of next 10 rows, 160 sts. Cont st st RC380.
Place marker at each side of centre 50 sts.
Using WY, k a few rows and release from machine.

Right front

MC2 E wrap cast on 65 sts, rep * to * as back panel.
RC000 MC2 cont in st st for 280 rows, at same time on L side edge inc 1st every 20th row, 5 times 75 sts remain.

Shawl Wrap Coat.

Shawl Wrap Coat.

Armhole shaping

COL dec 1st ff at beg of next alt rows, 10 times, at same time dec 1st every 10th row on front edge until 55 sts remain.

Cont in st st until RC380.

With knit side facing, replace 55 sts from R back shoulder onto corresponding Ns. Using MT+2, k 1 row. Latch off.

Left front

Work as for R front, reversing cast on and shaping by reading L for R and R for L.

Sleeves

With knit side facing, pick up 150 sts along armhole edge. C1, k 1 row, sl st 6 rows. RC000, C2 knit 10 rows.

Change C every 6 rows sl st and 10 rows k. At same time dec evenly until 70 sts remain.

Cont with striped sl st and k patt until RC154. Sl st 6 rows, k 2 rows, sl st 6 rows, k 2 rows and latch off.

Collar

MC3 E wrap cast on 120 sts and follow back border patt from * to *.

RC000 cont st st for 850 rows. Rep * to *. K 2 rows. Using MT+2, k 1 row. Cast off with latch tool.

Making up

Attach centre collar by picking up centre sts from back neck and place middle sts of collar onto these sts. MT+2, k 1 row, cast off.

Sew rest of collar in position stretching to fit. Join sides and sleeve seams.

Shawl Wrap Coat, colours changed to soft pale sage and grey.

A	86cm
B	34cm
C	21cm
D	25cm

G	21cm
H	31.5cm
I	48cm

E	200cm
F	61cm

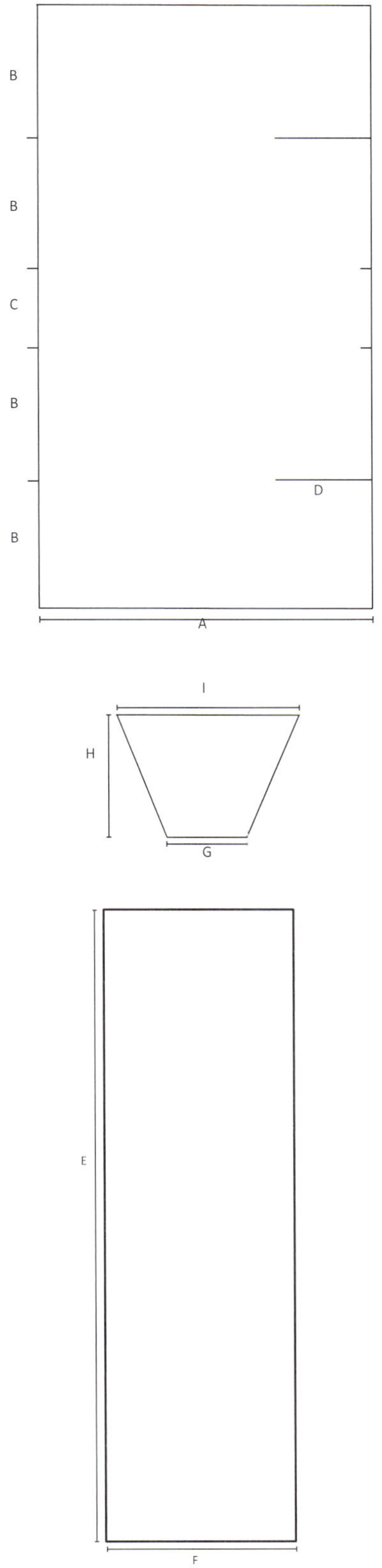

Shawl Wrap Coat schematic.

Tie-Front Cardigans in fuchsia, sea blue and autumn.

Materials

Finished weight 240g.

Cs: use 2/20s 2-ply yarn in various Cs depending on whether the back, fronts and sleeves are to change colour. Two Cs (C1, C2) for the slip stitch border pattern which remains the same throughout.

Measurements

The sizing is flexible. Around chest 108cm, length to shoulder 48cm, sleeve length 43cm.

Tension

Approx MT 6• 26 sts – 43 rows = 10cm.

Machine

Standard gauge electronic or punchcard.

Punchcard stitch pattern

0X0X0X0X

TIE-FRONT CARDIGAN

Blocks of colour can be very effective. These little tie-front cardigans change colour for the back and each front and sleeve, although obviously the back and sleeves can be the same colour. It's a great way to have fun and play with colour combinations.

Method

The purl side of the work is the right side.

Back

MC E wrap cast on 140 sts, k 4 rows, *C1 6 rows sl st, MC k 2 rows, C2 6 rows sl st*. RC000 cont in MC to RC120.

Armhole shaping

FF dec 1 st at beg of next 10 rows, cont to RC220, mark centre 40 sts, knit onto WY.

Right front

MC E wrap cast on 140 sts and k 4 rows, rep * to * as for back, cont in MC. RC000.

Dec 1 st FF on front edge every other row.

RC120.

Shape armhole

Dec 1 st ff on armhole edge at beg of every alt row 5 times.

Cont to dec on front edge until 45 sts remain.

RC220 pick up shoulder sts from back, k 1 row and cast off.

Rep, reversing shaping, for L front.

Sleeves

With p stitch side facing, pick up 130 sts around armhole.

MC k 170 rows, at same time dec 1 st at each end of every 3rd row until 60 sts remain.

Rep bottom border * to * reversing Cs. K 4 rows MC and latch off.

Rep for second sleeve.

Back of neck

Pick up 40 sts left on WY and C1 k 2 rows, C2 6 rows sl st, C1 k 2 rows and latch off.

Making up

Sew in ends around back of neck and sew side seams and sleeve seams together.

Tie-Front Cardigans in brown and sage, purple and lilac.

Tie-Front detail.

A	56cm
B	48cm
C	33cm
D	20.5cm
E	53cm

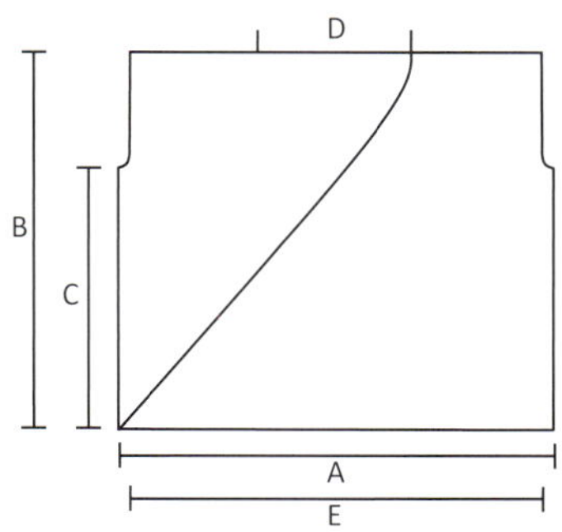

F	22cm
G	43cm
H	47cm

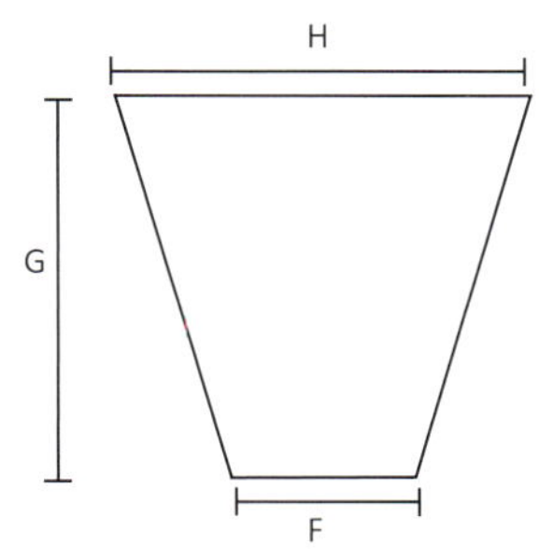

Tie-Front Cardigan schematic.

Sunburst Brown Coat.

Sunburst Coat, short grey variation.

SUNBURST COATS AND JACKETS

The Sunburst Coats and Jackets use the partial knitting technique to create lots of extra rows, thus giving added shape to a garment. The basics are that needles are placed into HP (holding position) and will not knit until they are placed back into WP (working position). Always wrap the yarn around the last needle in HP to prevent a hole. It can be a decorative technique to leave a hole, but not for these coats. The sunburst panels are created by gradually placing more needles into HP and then reversing this process.

When all 200 needles are used a coat can be made and the shaping enhanced by the change of colour for the panels. Knitted in the round, i.e. starting from the front edge and working around the back and finishing at the other front edge, the yarn will naturally pull in gently and mould to the body shape.

A shorter version can be made using the same pattern techniques; the only change is to use fewer stitches for the skirt panels. Various colour combinations can be used and various yarns.

Various yarns can be used, from fine silk to Donegal wool. Some yarn when knitted does tend to drop and add length so you will need to know the characteristics of the yarn you are using to account for this. For example, silk and fine yarn will drop more than a firm Donegal or Shetland yarn.

This coat shows in detail the coloured panels and colour changes. It is knitted using Knoll Donegal wool.

Marine Blue Sunburst Coat.

Materials
Finished weight approx 700g.
Knoll Donegal Soft wool.
MC: Sheridan 5539 (navy).
Cs: C1, C2, C3, etc.: Peacock 5564 (turquoise), Deep Blue 5565 (bright blue), Healy 5551 (purple).
3 buttons.

Measurement
The sizing is flexible. Finished measurements: around chest 95cm, length to shoulder 91cm, sleeve length 54cm.

Tension
MT 7• 20 sts – 39 rows = 10cm.

Machine
Standard gauge electronic or punchcard.

Punchcard stitch pattern
0X0X0X0X

Sunburst Coat, detail of coloured panels.

Method

E wrap cast using MC 190 sts, *k 6 rows, C2 rows sl st*. Rep * to * 5 times, changing C with set of each k and sl st rows.
MC k 34 rows.

Shape collar
COR. Cast off 20 sts.

Left front
MC k 20 rows. **Place 50 sts in HP, change C, k 1 row, place 10 sts into HP, k 1 row, wrap yarn around last N in HP, k 1 row. Place 10 Ns into HP, rep until all Ns are in HP. Place last 10 Ns into HP into WP and gradually place all HP Ns into WP**.
MC k 20 rows.
Rep ** to **.
MC k 20 rows. Rep ** to **. MC k 20 rows.

Armhole shaping
Cast off 60 sts, cast on 60 sts. Rep ** to **.

Back
MC k 20 rows. Cont to rep ** to **. Cont to rep plain rows and HP rows so there are 7 coloured panels in skirt. End with MC k 20 rows.

Shape armhole
Cast off 60 sts, cast on 60 sts. Rep ** to **.

Right front
Follow patt as for L front, ending with MC k 20 rows.

Collar shaping
Cast on 20 sts MC. K 34 rows and rep * to *, ending with 6 k rows. Cast off loosely.

Sleeves
E wrap cast on 50 sts using MC and *k 6 rows. Using C2, k 2 rows sl st.
Rep * to *, changing C each knit and slip row.
MC k 190 rows, at same time inc 1 st each end of every 4th row until 120 sts. Cast off.

Sunburst Coat, detail of sleeve.

Sunburst Coat, detail of front.

A	91cm
B	62cm
C	95cm
D	220cm
E	45cm
F	6.25cm
G	29cm
H	125cm

I	22cm
J	54cm
K	52cm

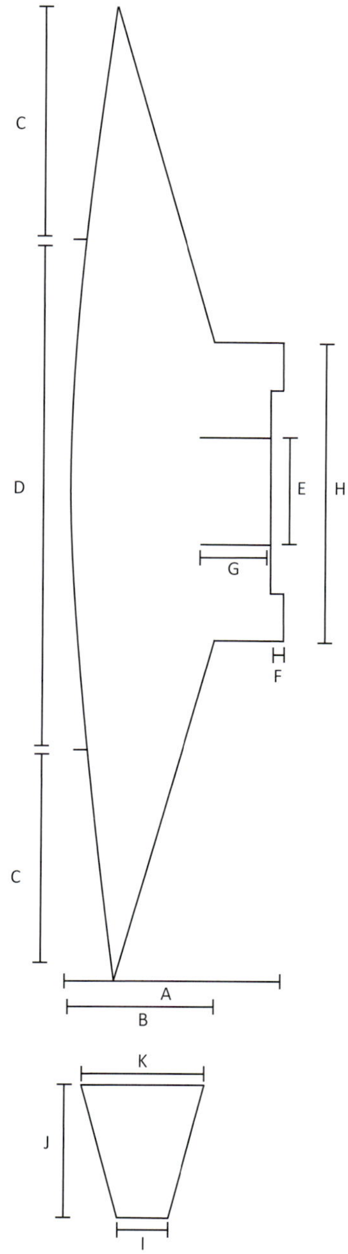

Sunburst Coat schematic.

Making up

Sew shoulder seams tog and back of collar. Gently gather collar onto back of neck and sew in place. Set in sleeves and sew down side seams. Turn back collar and sew down. Sew three loops for buttons, starting with top one level with armhole. Sew on buttons.

Adaptations are very easy with this pattern: more coloured panels can be added by knitting 10 plain rows between the shaped panels, so doubling the number, or you can use different coloured plain rows between the shaped panels.

A very short jacket can be made by placing needles into the HP every two stitches – there are endless variations for you to experiment with using this pattern.

St Mark's Rug, detail.

Frilly-Front Cardigan.

St Mark's Rug.

FRILLY-FRONT CARDIGAN

The Frilly-Front Cardigan is a combination of patterns from other garments. The back and front use the shape as the Honeycomb Cardigan with the bottom border from the Tie-Front Cardigan and the sleeve stitch pattern from the Shawl Wrap Coat. The partial knitting technique is used to make the long frilly border around the bands and neck. It is worked over twenty-five stitches and with three needles at a time, placed into and out of HP with the colour changing after each section has been completed. Make a length long enough to be picked up around the fronts and add the bands afterwards.

Playing around with shapes and patterns can be a risky business, but it is worthwhile as it allows you to expand your repertoire to make some stunning original designs and colourways.

ST MARK'S RUG

This design was inspired by the floor tiles in St Mark's Basilica in Venice, and shows how flat knitting can have a three-dimensional appearance merely through colour choice. It can be made larger, smaller or as a cushion cover so has various possibilities. Various ends of yarn can used up and other colours used completely.

The basic instructions are simple: E wrap cast on 24 sts, k 2 rows, ff dec at each end of every row until no sts are left. Change C halfway through. Make 4 and piece tog.

Using greys, black, white and shades of brown, the rug in the image has 165 squares, with four triangles in each so that there are 660 knitted pieces in total. Notice that the black and white are opposite each other and the two greys are opposite each other.

You can plan this out carefully or take a more random approach.

Yarns in the three primary colours.

Adding colours in between.

THE COLOUR WHEEL

The colour wheel is a tangible way in which to look at hues of colours organized around a circle and illustrates the relationship between the three primary colours (red, yellow and blue), the three secondary colours (orange, green and purple), and the tertiary colours made by mixing a primary colour with a secondary colour. Most colour wheels are based on the three primary colours, three secondary colours and the six tertiary colours, giving a total of twelve main divisions. There are many colour theorists who all have something to say on the subject but it does all get very over-complicated. For our purposes I therefore intend to keep it simple, but be aware that the colour wheel does not include 'non-colours' such as black, white or the many shades of grey.

It is a useful exercise to get out all your colours and place the primary colours separately around a circle, then start to fill the spaces between with all the colours which fit. For example, going in a clockwise direction starting with red, add the orange-red colours, through to orange, yellow, yellowy green, green, blue-green, blue, purple-blue, purple and red- purple. This will help you get to know some of the colours and where they are best placed. Complementary colours are opposite on the circle.

Having completed this exercise, use the colours selected to make a Colour Wheel Cowl. The stitch used is a slip stitch, which has an interesting texture on both sides of the fabric, and the colours are overlapped, which means that the colours blend around the cowl. The length is such that it will sit nicely as a collar around the neck.

Colour Wheel Cowl.

COLOUR WHEEL COWL

Method

Waste cast on 100 sts and start patt sequence as set out in chart.

Cont changing C until approx 372 rows completed or desired length reached, ending with 2 knit rows.

To join cowl, hook up first row knitted; with MT10 k 1 row and latch off loosely.

For a longer cowl which will wrap around twice, work 840 rows.

Materials
Finished weight 80g.
Cs: 31 Cs if you have them or you can repeat the sequence to use small amounts of as many Cs as you have.

Measurements
Width 29cm, length 31.5cm after folding over.

Tension
MT 8 32 sts – 54 rows = 10cm over slip stitch pattern.

Machine
Standard gauge electronic or punchcard.

Punchcard stitch pattern
X000000XX000000XX000000X
000XX000000XX000000XX000

Pattern sequence

Rows	Pattern Setting	Feeder 1
2	Knit	A
*10	Slip	A
2	Knit	A
10	Slip	B
2	Knit	B

Rep *, changing C after every 2 knit rows.

Lightly felted Colour Wheel Cowl.

Colour Wheel Sculpted Scarf

A larger version of this stitch pattern morphs into the sculpted scarf, which is chunky. Use a strong yarn as there is a strain on the plain row stitches after twenty rows slip. The stitch pattern is larger and to help take the strain the one slipped stitch becomes two.

Punchcard stitch pattern
X0000000000XX0000000000X
00000XX0000000000XX00000

Follow the pattern sequence as above but change the 10 rows sl st to 20 rows sl st.

Colour Wheel Sculpted Scarf in slip stitch.

CHAPTER 6

CIRCLES

A circle is a round plain figure whose circumference consists of points equidistant from a fixed point at its centre. The symbol of the circle is used across many cultures, and can represent the moon, the sun, the universe, as well as the cycle of nature. A circle has no beginning and no end. In many cultures it may take on mystical qualities and can be thought to represent the embodiment of the soul or the path of the spiritual journey through the field of consciousness and life. Some circles are seen as a saturated field of colour, others as a halo or nimbus. It is a non-threatening shape, not jagged or rough, but complete and almost other-worldly. It can represent a role model for our lives, as what goes around comes around!

Many designers have been inspired by circles. Look at the work of artist Polly Apfelbaum and her use of rich, active colours which pop and crackle, where some colours absorb other colours, shine, vibrate and lighten up the space around. She shows that dayglo colours do not need to have a synthetic appearance, as atonal and unexpected colours are constantly, and surprisingly, present in nature. With her depictions of suns, targets and moons – call them what you like – she does not represent true circles, but the eye is tricked into seeing them as circles. This deceit lends itself to the tuck stitch circles which can be made by machine, as the shape is the same. Notice also that the centre of every circle is yellow but the surrounding colours and their variety give each circle its own identity.

Polly Apfelbaum's circles.

When thinking about and analysing the circle, consider using colour like a composer uses notes for a musical composition. Each note of colour resonates with the surrounding colours, not just directly with those placed next to each other, but further apart like ripples on a pond. Colours can be repeated, alternated, and groups of colours repeated again. This in turn can stimulate cool areas which pulse through the knitted fabric and resonate with other areas.

Polly Apfelbaum's inspiration, detail.

Variety of knitted circles.

Fragments and Harris Scarves.

Yarn variations for circles inspired by garden flowers.

Consider which colour should be placed at the core and which around the outside; how thick should the halo be? Consider the scale, not just the size of the circle but the weight of the colours within. Circles can be bunched together and almost lose their identity in certain instances, like in the Fragments and Harris Scarves.

Using a thicker yarn on a finer background will create a solid core of colour, as compared with a slip stitch and a crunchy textured circle.

SEA MOON SCARF

The circles depicted in the Sea Moon Scarf were initially placed on a pale or dark background to represent a light shining through the sea mist or a dark night, with a halo diffusing a hard edge.

Some of the circles are in a different size to create movement and to depict the moon waxing and waning.

Sea Moon Scarves in Sand, Nocturne and Mist.

Method

E wrap cast on using MC and follow chart, rep as required.
K approx 700 rows or length required, making sure to finish after a section of k rows. Cast off.

Materials

Finished weight 120g.
Background C approx 70g and small amounts of the moon Cs.

Nocturne colourway

Dark and dramatic using a mix of threads for the background, a black 2/24s mixed with a navy 2/34s. All the other Cs are 2/34s to create a bubble when a tuck stitch is used. The moon Cs include maroon, brown, terracotta and ochre.

Mist colourway

Softer, using greys and blues on a white background; similar thickness yarns were used as the Nocturne Coat. The moon Cs include greys, cream and shades of blue.

Sand colourway

The background was a mix of off-white and ecru, 2/24s and 2/34s. The moon Cs include black, khaki, olive, terracotta, navy and brown.

Measurements

Width 26cm, length 158cm.

Tension

MT 8• 31 sts – 48 rows over 10cm tuck stitch pattern.

Machine

Standard gauge electronic or punchcard.

Punchcard stitch patterns

Moons are in three sizes; note that the circles are offset as this creates interest within the design.
1: 5 sts circle X00000X00000X
2: 7 sts circle 0000X0000000
3: 11 sts circle X00000000000

Pattern sequence

MC = background colour, HC = colour outside circle, or halo, C = colour inside the circle.

Rows	Circle No.	Pattern Setting	Feeder 1
14		Knit	MC
2	2	Tuck	HC
8	2	Tuck	C
2	2	Tuck	HC
14		Knit	MC
2	2	Tuck	HC
8	2	Tuck	C
2	2	Tuck	HC
14		Knit	MC
2	3	Tuck	HC
8	3	Tuck	C
2	3	Tuck	HC
14		Knit	MC
2	1	Tuck	HC
8	1	Tuck	C
2	1	Tuck	HC
14		Knit	MC
2	3	Tuck	HC
8	3	Tuck	C
2	3	Tuck	HC
16		Knit	MC
2	3	Tuck	HC
8	3	Tuck	C
2	3	Tuck	HC
16		Knit	MC
2	1	Tuck	HC
8	1	Tuck	C
2	1	Tuck	HC
14		Knit	MC
2	2	Tuck	HC
8	2	Tuck	C
2	2	Tuck	HC

Sunset Moon Scarves in Black, Cream and Navy.

SUNSET MOON SCARF

The colours in the Sunset Moon design are influenced and inspired by the works of Sonia Delaunay, the co-founder of Orphic Cubism, an art movement which studied geometry and colour in Paris in the early twentieth century. Many of her paintings show various rainbows sweeping and zigzagging across the surface. The challenge was how to distil all the *joie de vivre* into the constraints of the knitting machine. The colours within the circles reflect the work and spirit of Sonia Delaunay and the way in which she married colours together.

Many designers and artists alike work in a series of designs using a common theme, which means that ideas can be pursued, developed and expanded. It also facilitates working on more than one idea at a time, and keeps the mind and imagination open to other ideas of experimentation, and therefore discovery. A great deal can be learnt from failure as well as successful projects, as one idea stimulates another – which is all part of the ongoing, constant journey which can be intense but also exhilarating.

To extend the idea of the Sea Moon design into a series, add yet another colour to the circles, so that each circle now has three colours within it.

The Black colourway uses two threads mixed for the main colour and various bright Sonia Delaunay-influenced shades for the circles. The Cream colourway uses almost the same coloured circles as the Black colourway, but they appear quite different. The Navy colourway mixes black and a dark blue for the main colour – note how this colour appears to ghost around the circles as it lightly distorts the fabric and creates a sense of movement.

The chart for Sea Moon was used but extended to add an extra colour.

HC = halo colour, C1 the first colour, C2 the middle colour.

For example:

Rows	Circle No.	Pattern Setting	Feeder 1
14		Knit	MC
2	3	Tuck	HC
2	3	Tuck	C1
2	3	Tuck	C2
2	3	Tuck	C1
2	3	Tuck	HC
14		Knit	MC

To still further develop the series yet another colour was added to the inner circle.

Summer Sun Scarf in Navy.

Summer Sun Scarf, detail of circles.

Summer Sun Scarf, detail of circles.

SUMMER SUN SCARF

The process of using so many colours in close proximity is not only challenging technically, but also an interesting design exercise. The side stitches next to the circles had to be constantly checked to make sure they had not dropped. The small five-stitch and medium seven-stitch circles were dropped from the design as they were deemed too small. So the eleven-stitch larger circle was used and offset with the second one. The process was time-consuming to begin with but, as always, with practice speed was picked up.

Halzephron Scarves in Yellow and Blue.

Halzephron Scarf, Yellow colourway detail.

Halzephron Scarf, Blue colourway detail.

Halzephron Scarf and Cardigan

Halzephron is a secluded sandy beach in Cornwall, and the colours used in this design reflect the sea and sand, with the intense sun shining and creating patterns of light dancing over the waves of a sapphire blue sea. It was an obvious development to include this idea as one of the many variations on the circle set motif. The colours chosen were all bright and cheerful and the shape of the circle and its size are in harmony: neither dominates. The background threads in Halzephron and the accidental way in which they produce a wavy stripe give the effect of spatial movement by appearing to squeeze the background as the circle expands, and so give the impression of producing a gentle, calm movement.

Scarf materials

Yellow colourway

MC: cream 2/28s mixed with yellow 2/34s.

Cs for circles: 2/32s in purple, lime, turquoise, navy, green, red, orange, denim blue and terracotta.

Blue colourway

MC: cream 2/28s mixed with pale blue 2/34s.

Cs for circles: 2/32s in bright green, ochre, bright pink, denim blue, amethyst, red and orange.

Measurements

Width 36cm, length 80cm.

Tension

MT 8 42 sts – 31 rows = 10cm.

Machine

Standard gauge electronic or punchcard.

Punchcard stitch pattern

Offset 11 sts circles.

X0000000000X0000000000

00000X0000000000X000000

Pattern sequence

MC = main colour, C1 = outside circle colour, C2 = inside circle colour.

Rows	Pattern Setting	Feeder 1
14	Knit	MC
*2	Tuck	C1
8	Tuck	C2
2	Tuck	C1
14	Knit	MC

Rep rows, from * changing circle Cs as you decide.

Scarf method

E wrap cast on using MC and follow chart until approx 670 rows or required length reached, ending with 14 rows MC. Cast off.

Halzephron Cardigan in cashmere and silk.

Cardigan materials

Finished weight approx 240g.

Yellow colourway

MC: cream 2/20s or 2-ply yarn mixed with 2/32s 1-ply yarn in yellow.

Cs for circles: small amounts of 2/32s 1-ply in purple, lime, turquoise, navy, green, red, orange, denim blue and terracotta.

Blue colourway

MC: cream 2/20s or 2-ply yarn mixed with pale blue 2/32s.

Cs for circles: 2/32s in bright green, ochre, bright pink, denim blue, amethyst, red and orange.

Measurements

The sizing is flexible. Finished measurements: chest 116cm, length to shoulder 52cm, sleeve length 39cm.

Tension

MT 8 42 sts – 31 rows = 10cm.

Machine

Standard gauge electronic or punchcard.

Punchcard stitch pattern and sequence

See Halzephron Scarf.

A	58cm
B	52cm
C	30cm
D	49cm
E	20cm

F	44cm
G	20cm
H	39cm

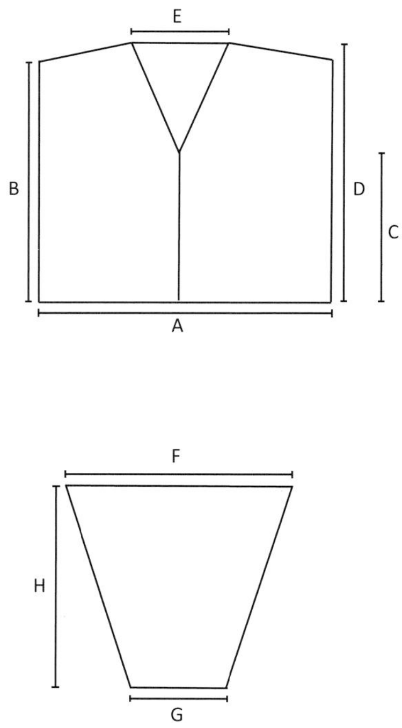

Halzephron Cardigan schematic.

Cardigan method

Back

E wrap cast on 118 sts using two threads of MC and follow patt sequence to RC130.

Mark with contrasting thread for armhole, cont k until RC242.

Shape shoulder

Use HP at R and L sides and bring forward 15 sts 6 times and 7 sts 2 times. Wrap last needle in HP to prevent a hole.

Knit the two shoulders of 52 sts onto WY and do same with central 40 sts.

Right front

MC cast on 72 sts and work to RC130, mark armhole edge with contrasting yarn.

K RC132.

Shape front edge

FF dec every 4th row until 20 sts have been dec.

K RC242, shape shoulder. Bring 15 sts to HP every alt row until 7 sts are L WP. K these stitches and bring all Ns to HP.

Attach back shoulder to front.

With right side facing, pick up sts from R shoulder, remove WY, k l row MT+1 and latch off. The join seam will be on the outside of the top of the shoulder.

Rep for L front reversing all shaping.

Sleeve

With right side of cardigan facing, place edge sts from shoulder seam on centre Ns of machine and pick up 65 sts on front side of armhole to marked thread. Do same on back RC000. 130 sts in total.

Follow patt sequence dec 1 st at each end of every 4th row until 60 sts remain.

K RC186. Cast off.

Rep for second sleeve.

Neckband

With right side facing, pick up 40 sts on WY across back neck and 130 sts down L front. MC k 7 rows, k l row T 10, latch off.

Button band

Pick up 130 sts from R front edge and MC k 4 rows; using circles as guide, place buttonholes by each one, transfer one st to another. Leaving empty N in WP, k 3 rows.

K 1 row T 10 and latch off.

Making up

Sew down sleeve and side seam. Join bands tog on shoulder. Sew on buttons.

TAMBOURINE SCARF

Circles can be placed in large or small stripes and this anchors them to the background, as in the Tambourine design, which contrasts with the previous circles in Sea Moon and Halzephron. If the circles are placed on a single colour or mildly contrasting background they appear to float, expand and breathe.

By increasing the scale of the circle and the rows between them they take on a more circular appearance. Adding a contrasting background enhances this effect. Adding a darker or lighter outline creates a halo. The only constraint is due to the process: you are always working from the outside to the centre.

With Tambourine the bright colours clash and encircle, creating a movement from a static design of a sun or moon.

The Cornish artist Terry Frost expertly used circles to create bright tambourine shapes and halos around circles. American artist Kenneth Noland strove to capture the line between water and the land by painting circles. The Danish artist Poul Gernes also studied circles or, as he calls them, targets. His use of bright vibrant colours confirm that this is a rich seam of inspiration to plunder. The Tambourine design is a distillation of all their ideas and use of colour.

Tambourine Scarves in Orchard, Moon and Forest colourways.

Method

E wrap cast on 80 sts MC1 and follow patt sequence.

Cont changing Cs until approx 650 rows completed or required length reached. Finish after a completed section.

Final row MT 10 and latch off.

Materials

Finished weight 100g.

Similar weight yarns 2/20s about 2-ply.

Orchard colourway

Cs: British fruit colours such as apples, pears, redcurrants, blackberries are all reflected in the colour choice. Use small amounts of various Cs.

Moon colourway

Cs: this uses softer Cs than the vibrant Orchard: blues, pale yellow and greens. Find small amounts of various shades in this range.

Forest colourway

Cs: darker Cs are used to create a contrast with the other colourways. There are autumnal shades of brown, dark green and black but highlights of yellow and white. Use small amounts of various Cs.

Measurements

Width 36cm, length 80cm.

Tension

MT 7• 22 sts – 40 rows = 10cm.

Machine

Standard gauge electronic or punchcard.

Punchcard stitch pattern

X0000000X0000000X0000000

The circles are placed one above the other.

Pattern sequence

Row	Pattern Setting	Feeder 1
12	Knit	MC1
2	Tuck	C1
8	Tuck	C2
2	Tuck	C1
12	Knit	MC1
12	Knit	MC2
2	Tuck	C3
8	Tuck	C4
2	Tuck	C3
12	Knit	MC2

Bubble Scarf, Dark colourway detail.

Bubble Scarf in Blue colourway.

Bubble Scarves in Blue, Cream, Araby and Brown colourways.

BUBBLE SCARF

This was one of the first designs I made, and it came as a breakthrough moment. The contrast between the soft lightly felted cashmere and the fine non-felted background stripes was a revelation. I have used it many times since and it is still a favourite of mine. It has led onto many other developments, not least the Garden Flowers and Cottage Garden series of patterns, which are the next designs in the chapter.

Method

E wrap cast on 80 sts MC1. Follow the pattern sequence. Rep * working through Cs for approx 600 rows or until required length reached, ending with 6 tuck rows, 2 k MC, 2 C rows and latch off.

The colour palette used in the Bubble Scarf variations shown in the picture are:

Bright: navy, yellow, orange, pink, blue, white, emerald green and any other clear bright shades.

Red/Blue: tomato, purple, cherry, emerald green, amethyst, red and navy.

Brown: olive green, beige, putty, ochre, pale yellow, terracotta, orange, rust, brown, dark brown and bright green.

For a variation on the previous pattern, and using the same card, alternate each colour change with a different texture yarn. The bottom border consists of k 6 rows, T 6 rows, rep 5 times. For main length of the scarf and using any C, *k 14 rows, T 6 rows, change C, rep from *, RC approx 450 rows. Then rep bottom border rows.

The width of the scarf is 80 stitches and the length about 500 rows depending on the length you require. If you have used alternate felting and non-felting yarns this will add an extra textural dimension to the finished fabric.

The Cottage Garden and Garden Flowers series are a variation of the Bubble design.

Materials

In each of the scarves you need various Cs of yarn that will lightly felt, such as lambswool, wool and cashmere. Use 2/14s weight 3-ply; for the background Cs use a yarn which is felting-resistant such as fine silk, cotton or linen yarn, 2/34s 1-ply or less. Use as many Cs of each yarn as you can find within the range you are using. See the photographs to help in colour choice.

Blue colourway

MCs: MC1, MC2, MC3, MC4, etc., in non-felting fine yarn in shades of blue.

Cs: C1, C2, C3, C4, etc., in thicker felted yarn in shades of blue and cream.

Cream colourway

MC: fine cream silk.

Cs: C1, C2, C3, C4, etc., in thicker felted yarns in bright primary Cs like Smarties.

Araby colourway

MCs: MC1, MC2, MC3, MC4, etc., in fine non-felting yarn in dark purple, greens, blues and ochre.

Cs: C1, C2, C3, C4, etc., in thicker felted yarns in red, black, navy and green.

Brown colourway

MCs: MC1, MC2, MC3, MC4, etc., in fine non-felting yarn in shades of brown and beige.

Cs: C1, C2, C3, C4, etc., in orange, cream and dark green.

Measurements

Width 36cm, length 80cm.

Tension

Approx T 7• 22 sts – 40 rows = 10cm.

Machine

Standard gauge electronic or punchcard.

Punchcard stitch pattern

X000X000X000X000X000X000

The bubbles are one above the other.

Pattern sequence

Row	Pattern Setting	Feeder 1
2	Knit	C1
2	Knit	MC1
*6	Tuck	C2
10	Knit	MC2

Variation on the Bubble Scarf, with bobbles in Bright, Red/Blue and Brown.

Cottage Garden Scarves in Pansy, Aster and Daisy.

COTTAGE GARDEN SCARF

The Cottage Garden colourways were based on three flowers: the Daisy which is full of pink bright, light colours; the Aster which uses every shade of blue; and the Pansy which uses up darker colours but with bright accents of red and orange. The felted yarn for the circles is Knoll Soft Donegal and the fine yarn a 2/34s industrial silk mix.

Method

E wrap cast on 80 sts C1. Follow the pattern sequence.
Rep from ** for approx 640 rows ending with 10 rows knit.
Rep bottom border, using Punchcard A reversing patt sequence.
Cut off ends.
Machine wash at 40°, 800 spin speed, to felt the Donegal wool.

Materials

Similar amounts of yarn to the Bubble Scarf.

Daisy colourway

MCs: MC1, MC2, MC3, MC4, etc., in pink, turquoise, orange and bright purple.

Cs: C1, C2, C3, C4, etc., in Knoll Soft Donegal in Liscannor 5526 (bright purple), Ahearne 5541 (pink), Brosna 5522 (bright pink), Bann 5505 (pale green), Clare 5530 (orange), Healy 5551 (lilac), Abbert 5524 (red) and Gara 5534 (yellow).

Aster colourway

MCs: MC1, MC2, MC3, MC4, etc., in turquoise, olive, lime, violet and blue.

Cs: C1, C2, C3, C4, etc., in Knoll Soft Donegal in Killala 5536 (grass green), O'Byrne 5550 (lime green), Dariana 5532 (purple), Gara 5534 (yellow), Roe 5527 (dark blue), Beltra 5528 (green-blue), Malone 5548 (pale blue) and Moy 5519 (pale green).

Pansy colourway

MCs: MC1, MC2, MC3, MC4 in ochre, orange, dark green, terracotta and olive.

Cs: C1, C2, C3, etc., in Knoll Soft Donegal in Abbert 5524 (red), Fitzgerald 5538 (wine red), Dingle 5516 (dark red), Beltra 5528 (green-blue), Bantry 5531 (dark purple), Liscannor 5526 (bright purple), Brosna 5522 (bright pink), Roe 5527 (dark blue) and Sheelin 5520 (black).

Measurements

Width 36cm, length 80cm.

Tension

Approx T 7• 22 sts – 40 rows = 10cm.

Machine

Standard gauge electronic or punchcard.

Punchcard stitch pattern

Punchcard A	Punchcard B
X000X000X000X000X000X000	00000X00000X00000X00000X
00X000X000X000X000X000X0	00X00000X00000X00000X000

Pattern sequence

Row	Pattern Setting	Punchcard	Feeder 1
2	Knit		C1
2	Knit		MC1
*6	Tuck	A	C2
2	Knit		MC2
6	Tuck	A offset	C3
2	Knit		MC3
6	Tuck	A offset	C4
Rep * × 4			
**10	Knit		MC
8	Tuck	B	C
10	Knit		MC
8	Tuck	B offset	C

Cottage Garden and Garden Flowers Scarves.

Fragments Scarves in Ruby and Gems colourways.

GARDEN FLOWERS SCARF

This uses the same pattern chart as Tambourine but the background colours are Knoll Soft Donegal and the circles a fine non-felting yarn. The colours used are the same as for Cottage Garden but the effect is thicker and more rugged. Some of the circles have changed size to add interest and a change in texture.

Fragments Scarves in Sapphire and Opal colourways.

FRAGMENTS SCARF

Your imagination is the only boundary to using this tuck stitch pattern to its full extent. It requires copious amounts of colour changing but is well worth the effort. Use a wool yarn for the knit rows and a fine non-felting yarn for the tuck rows. Change the colour of the tuck rows every time and the two knit rows between the tuck rows every eight or nine times, as in the Ruby, Gems and Opal samples. A variation is to continue throughout with the same colour, as shown in the Sapphire sample.

Depending how many colours are used a rhythm is set up while running through the colours and this can be interrupted and changed by the introduction of another colour into the knit rows. How the colours react to other colours is the key to making this scarf bright and cheerful, or calm and sophisticated.

Method

E wrap cast on MC 76 sts, k 1 row.

Changing C as previously described, 6 rows tuck, 2 rows k, rep.

Wrap cut ends of yarn around first N.

Complete approx 700 rows, ending with 2 rows k, and latch off.

Materials
Finished weight 120g.

Ruby colourway
Cs: various shades of red, terracotta, mustard, dark, blue and maroon.

Gems colourway
Cs: bright shades of purple, yellow, blue, turquoise, coral and lime.

Sapphire colourway
Cs: cream for the k rows. Lilac, purple, bright blue, sky and amethyst.

Opal colourway
Cs: cream, beige, brown, pale green, vanilla, grey and putty.

Measurements
Width 34 cm, length 140 cm.

Tension
MT 7• 22 sts and 48 rows = 10 cm.

Machine
Standard gauge electronic or punchcard.

Punchcard stitch pattern

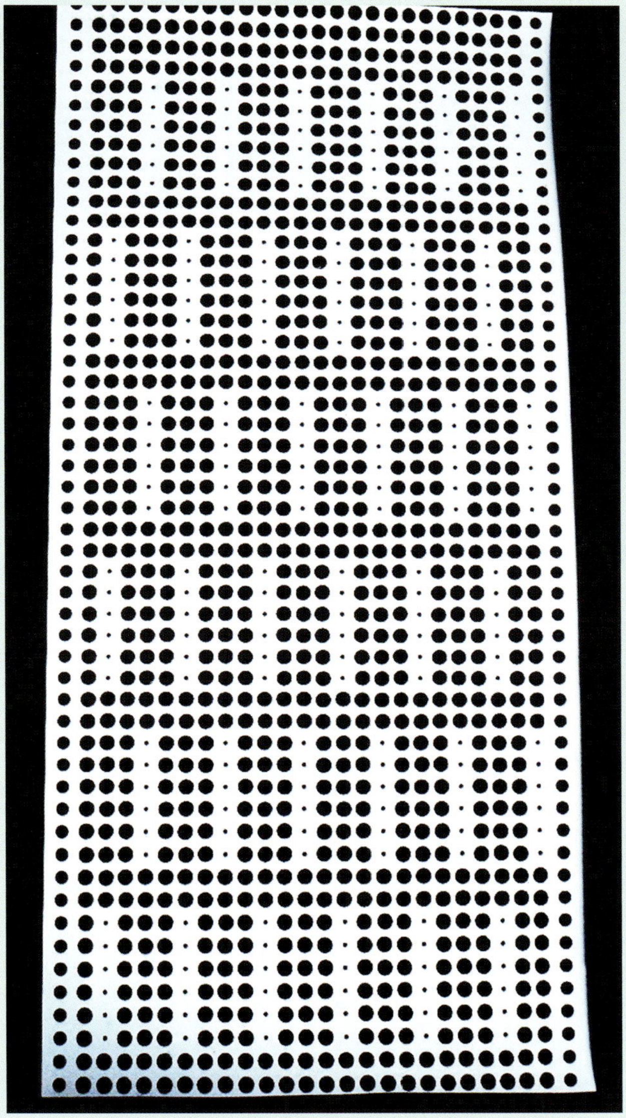

Punchcard stitch pattern for Fragments Scarf.

Dotty Scarves in Blue and Lemon colourways.

DOTTY SCARF

The Dotty samples, with only two colours used, show clearly how the circles move away from each other and have extra knit rows between. It is a gradual process, with the knit rows starting at two, progressing to four, six and eight and then working back to six, four and two. This creates movement on the fabric surface and when many other colours are used the intensity of these comes and goes in waves as the plain rows extend and retract. The circles remain the same size and are created by slip stitch for twelve rows.

Method

Note: from RC84 you will need to lock or reselect the card periodically and make sure you are selecting the correct slip circle.

E wrap cast on MC 60 sts, RC000*. MC k 2 rows.
C 12 rows sl st, rep from * RC84.
** MC k 4 rows, C 12 sl st, rep from ** RC180.
Cont C sequence and sl st rows, change to 6 k rows RC228.
Keep C sequence and sl st rows, change to 8 k rows RC488.
Keep C sequence and sl st rows, change to 6 k rows RC594.
Keep C sequence and sl st rows, change to 4 k rows RC690.
Finally, change to 2 k rows RC776 and cast off.

Materials
Finished weight 100g.
The same thickness of yarn is used throughout – 2/20s 2-ply.
Choose two Cs; the blue sample shows MC chilli, C denim blue (50g of each).

Measurements
Width 36cm, length 70cm.

Tension
Approx MT 7• 22 sts – 40 rows = 10cm.

Machine
Standard gauge electronic or punchcard.

Punchcard stitch pattern

Punchcard stitch pattern for Dotty, Sliding Circles, Florentine and Luskentyre.

Sliding Circles Scarves in Spring Greens, Pale, Dark, Multi and Bright colourways.

SLIDING CIRCLES SCARF

This scarf shows clearly how with the addition of many colours the design becomes more interesting. Each colourway has its own characteristic. The yarn used can include a thicker or finer thread used within the same sample, also feltable and non-feltable yarns.

Choose an odd number of colours as the slip stitch colours will be the knit colours when the sequence is repeated; this makes for a more interesting and vibrant fabric.

Spring Greens colourway
This is bright and fresh, with inspiration sparked by spring flowers and colours which have an energy and clarity.

Pale colourway
Inspired by pebbles and minimal colour contrast, using beige, grey and off-white.

Dark colourway
Here is a palette of dark wood brown, ruby, navy, maroon and dark green, with highlights of black that will sharpen up the dull colours.

Multi colourway
Colours across the spectrum are used and the pattern stopped in places so the circles become mirrored arch shapes. To do this randomly creates interest, and the colours will react together in a different way.

Bright colourway
This is full of joy and has a carnival feel, using every bright colour on the shelf; use these as you want, rather than planning carefully.

If you are using many colours, thread up the ones you can through the yarn brake, place the remaining cones in a row by the side of the machine within reach, and feed them up from the floor, creating tension by running the thread through your fingers. When you have cut off an end place it on top of the cone so it won't get knotted and carried up with the next colour, otherwise it can be very frustrating and time-consuming to unravel.

Follow the instructions for the Dotty sample; however, change colour every time you move from knit to slip.

Luskentyre Scarves in Seaweed and Sea.

Cashmere variations on Luskentyre Scarves.

LUSKENTYRE SCARF

The two colourways of these scarves were inspired by the waves of the sea and glimpsing bright orange seaweed amongst the rocks. The delicate flame gradations of the Bargello embroidery stitch pattern reminded me of the waves tirelessly breaking on the shore, with splashes of winter sun playing on one of the most beautiful beaches in the world at Luskentyre, on the Isle of Harris in the Hebrides. Peering down through a cold but crystal-clear sea I could see fronds of seaweed toing and froing under the waves. The colours were mesmerizing – bright orange, acid yellow, lime green and black-brown – and this scene inspired the Seaweed colourway.

There are an odd number of colours used in this pattern so that, as the pattern is repeated, the small two-row colour becomes a twelve-row colour when repeated. This has the effect of the colours moving and travelling up the work and makes it more interesting. It also evokes the ebb and flow of the waves. Sea uses nine colours while Seaweed uses eleven; the pattern is the same for both but just extend the colour sequence in feeder 1.

Method

E wrap cast on 80 sts using A.

Wrap yarn ends twice around first N; ends can then be cut off when work is completed.

Follow patt sequence as set out in chart and rep from *. Cont until 800 rows have been completed or length required reached.

K last row TD10 and latch off.

The cashmere variations of colourways shown here use bright and light colours, the expression of dark winter days with amethyst, maroon and midnight and, finally, a variety of marbled yarn in many colours which all seem to meld together.

Materials

Finished weight 100g using 2/34s fine 1-ply yarn.

Sea colourway

Cs: A navy, B white, C sky blue, D bright blue, E amethyst, F cream, G pale green, H purple, I lilac.

Seaweed colourway

This colourway has more Cs than Sea; however, the pattern sequence is the same, so just extend the C sequence in feeder 1.

Cs: A navy, B terracotta, C olive green, D dark pink, E ochre, F grey, G cherry red, H purple, I brown, J mid-green, K amethyst.

Measurements

Width 30cm, length 180 cm.

Tension

MT 8 27 sts – 46 rows = 10 cm.

Machine

Standard gauge electronic or punchcard.

Punchcard stitch pattern

Use the same stitch pattern as Sliding Circles.

Pattern sequence

Rows	Pattern Setting	Feeder 1
2	Knit	A
2	Slip	B
10	Slip	C
2	Knit	C
2	Slip	D
*10	Slip	E
2	Knit	E
2	Slip	F
10	Slip	G
2	Knit	G
2	Slip	H
10	Slip	I
2	Knit	I
2	Slip	A
10	Slip	B
2	Knit	B
2	Slip	C
10	Slip	D
2	Knit	D
2	Slip	E
10	Slip	F
2	Knit	F
2	Slip	G
10	Slip	H
2	Knit	H
2	Slip	I
10	Slip	A
2	Knit	A
2	Slip	B
10	Slip	C
2	Knit	C
2	Slip	D

Luskentyre Jacket and Scarf in Sea.

Luskentyre Jacket and Scarf in Seaweed.

LUSKENTYRE JACKET

The yarn used for the scarves is doubled up to make these jackets. Knitted in the round, the slip stitch pattern naturally pulls the fabric together so it gently moulds to the body shape. The fronts and back of the neck have a facing.

Materials
Finished weight 310g.
The yarn used is an industrial count 2/34s which has been doubled.
7 buttons plus 1 spare.

Measurements
The sizing is flexible. Finished measurements: chest 96cm, length to shoulder 64cm, sleeve length 35cm.

Tension
Approx TD 8 24 sts – 54 rows = 10cm over pattern.

Stitch pattern
Follow the same stitch pattern and colour changes as for the scarves above.

Machine
Standard gauge electronic or punchcard.

Method

Fronts and back

E wrap cast on with C 150 sts and k 20 rows for facing. RC000 COR.

Start to work stitch patt and C changes as shown in scarf chart, work to RC138.

Shape armhole

Cast off 60 sts, cast on 60 sts, cont to patt RC448.

A	64cm
B	40.5cm
C	25cm
D	26.5cm
E	7cm

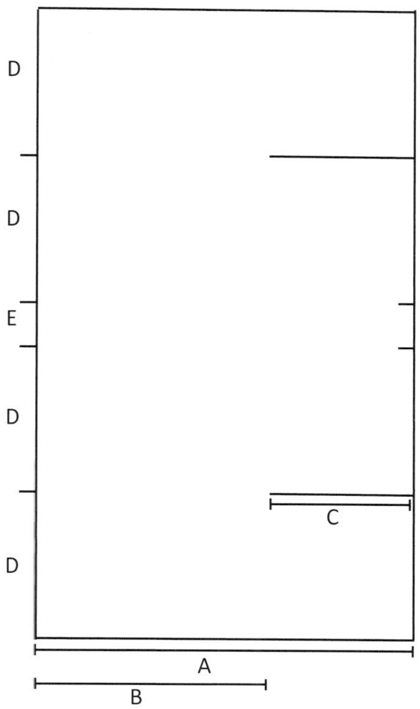

F	23cm
G	35cm
H	48cm

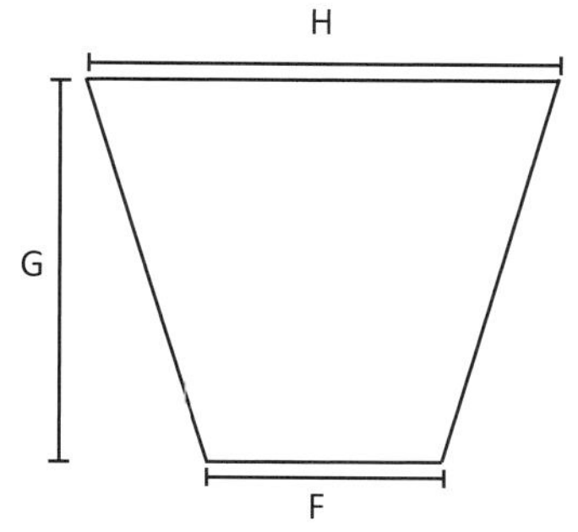

Luskentyre Jacket schematic.

Shape armhole

Cast off 60 sts, cast on 60 sts.

Cont to patt RC580, place 7 buttonholes evenly down front and follow instructions for buttonholes below.

Cont to patt RC588.

Knit 20-row facing, completing buttonholes on relevant rows. Cast off loosely.

Sleeves

Cast on 60 sts using WY. K 12 rows for facing in C RC000.

Start to follow stitch patt. RC13 pick up facing stitches and remove WY.

Cont to work patt, at same time inc 1 st each end of every 3rd row until 130 sts.

Cont to RC184 and cast off.

Back neck facing

With wrong side towards you, pick up 30 sts across centre back neck. K 20 rows and cast off.

Making up

Fold facings to inside of jacket and sew down. Join shoulder seams and sew down back neck facing.

Insert sleeves and sew down side seams.

Note: the hat worn with the Seaweed jacket is an ordinary felt hat with a scarf wound round it.

Buttonholes

Look at the pictures here and follow the instructions; this makes a neat buttonhole and can be used over one stitch or as many as needed.

Step 1: Using contrast yarn, knit the stitches back by hand.

Step 2: Continue to knit the required number of rows.

Step 3: Pick up the stitches between the contrast yarn.

Step 4: Cast off the stitches behind the sinker gate.

Step 5: Lift the cast-off stitches to the front of the sinker gate.

Step 6: Pick up the stitches between the contrast yarn and place on the empty needles, pull out the contrast yarn.

Completed buttonhole.

FLORENTINE SCARF AND COAT

This design really should be called Bargello as it describes the traditional embroidery technique which uses many shades of one colour to produce a flame-like effect. It has been called Florentine work because a set of chairs with embroidered covers was found in the Bargello Palace in Florence.

As with many of these traditional techniques the accurate history is lost in the mists of time, although there is evidence from the Bargello Museum in Florence that a set of seventeenth-century chairs with backs and seats was embroidered with Hungarian Point. Also, in the eighteenth century Queen Maria Teresa of Hungary worked pieces in this style, and these are part of the archive in the Hungarian National Museum.

Florentine Scarf detail.

Materials

Finished weight 100g.

Cs: A in amethyst, B in ochre, C in navy, D in cream, E in rusty red, F in lilac, G in beige, H in dark purple, I in terracotta, J in lemon, K in brown, L in grey, M in pale yellow, N in pale green and O in pale grey.

Measurements

Width 30cm, length 180cm.

Tension

MT 8 27 sts – 52 rows = 10 cm.

Machine

Standard gauge electronic or punchcard.

Punchcard stitch pattern

Use the same card as Sliding Circles.

Pattern sequence

Row	Pattern Setting	Feeder 1
2	Knit	A
2	Knit	B
10	Slip	C
2	Slip	C
2	Knit	D
*10	Slip	E
2	Knit	E
2	Slip	F
10	Slip	G
2	Knit	G
2	Slip	H
10	Slip	I
2	Knit	I
2	Slip	J
10	Slip	K
2	Knit	K
2	Slip	L
10	Slip	F
2	Knit	F
2	Slip	M
10	Slip	B
2	Knit	B
2	Slip	N
10	Slip	A
2	Knit	A
2	Slip	O
10	Slip	M
2	Knit	M
2	Slip	C
10	Slip	L
2	Knit	L
2	Slip	N
10	Slip	C
2	Knit	C
2	Slip	D

Rep from *.

Florentine Coat.

Detail of the larger circles used in the Florentine Coat.

Which came first, Bargello or Hungarian Point, is debatable; however, they are both intricate and exquisite in their use of many shades of one colour, and there is an obvious cross-fertilization of pattern and colour use.

The geometric patterns naturally lend themselves to knitting, and the results include stylized fruits, shells and flowers; they also inspire the use of natural colours.

The colours used for the Florentine Old Gold slip stitch design were chosen to emulate antique shades, sun-bleached but precious textiles, to be found in the dusty corners of an old country house.

Method

E wrap cast on 80 sts using A.

Wrap yarn ends twice around first N; ends can then be cut off when work is completed.

Follow patt sequence as set out in chart and rep from *. Cont until 600 rows have been completed or length required reached, making sure to finish on k 2 rows.

K last row TD10 and latch off.

Florentine in autumn and blue shades.

The versatility of this pattern can be seen here. By doubling up the yarn to make a thicker-quality thread and altering the slip stitch circles to make them eleven stitches across and twelve rows in depth, a bolder pattern emerges.

Follow any of the coat patterns to make a coat, or to make a shorter cardigan version follow the Luskentyre pattern.

Change the yarn and the colours to warm autumn shades or choppy sea blues and keep to the larger eleven-stitch circle and yet other colour combinations emerge.

Honeycomb Scarf in Jolly, Pale and Bright colourways.

Honeycomb Scarf using autumnal colours.

HONEYCOMB SCARF AND CARDIGAN

This uses a versatile stitch which can be employed in many different ways and which lends itself to colour exploration.

The image shows three very different colourways of the Honeycomb Scarf, so called because when the shape of the circle becomes more like a hexagon and when knitted in a piece, it is reminiscent of a honeycomb. The colour changes for the slip stitch hexagon and the background knit rows.

The Jolly colourway uses colours to swing back and forth around the hexagon, creating a halo around it. While the Pale colours are more soft and subdued, the third, Bright, colourway contrasts by using different yarn and bright light colours.

Method

E wrap cast on 70 sts and follow chart for approx 600 rows or required length reached.

Wrap cut ends around first N and cut off when completed. Cast off.

You can achieve an equally colourful scarf by only changing the colours of the slip stitch hexagons. This can in turn be worked into a cardigan. The shape of the cardigan is dropped shoulder with minimal shaping. It drapes from the shoulder and covers the waist, so is flattering for many sizes.

Materials
Finished weight 40g.
Fine yarn in various Cs, 2/28s.
Use an odd number so the knit stitches will become the slip stitches as you run through the Cs, creating interest.

Jolly colourway
Cs: C1, C2, C3, C4 in turquoise, marine blue, tomato, olive green, black, purple, green, ochre, chilli, yellow and grey.

Pale colourway
Cs: C1, C2, C3, C4 in soft green, lemon, cream, pale blue, green, beige, pink, mint green and lilac.

Bright colourway
Cs: C1, C2, C3, C4 in yellow, red, green, blue, orange, pink and pale blue.

Measurements
Width 27cm, length 80cm.

Tension
Approx MT 7• 26 sts – 42 rows = 10cm over pattern.

Machine
Standard gauge electronic or punchcard.

Pattern sequence

Row	Pattern Setting	Feeder 1
2	Knit	C1
10	Slip	C2
2	Knit	C3
10	Slip	C4

Rep through all Cs.

Punchcard stitch pattern

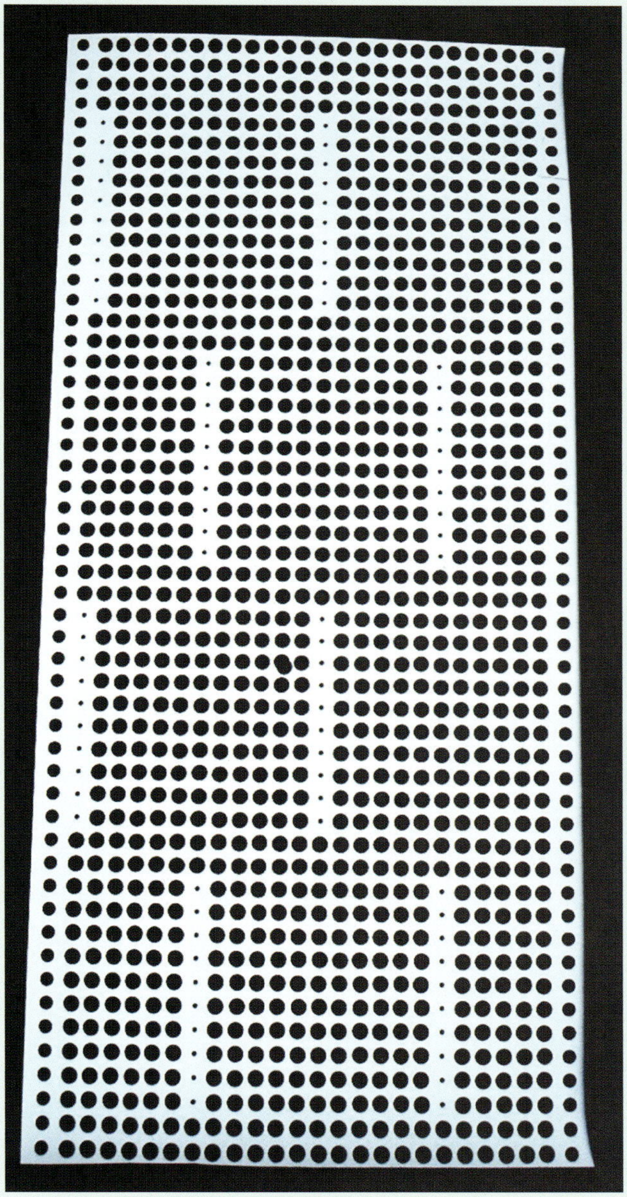

Punchcard stitch pattern for Honeycomb Scarf.

Honeycomb Cardigan using autumnal colours.

Honeycomb Cardigan

Method

Back

E wrap cast on C 140 sts and k 4 rows RC000.

Follow patt sequence.

K 160 rows inc 1st each end of every 20th row, 5 times (150 sts).

Armhole shaping

FF dec 1 st at beg of each row 10 times (140 sts).

Cont to RC258.

Materials

Finished weight 210g.

Choose which colourway you intend to work and gather the yarn together.

7 buttons plus 1 spare.

Measurements

See schematic. The pattern fits several sizes due to its loose fitting and dropped shoulder.

Tension

MT 7• 23 sts – 46 rows = 10 cm.

Machine

Standard gauge electronic or punchcard.

Shape shoulder

At beg of each row place 15 Ns into HP, 15 sts 4 times and 20 sts twice.

This will leave 40 sts for back of neck. Strip off onto WY the back neck, R shoulder and L shoulder.

Right front

E wrap cast on MC 70 sts and k 4 rows RC000.

Follow patt sequence. K 160 rows inc 1 st on RHS edge every 20 rows 5 times (75 sts).

Armhole shaping

FF dec 1 st at RHS on next 10 alt rows (70 sts).

Front shaping dec 1 st on front edge every 4th row until 20 sts are dec in total (50 sts remain).

Cont to RC258.

Shape shoulder

As for back, but do not place onto WY.

Pick up R shoulder stitches from back with RS facing. K 1 row MT+1 and cast off.

Left front

As for R front but reverse all shapings.

Sleeve

With wrong side facing, pick up 65 sts either side of centre (130 sts) from armhole of back and front.

K 2 rows.

RC000. Cont to follow chart and dec 1 st each end every 4th row until 60 sts remain.
Cont RC190 ending with k rows and cast off.

Front bands

Pick up 40 sts from back of neck and 130 sts down L front. MC k 8 rows and cast off loosely.
Pick up 130 sts from R front and k 4 rows. Place 7 buttonholes at even intervals down front by transferring one st to another, leaving the empty Ns in WP. K 4 rows, cast off.
For a shorter length cardigan k 140 rows to armhole and shape shoulder on RC256. All else remains the same as the shorter version.

Honeycomb Storm Cardigan

The Storm cardigan used the same chart stitch pattern but the slipped stitches were tucked to gain a different texture. The colours used were dark green, maroon, dark blue, navy, mid-blue, blue-green, grey, dark brown and purple – the colours of a stormy sea. The cardigan is made as the previous one, working through the colours and a changing background. There is no difference in the measurements between the tucked and slipped versions of this cardigan.

Honeycomb Pebble Cardigan

A smaller five-stitch circle was used for the Pebble cardigan – the slip stitch for eight rows – to create the look of a pebbly beach. The colours used were very restrained: various shades of grey, cream and beige with the background knit rows a pale grey, which was not changed.

A	64cm
B	33.5cm
C	52cm
D	20cm
E	61cm
F	27cm
G	22cm
H	42cm
I	42cm

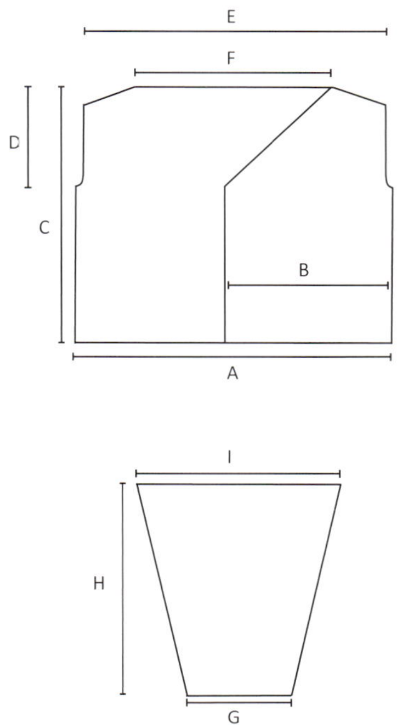

Honeycomb Cardigan schematic.

Honeycomb Pebble Cardigan.

Honeycomb Storm Cardigan.

Honeycomb Autumn Cardigan.

Honeycomb Turquoise Cardigan.

Honeycomb Autumn Cardigan

The background is worked in pale grey and the seven-stitch circles were slipped for eight rows. The autumnal colours can be seen clearly and the overall feel is summery.

Honeycomb Turquoise Cardigan

The background is turquoise and does not change colour; the eleven-stitch circles are tucked with lots of summery colours.

Honeycomb Spring Greens Cardigan.

Variation on the Honeycomb Cardigan.

Honeycomb Spring Greens Cardigan

This one uses the colourway of the scarf described in Sliding Circles; however, there are five-stitch circles which are tucked for eight rows and the background colour changes every two knit rows – the overall result is an intricate and vibrant cardigan.

Note: the button bands also use the tuck stitch to create a different finish. Make sure that the button holes are placed centrally within the pattern for a neat finish.

The unstructured loose-fitting Honeycomb cardigan is a good basic pattern for any stitch. This cardigan uses the amazingly versatile Card 3 from the Silver Reed basic set and slip stitch. This involves changing colour every four rows; in this case the colour sequence is purple, maroon, navy, yellow, dark red and lilac.

Honeycomb Water Scarves in Aqua, Shady and Malachite.

HONEYCOMB WATER SCARF

This design was inspired by a picture by Laura Knight and her interpretation of light playing on the Cornish sea. The colours which she uses are mesmerizing and this was my attempt to capture some of her magic. The Aqua colourway depicts the light on the water and gently lapping waves. The Malachite colourway conveys the rocks under the sea with the water overhead and the Shady is inspired by how the water looks much darker under a cloudy day and with the reflection of trees and leaves on the water.

The background uses a thicker yarn, about 4-ply, for the knit rows, and the tuck stitch circles are a much finer 1-ply yarn. I have given all the colours I have used and tried to describe them so you can choose what shades to use and what yarn spinner. Of course you can use fewer colours and the design will still look good; just keep in mind the sea and wave colours when choosing.

Inspiration for Honeycomb Water Scarf in Shady from the water colours in a river at Blair Atholl.

Method

Bring forward 80 Ns to WP.

Insert punchcard joined into a circle and lock.

E wrap cast on with B and knit 2 rows.

Release card.

Follow patt sequence from * as in chart.

When there are two ends of yarn at row end due to C changeover, wrap these twice around end N. They can then be cut off when the piece is completed and this will save a great deal of time sewing in ends.

Keeping to sequence of Cs as shown, work to about 730 rows or as long as you decide.

Work 2 rows knit, and further 2 k rows in next C sequence yarn and cast off.

Although the original idea came from a seascape, river water can be equally inspirational; here the colour of the water is brown and yellow from the peat it has washed through.

Materials

Finished weight 100g.

Aqua colourway

Cs for knit rows: thicker 4-ply yarn 2/10s: A mint green, B pale grey, C sea green, D mid-grey, E cream, F aqua green, G pale beige.

Cs for tuck stitch rows: finer 1-ply yarn 2/28s: H sky blue, I denim blue, J purple, K turquoise, L white, M violet, N cream, O lilac.

Shady colourway

Cs for knit rows: thicker 4-ply yarn: A brown, B yellow ochre, C orange, D chocolate brown, E yellow, F marmalade, G light brown, H cream.

Cs for tuck stitch rows: finer 1-ply yarn for the tuck stitch rows: I pale green, J dark green, K lilac, L brown, M pale mint green, N terracotta, O lime green, P flamingo pink, Q beige.

Malachite colourway

Cs for knit rows: thicker 4-ply yarn: A marine blue, B bright green, C turquoise, D mint green, E orange, F cream, G pale aqua green.

Cs for tuck stitch rows: finer 1-ply yarn: H sky blue, I pale green, J lilac, K white, L blue, M slate grey, N pale green, O denim blue, P mid forest green, Q violet, R olive green, S yellow ochre.

Measurements

Width 30cm, length 180 cm.

Tension

MT 7• 20 sts – 44 rows = 10cm over tuck stitch pattern.

Machine

Standard gauge electronic or punchcard.

Punchcard stitch pattern

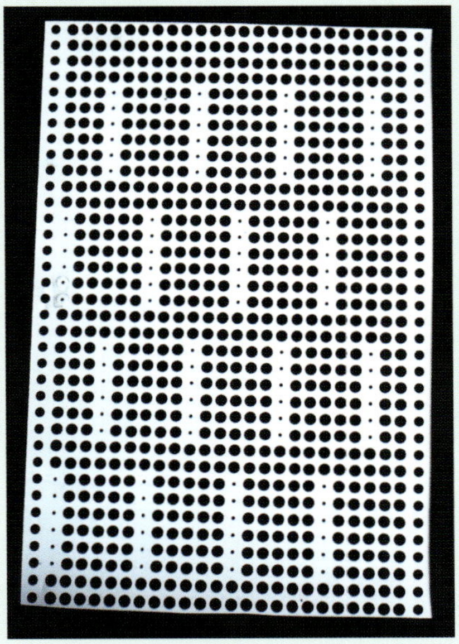

Punchcard stitch pattern for Honeycomb Water Scarf.

Pattern sequence

Rows	Pattern setting	Feeder 1
*2	Knit	A
6	Tuck	H
2	Knit	A
6	Tuck	I
2	Knit	A
6	Tuck	J
2	Knit	A
6	Tuck	K
2	Knit	A
6	Tuck	L
2	Knit	B
6	Tuck	M
2	Knit	B
6	Tuck	N
2	Knit	B
6	Tuck	O
2	Knit	B
6	Tuck	H
2	Knit	B
6	Tuck	I

Rep from * using C for 5 reps of knit rows, while cont C sequence for J, K, L, M, N, etc.

Snow, Moon, Redcurrant and Summer Berry Scarves.

Berry Scarves

The contrast between soft cashmere and finer yarn creates an interesting texture. Snow Berry uses pared-back pale subtle shades, the inspiration being the white snow berries on the hedge in the winter which shine out when all around is shrouded in mist. Moon Berry is also pale in shades, looking at a misty sky with the moon peering out from behind the clouds, almost milky in appearance. Summer Berry is a bright lively colourway reminiscent of hot summer days and soft fruit in abundance, like raspberries, blueberries and the red-, white- and blackcurrants. The Redcurrant colourway uses dark rich colours including amethyst, gold and plum.

Materials

Finished weight: large size 120g, small size 100g.

Snow Berry colourway

Cs for thicker 4-ply yarn which will lightly felt when washed: A beige, B cream.

Cs for finer 1-ply yarn in fine cotton, silk or linen which is resistant to felting when washed: C white, D lilac, E pale mint green, F leaf, G sky blue, H pale vanilla.

Moon Berry colourway

Cs for thicker 4-ply weight of yarn which will lightly felt: A lilac, B grey.

Cs for finer 1-ply which is resistant to felting: C white, D sky blue, E pale grey, F mauve, G pale green.

Summer Berry colourway

Cs for thicker 4-ply yarn in berry Cs which will lightly felt: A dark red, B lilac, C orange, D yellow, E apricot, F flame red, G cerise. Also leaf Cs same weight: H emerald green, I light green, J mid-green.

Cs for finer 1-ply yarn which is resistant to felting: K in bright blue, L in pale blue, M mid-blue, N green, O pale green.

Redcurrant colourway

Cs for thicker 4-ply yarn which will lightly felt: A dark red, B maroon, C plum, D cerise, E flame red.

Cs for leaf motifs: F gold, G dark green, H lime green.

Cs for finer 1-ply yarn resistant to felting: I navy, J dark green, K maroon, L slate grey, M amethyst.

Measurements

Large: width 38cm, length 192cm.

Small: width 30cm, length 170cm.

Tension

MT 7 33 sts – 38 rows = 10cm.

Punchcard stitch pattern

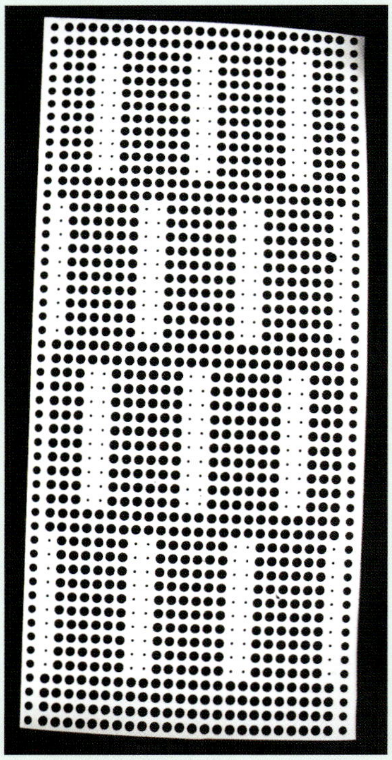

Punchcard stitch pattern for Snow, Moon and Summer Berry and Redcurrant Scarves.

Pattern sequences

Snow Berry colourway

E wrap cast on with B, then follow patt sequence.

Rows	Pattern Setting	Feeder 1
2	Knit	A
*10	Slip	C
2	Knit	C
10	Slip	D
2	Knit	D
8	Slip	B
2	Slip	A
2	Knit	A
10	Slip	E
2	Knit	E
10	Slip	F
2	Knit	F
8	Slip	B
2	Slip	A
2	Knit	A
10	Slip	G
2	Knit	G
10	Slip	H
2	Knit	H
8	Slip	B
2	Slip	A
2	Knit	A

Rep this C sequence from * until required length reached. Cast off.

Moon Berry colourway

E wrap cast on with A, then follow patt sequence.

Rows	Pattern Setting	Feeder 1
2	Knit	B
*10	Slip	C
2	Knit	C
10	Slip	D
2	Knit	D
8	Slip	A
2	Slip	B
2	Knit	B
10	Slip	E
2	Knit	E
10	Slip	F
2	Knit	F
8	Slip	A
2	Slip	B
2	Knit	B
10	Slip	G
2	Knit	G
10	Slip	C
2	Knit	C
8	Slip	A
2	Slip	B
2	Knit	B
10	Slip	D
2	Knit	D
10	Slip	E
2	Knit	E
8	Slip	A
2	Slip	B
2	Knit	B
10	Slip	F
2	Knit	F
10	Slip	G
2	Knit	G
8	Slip	A
2	Slip	B
2	Knit	B

Rep from *.

Summer Berry colourway

E wrap cast on in A. K 2 rows with G, then follow this chart.

Rows	Pattern Selection	Feeder 1
10	Slip	K
2	Knit	K
10	Slip	L
2	Knit	L
8	Slip	A
2	Slip	H
2	Knit	H
10	Slip	M
2	Knit	M
10	Slip	N
2	Knit	N
8	Slip	B
2	Slip	I
2	Knit	I
10	Slip	O
2	Knit	O
10	Slip	K
2	Knit	K
8	Slip	C
2	Slip	J
2	Knit	J
10	Slip	L
2	Knit	L
10	Slip	M
2	Knit	M
8	Slip	D
2	Slip	H
2	Knit	H

Cont in patt sequence using combination of 10 sl st and 2 k rows in order K, L, M, N, O.

Using leaf Cs, use combination of 2 sl st and 2 k rows in order H, I, J.

For 8-row reps, use A, B, C, D, E, F, G.

Redcurrant colourway

E wrap cast on in A, k 2 rows.

Rows	Pattern Setting	Feeder 1
10	Slip	I
2	Knit	I
10	Slip	J
2	Knit	J
8	Slip	A
2	Slip	F
2	Knit	F
10	Slip	K
2	Knit	K
10	Slip	L
2	Knit	L
8	Slip	B
2	Slip	G
2	Knit	G
10	Slip	M
2	Knit	M
10	Slip	I
2	Knit	I
8	Slip	C
2	Slip	H
2	Knit	H
10	Slip	J
2	Knit	J
10	Slip	K
2	Knit	K
8	Slip	D
2	Slip	F
2	Knit	F

Cont in patt sequence using I, J, K, L, M for the 12-row reps.

For the 4 leaf rows use F, G, H.

For the 8-row berry reps use A, B, C, D, E.

Method

Small

E wrap cast on 76 sts as shown in appropriate C sequence.

Work through chart until 760 rows completed.

K 2 rows of last C in sequence and latch off.

Large

E wrap cast 100 sts as shown in appropriate C sequence.

Work through chart until 890 rows completed.

K final 2 rows and latch off.

Snow Berry Scarf using cashmere and silk.

Moon Berry Scarf and pebbles.

Rosebud Scarves in Dark, Green and Blue silk yarn.

Pale Rose Garden Scarf.

ROSEBUD SCARF

The Rosebud pattern is the Berry pattern turned upside down, so it makes sense that it should follow on here. The Rose Garden pattern is a larger version of this.

Method

Dark Rosebud colourway in fine silk

E wrap cast on 80 sts using F, k 2 rows.

Follow patt sequence as set out.

Cont to work through patt sequence for 700 rows ending with 3 sequences of background Cs.

K 2 rows in next dark background C.

K 2 rows F and cast off with latch tool.

Blue Rosebud colourway in fine silk

E wrap cast on 80 sts using D, k 2 rows.

Follow patt sequence as set out.

Cont to work through patt sequence for 700 rows ending with 3 sequences of background Cs.

K 2 rows in next background C.

K 2 rows in next background C and cast off with latch tool.

The Pale, Blue and Brown Rosebud Scarves in the photos have all been knitted with cashmere/wool ranging in weight from 2/10s 4-ply to 2/20s 2-ply and a finished weight of 120g. They measure 150cm long and 28cm wide with a tension of approximately MT 8 and 34 sts – 38 rows = 10cm. They are heavier in weight and produce a warm winter fabric. Follow the above pattern but knit about an extra 50 rows.

Materials

Finished weight 100g.

Note: lightweight fine yarn was used; however, the design works just as well in a thicker yarn.

Dark Rosebud colourway

Background Cs: A amethyst, B dark red, C brown, D dark green, E slate grey.

Rosebud Cs: F bright pink, G violet, I orange, J maroon.

Leaf Cs: H bright green, K leaf green.

Blue Rosebud colourway

Background Cs: A sky blue, B turquoise blue, C mid-blue, D ineen-blue, E inright blue.

Rosebud Cs: F bright pink, G violet, H orange, I maroon.

Leaf Cs: J bright green, K leaf green.

Measurements

Width 30cm, length 170cm.

Tension

MT 7 33 sts – 38 rows = 10cm.

Machine

Standard gauge electronic or punchcard.

Punchcard stitch pattern

The same punchcard stitch is used as for the *Berry* designs.

Rosebud Scarf in Pale cashmere.

Rosebud Scarf in Blue cashmere.

Rosebud Scarf in Brown cashmere.

Pattern sequences

Dark Rosebud colourway

Rows	Pattern Setting	Feeder 1
2	Knit	A
*10	Slip	B
2	Knit	B
10	Slip	C
2	Knit	C
10	Slip	D
2	Knit	D
4	Slip	F
4	Slip	G
2	Slip	H
2	Knit	H
10	Slip	E
2	Knit	E
10	Slip	A
2	Knit	A
10	Slip	B
2	Knit	E
4	Slip	I
4	Slip	J
2	Slip	K
2	Knit	K
10	Slip	C
2	Knit	C
10	Slip	D
2	Knit	D
10	Slip	E
2	Knit	E
4	Slip	F
4	Slip	G
2	Slip	H
2	Knit	H

Rep from *.

Blue Rosebud colourway

Rows	Pattern Setting	Feeder 1
2	Slip	E
*10	Slip	A
2	Knit	A
10	Slip	B
2	Knit	B
10	Slip	C
2	Knit	C
4	Slip	F
4	Slip	G
2	Slip	J
2	Knit	J
10	Slip	D
2	Knit	D
10	Slip	E
2	Knit	E
10	Slip	A
2	Knit	A
4	Slip	H
4	Slip	I
2	Slip	K
2	Knit	K
10	Slip	B
2	Knit	B
10	Slip	C
2	Knit	C
10	Slip	D
2	Knit	D
4	Slip	F
4	Slip	G
2	Slip	J
2	Knit	J

Rep from *.

Dark Rose Garden Scarf knitted in wool.

Rose Garden in blue, grey and dark shades using a silk mix yarn.

ROSE GARDEN SCARF

The Rose Garden design is a larger version of the Rosebud and uses a bigger bolder circle. The background colours which are chosen will need to be subtle so that the roses and leaves show up.

Method

E wrap cast on MC1 118 sts and follow chart RC000.
Cont until RC1034 ending with one MC sequence. K 2 rows and cast off.
The sample has been lightly felted in a washing machine at 40° wash, 800 spin speed.

A finer yarn has been used for the Rose Garden Scarves pictured in blue, grey and dark – a silk mix yarn 2/20s 2-ply. There are many ways in which this pattern can be developed. Add two or three extra colours to the roses, or change the colour of the knit rows to add a stripe. Some will work and for others the rose pattern will disappear and become a melange of colour chaos, which is not necessarily a bad outcome as the design will have moved on and become a more abstract colour exercise. Nothing is ever wasted.

Materials

Finished weight 200g.

The dark version uses background Cs of black and blue (MC), while the roses are bright red (C1) and flame (C2) with lime green leaves (C3). You can add an extra background C between the roses; however, they will then appear in a line, one above the other, and I prefer to offset them. Use other Cs for the roses; they must be bright to stand out.

Measurements

Width 35cm, length 180cm.

Tension

MT 8.

Machine

Standard gauge electronic or punchcard.

Pattern sequence

Row	Pattern Setting	Feeder 1
2	Knit	MC1
*10	Slip	MC2
2	Knit	MC2
4	Slip	C1
4	Slip	C2
2	Slip	C3
2	Knit	C3
10	Slip	MC1
2	Knit	MC1

Rep from *.

Punchcard stitch pattern

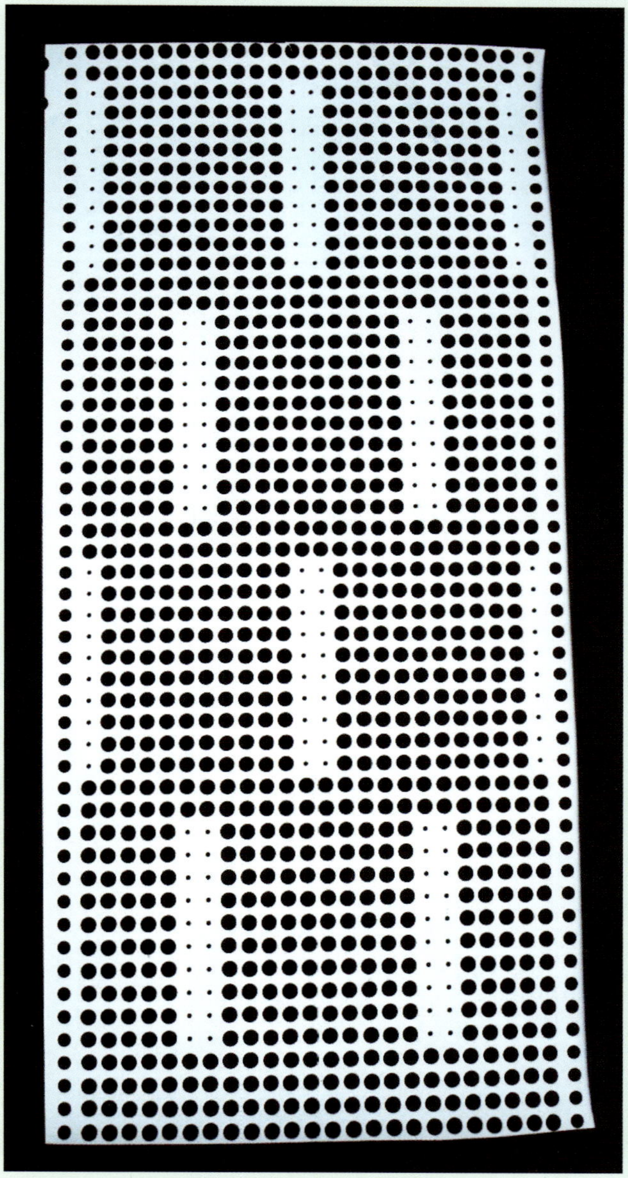

Punchcard stitch pattern for Rose Garden Scarf.

Monet Scarves in Green, Red and Pink.

MONET SCARF

Having been utterly mesmerized by the wonderful texture and colours in the series of lily pond pictures painted by Claude Monet, I wanted to try and capture some of their magic in this design. The light reflected on the water had been an inspiration for many years, but the difference of light on seawater and on inland pond water proved to be a challenge. The three colourways are the results of this inspiration, using approximately 10cm of the original paintings.

Method

For all colourways, E wrap cast on 80 sts using C, k 2 rows.

Follow patt sequence as set out for rows and pattern setting, working through Cs A–J for Green, A–G for Pink and A–K for Red.

Cont to rep C sequence until approx 700 rows completed or desired length reached.

Work 2 k rows last row TD10 and latch off.

Materials
Finished weight 60g.
Fine yarn 2/32s 1-ply.

Green colourway
Cs: A amethyst, B dark green, C midgreen, D olive green, E pale green, F lilac, G moss green, H lime green, I beige, J dark dull pink.

Red colourway
Cs: A orange, B dark maroon, C dull pink, D bright blue, E turquoise, F lilac, G olive green, H lime green, I mid-blue, J dark green, K amethyst.

Pink colourway
Cs: A navy, B off-white, C pink, D beige, E grey, F dull pink, G pale yellow.

Measurements
Width 26cm, length 162cm.

Tension
MT 7 24 sts – 42 rows = 10cm over slip stitch pattern.

Machine
Standard gauge electronic or punchcard.

Pattern sequences
Green colourway

Rows	Pattern Setting	Feeder 1
*2	Knit	A
8	Slip	B
4	Slip	C
2	Knit	D
8	Slip	E
4	Slip	F
2	Knit	G
8	Slip	H
4	Slip	I
2	Knit	J
8	Slip	A
4	Slip	B
2	Knit	C
8	Slip	D
4	Slip	E
2	Knit	F
8	Slip	G
4	Slip	H

Rep from *.

Punchcard stitch pattern

Punchcard stitch pattern for Monet Scarves.

Tiles design in Orange, Red and Blue.

TILES SCARF

The same stitch pattern is used; however, when the colours are arranged in a different way, new ones added and the pattern is tucked, the whole design changes completely.

Method

E wrap cast on 80 sts MC1 RC000, k 2 rows.

Follow patt sequence, working through all Cs, and cont until RC700 or required length reached, ending with 2 k rows. Cast off.

Materials

Finished weight 110g.

The MC knit rows require 2/20s 2-ply, the C 2/28s 1-ply.

Orange colourway

MCs: small amounts: 1 dark green, 2 brown, 3 black, 4 red, 5 apricot.

Cs: A ochre, B yellow, C emerald green, D pale green, E pale yellow, F grey, G cinnamon.

Blue colourway

MCs: small amounts: 1 lilac, 2 grey and 3 bright blue.

Cs: A pale blue, B amethyst, C slate grey, D purple, E mint green, F denim blue.

Red colourway

MCs: small amounts: 1 red, 2 maroon, 3 black.

Cs: A bright pink, B dark blue, C purple, D orange, E cerise, F ochre, G turquoise.

Measurements

Width 32.5cm, length 184cm.

Tension

MT 7 24 sts – 43 rows = 10cm.

Machine

Standard gauge electronic or punchcard.

Punchcard stitch pattern

The punchcard stitch pattern is the same as for the Monet Scarves.

Pattern sequence

Rows	Pattern Setting	Feeder 1
2	Knit	MC1
6	Tuck	A
6	Tuck	B
2	Knit	MC1
6	Tuck	C
6	Tuck	D

Rep chart, changing MC after every 5th tuck circle.

Shells Scarves in Cream, Sand and Black.

SHELLS SCARF

Colour is the key to the Shells design. Looking at shells on a beach and their delicate colours and stripes, each one included several shades of purple, pink, beige and charcoal. The challenge was how to interpret this into a knitted fabric. Several examples of different sizes, colours and shapes of shells were collected from the beach and studied. They were left on a window sill in my workroom so I would see them every day and really look at the colours and the shapes. How to express the myriad of shades on the inside of a mussel shell became a challenge. I collected yarns together while constantly referring back to my design source.

The shape of the tuck stitch pattern reflects the shape of the shell. To use a slip stitch did not give the shape I wanted it as was too rounded. The colours needed to have a variety of textures and merge softly together. This design is the result. The Cream and Black versions use the same blue/grey shell colours with only the background changing. The Sand colourway, in the other sample, represents the sand on a beach and the shell is more lilac and purple like a mussel shell.

The background main colour is lightly felted so this pulls the colours inside the circle to produce a more shell-like shape.

Method

E wrap cast on MC 80 sts RC000.

Follow patt sequence to RC700 or desired length. End with k rows. Cast off.

Cream Shells detail.

Materials

Finished weight 110g.

Cream and Black colourways

MC: 60g 2/20s 2-ply cream or black yarn which will lightly felt.

Cs: various small amounts of non-felting yarn: A pale green, B denim blue, C navy, D pale blue, E vanilla, F silver grey, G lilac, H pink, I slate grey, J amethyst, K turquoise, L mid-green.

Sand colourway

MC: 60g 2/20s 2-ply camel/sand yarn which will lightly felt.

Cs: various small amounts of non-felting yarn: A white, B pale blue, C denim blue, D purple, E bright purple, F navy, G slate grey, H lilac, I pink, J turquoise, K leaf green, L amethyst.

Measurements

Width 30cm, length 180cm.

Tension

MT 24 sts – 38 rows = 10 cm over tuck stitch pattern.

Machine

Standard gauge electronic or punchcard.

Pattern sequence

Rows	Pattern Setting	Feeder 1
*2	Knit	MC
2	Tuck	A
4	Tuck	B
2	Tuck	C
2	Knit	MC
2	Tuck	D
4	Tuck	E
2	Tuck	F
2	Knit	MC
2	Tuck	G
4	Tuck	H
2	Tuck	I
2	Knit	MC
2	Tuck	J
4	Tuck	K
2	Tuck	L

Rep from *.

Punchcard stitch pattern

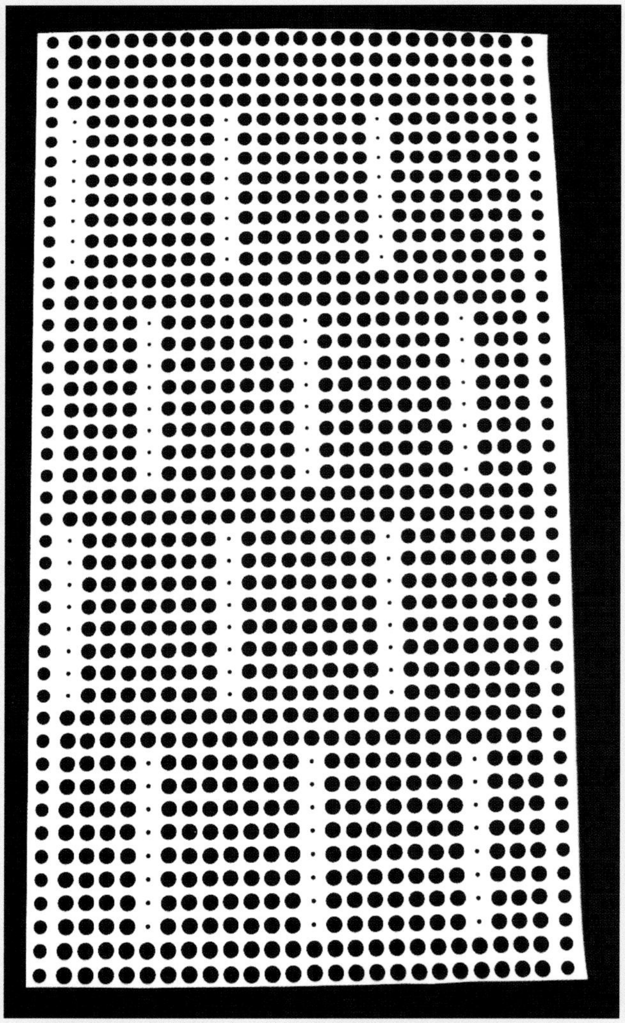

Punchcard stitch pattern for Shells Scarves.

Harbour Lights Scarves in Red, Blue and Gold.

Harbour Lights Scarves, Red detail.

Harbour Lights Scarf, Gold detail.

HARBOUR LIGHTS SCARF

The water reflections on a dark night in St Ives harbour were the starting point for the *Harbour Lights* design. The reflections of the bright coloured boats and the neon lights from the restaurants and cafes around the bay, broken up by the waves breaking on the shoreline, conjured up shades of red, gold, green and several shades of blue. Many photographs were taken to help with the colour analysis and final choice.

Method

E wrap cast on 80 sts using C A, RC000.

Follow chart to RC700 or until desired length reached, ending with 4 k rows. Cast off.

Materials
Finished weight 110g.
Fine yarn 2/28s 1-ply.

Red colourway
Cs: small amounts: A lime green, B dark brown, C purple, D bright purple, E sea green, F dark green, H mid-green, I emerald green, J bright blue, K denim blue, L turquoise, M orange, N red, O terracotta.

Gold colourway
Cs: small amounts: A lime green, B yellow, C khaki, D olive, E dark brown, F purple, G bright purple, H sea green, I ochre, J dark green, K mid-green, L denim blue, M emerald green, N terracotta, O bright blue.

Measurements
Width 32.5cm, length 184cm.

Tension
MT 7 24 sts – 43 rows = 10 cm over tuck stitch pattern.

Machine
Standard gauge electronic or punchcard.

Pattern sequence

Rows	Pattern Setting	Feeder 1
3	Knit	A
*4	Knit	B
4	Tuck	C
4	Tuck	D
4	Knit	E
4	Tuck	A
4	Tuck	F
4	Knit	G
4	Tuck	H
4	Tuck	I
4	Knit	J
4	Tuck	K
4	Tuck	L
4	Knit	M
4	Tuck	N
4	Tuck	O

Rep from *.

Punchcard stitch pattern

Punchcard stitch pattern for Harbour Lights Scarf.

Rockpools Scarves in Red and Blue.

ROCKPOOLS SCARF

I am not too sure which came first, the idea of wanting to express a lovely seaside scene with the tide out and a myriad of treasure boxes of sea life called rock pools, or the ability to be able to slip twenty rows at a time and the resulting textured pattern. Either way, this stitch pattern will require a little practice to make sure the slipped rows do not tangle up and drop side stitches, so care must be taken and you must work slowly. Choose the yarn carefully; it must be fine but strong, otherwise it will break on the knit rows when the slipped rows are being worked on, and the weights must be even. It is a very worthwhile pattern once you have mastered it.

The knit row colours are the lighter ones and the slipped rock pools are the dark ones, so bear this in mind when choosing your own colours. The two colourways emulate the sea with blues and green; the red evokes the rocks and seaweed.

Method

It is much easier if you line up the lighter colours, place the darker ones in front and feed them up from the floor. Work through the light colours for the knit rows and the dark ones for the slipped rows.

E wrap cast on 80 sts using B, k 2 rows.
Wrap all yarn ends around first N.
Follow C sequence as set out in chart until approx 700 rows have been completed or required length reached, having completed a 14-row sequence.
K 2 rows with required C.
TD10 k 1 row and latch off.

Materials
Finished weight 40g.
Various fine yarns 2/28s 1-ply.

Blue colourway
Light Cs: A lemon, B sky blue, C lilac, D cream, E pale green, F pale grey.
Dark Cs: G dark green, H mid-green, I bright blue, J navy, K olive green, L amethyst.

Red colourway
Light Cs: A cream, B lilac, C sky blue, D lemon, E pale green, F white, G pale grey.
Darker Cs: H cherry red, I amethyst, J dark pink, K ochre, L dark red, M terracotta, N brown, O purple.

Measurements
Width 27cm, length 160cm.

Tension
MT 7 26 sts – 42 rows = 10cm over slip stitch pattern.

Machine
Standard gauge electronic or punchcard.

Pattern sequences
Blue colourway

Rows	Pattern Setting	Feeder 1
2	Knit	A
14	Slip	G
2	Knit	B
14	Slip	H
2	Knit	C
14	Slip	I
2	Knit	D
14	Slip	J
2	Knit	E
14	Slip	K
2	Knit	F
14	Slip	L

Red colourway

Rows	Pattern Setting	Feeder 1
2	Knit	A
14	Slip	H
2	Knit	B
14	Slip	I
2	Knit	C
14	Slip	J
2	Knit	D
14	Slip	K
2	Knit	E
14	Slip	L
2	Knit	F
14	Slip	M
2	Knit	G
14	Slip	N
2	Knit	A
14	Slip	O
2	Knit	B
14	Slip	H
2	Knit	C
14	Slip	I

Punchcard stitch pattern

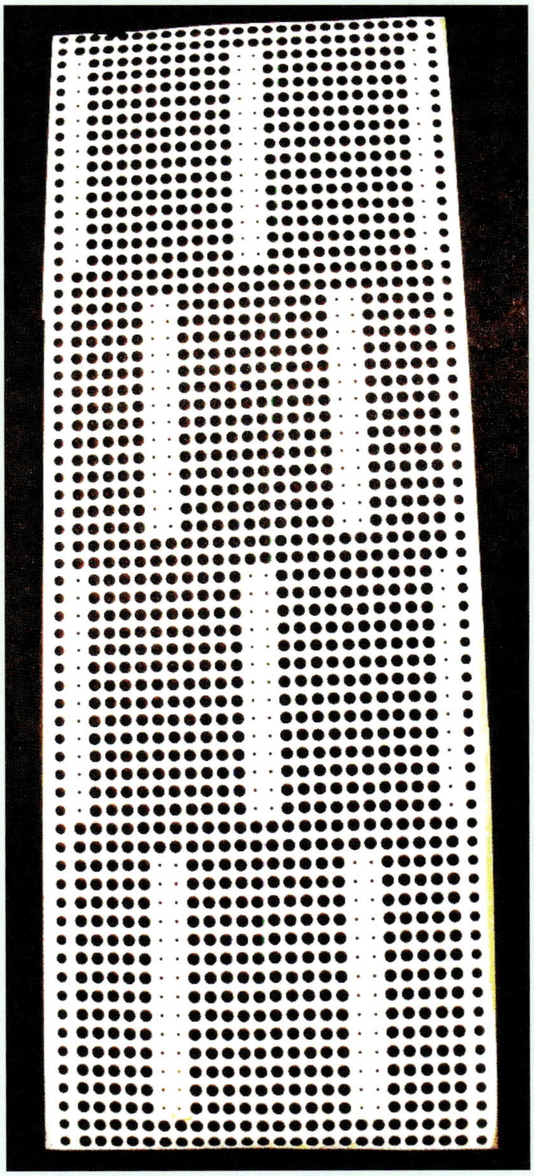

Punchcard stitch pattern for Rockpools Scarf.

Rockpools Scarf, Blue detail and inspiration.

Rockpools Scarf, Red detail and inspiration.

Spun yarn at Drinishader.

Harris landscape.

Harris seascape.

Harris Scarves in Heather, Grose Bay and Northton.

Harris Grose Bay Scarf, detail.

HARRIS SCARF

Having spent many happy holidays with my aunt on the Isle of Harris, I wanted to try and capture the atmosphere of our favourite places and the scenery of the bays and landscape. To stand on a Scottish island beach and know there is nothing between you and America is quite something! It is utterly inspiring to look at all the wonderful colours of the heather, and the green and turquoise sea of Grose Bay, and then move down south through an almost lunar landscape following the Golden Road, passing the seals languishing on the rocks like grey bananas on the way to Northton, while noting the darker shades around you. To express all this in a knitted fabric is a wonderful souvenir of quiet reflective holidays.

Method

E wrap cast on 80 sts C A, RC000.
Follow patt sequence, changing Cs as required.
At RC 850 or desired length, end with 2 k rows, cast off.

Materials

Finished weight 60g.

Fine yarn 2/34s 1-ply.

Small amounts of various Cs.

Heather colourway

Cs: A bright pink, B amethyst, C lilac, D vanilla, E pink, F purple, G cherry, H cream.

Grose Bay colourway

Cs: A lilac, B mid-green, C olive green, D amethyst, E mint green, F lilac, G beige, H purple.

Northton colourway

Cs: A mid-green, B brown, C rusty, D purple, E amethyst, F cream, G slate grey, H navy.

Measurements

Width 26.5cm, length 148cm.

Tension

MT 6• 30 sts – 36 rows = 10cm.

Machine

Standard gauge electronic or punchcard.

Pattern sequence

Row	Pattern Setting	Feeder 1
2	Knit	A
2	Slip	B
*6	Slip	C
2	Knit	C
2	Slip	D
6	Slip	E
2	Knit	E
2	Slip	F
6	Slip	G
2	Knit	G
2	Slip	H

Rep from *, working through the Cs selected.

Punchcard stitch pattern

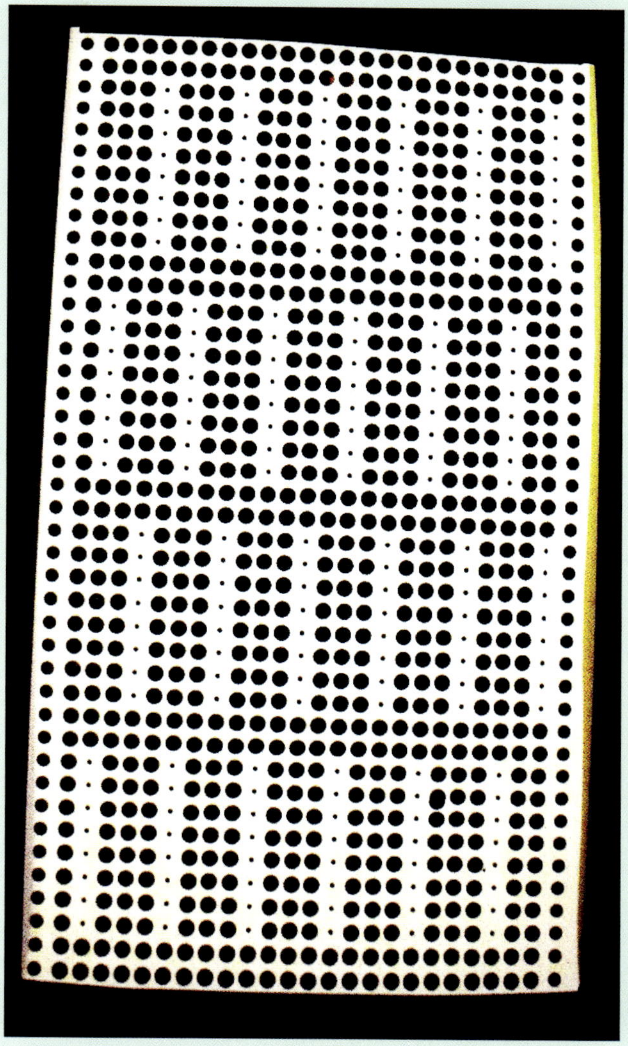

Punchcard stitch pattern for Harris Scarves.

Mosaic Scarves in blue, gold and pale variations.

Contrasting colours of mosaics from the Alhambra.

MOSAIC SCARF

This pattern emerged one day while experimenting and playing with pattern and punchcards and stitches. It is a simple slip stitch pattern which weaves the colours up and under other colours to create an interesting depth and a textured surface. Colour choice is vital with this pattern to really exploit the tessellated look of the finished fabric.

The slip stitch pattern will be pulled up so you will have to knit extra rows to obtain a required length.

Method

E wrap cast on 80 sts using B, k 2 rows.
Wrap all yarn ends around first N.
Follow patt sequence as set out and cont to work through Cs until approx 738 rows and an 8-row patt has been completed.
K 2 rows with another C, last row TD10 and latch off.

Looking at the mosaics at the Alhambra in Granada it became clear that with a very few dramatic colours a strong design can emerge. Here, only four colours have been used: ochre, denim blue, mid-green and navy.

Contrasting colours of mosaic from the Alhambra, detail.

Mosaic Scarf based on the Alhambra's mosaic colours.

Materials

Finished weight 40g.

Fine yarn 2/28s 1-ply.

Choose an odd number of colours so they will appear offset and not in a straight line.

Gold colourway

Cs: A in cherry red, B in dark green, C in beige, D in brown, E in olive green, F in terracotta, G in amethyst, H in grey, I in dark pink, J in ochre, K in navy.

Measurements

Width 27cm, length 160cm.

Tension

MT 7 26 sts – 42 rows = 10cm over slip stitch pattern.

Machine

Standard gauge electronic or punchcard.

Pattern sequence

Rows	Pattern Setting	Feeder 1
8	Slip	A
8	Slip	B
8	Slip	C
8	Slip	D
8	Slip	E
8	Slip	F

Punchcard stitch pattern

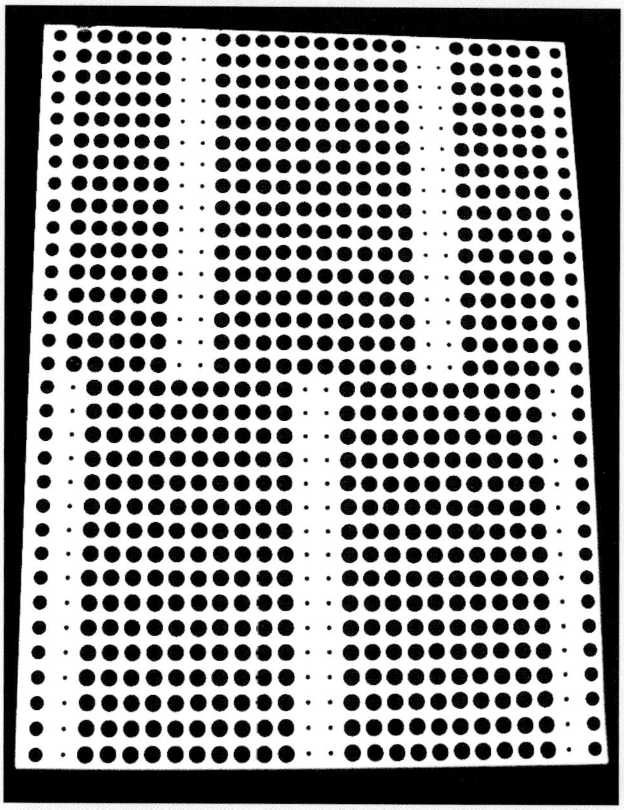

Punchcard stitch pattern for Mosaic Scarf.

Geneva Scarves in blue, bright and red.

Geneva bright pink scarf.

GENEVA SCARF

The Geneva Scarf has been knitted dozens of times and lends itself to the use of many varying colourways. The background colours are a mix of a thicker wool yarn (2/20s 2-ply) and a fine one (2/34s 1-ply). The colours are the same (for example, two threads of blue) but note that they will react differently when knitted depending which twists to the front of the fabric. The circles are knitted with a tuck stitch using the fine 1-ply yarn. The background yarn changes straight after a circle has been tucked, thus avoiding a hard edge to the stripe.

The size of the circles can vary but I tend to keep them the same size: 7 stitches, 10 rows tuck circles with 14 stocking stitch rows between. Keep checking that the side stitches either side of the circle tuck rows have not dropped.

Materials

Finished weight 150g.

All colourways require various Cs of fine and thicker yarns, based on whatever colour palette you are using. Clash Cs together and really go to town and have fun putting them together.

Geneva autumn colours.

Measurements

Width 27cm, length 186cm.

Tension

MT 8 36 sts – 42 rows = 10cm over pattern and after lightly felting.

Machine

Standard gauge electronic or punchcard.

Punchcard stitch pattern

X0000000X0000000X0000000

Pattern sequence

Rows	Pattern Setting	Feeder 1
14	Knit	MC1
10	Tuck	C1
14	Knit	MC2
10	Tuck	C2

Rep, working through all Cs chosen.

Method

E wrap cast on MC 80 sts, RC000.

Follow patt sequence until about RC720 or required length reached, ending with 14 rows k. Cast off.

Inspiration for the Porthminster Pebbles design.

Porthminster Pebbles in blue and grey.

PORTHMINSTER PEBBLES SCARF

This design is a development from the Geneva pattern. With more colour changing and careful choice of yarns it takes on a more sculptural feel. The circles become pebbles with changes of colour within the circles.

Blue Porthminster Pebbles Scarf with a St Ives Landscape Jacket.

Materials

Finished weight 170g.

Grey colourway

MCs: various weights of yarn and various Cs within the pebble spectrum. The MC here is 2/20s 2-ply wool yarn which is used throughout but mixed with similar Cs of 2/32s 1-ply fine yarn which are changed after five circles/pebbles have been completed. The pebbles are 2/30s–2/20s, 1-ply to 2-ply:

MC1 cream/pale blue, MC2 cream/grey, MC 3 cream/white.

Cs: A grey, B cream, C slate grey, D mid-blue, E lilac, F silver, G pale grey, H dark grey, I navy.

Tension

MT 8 36 sts – 27 rows = 10cm after felting.

Machine

Standard gauge electronic or punchcard.

Punchcard stitch pattern

Use the same as for the Geneva Scarf.

Pattern sequence

Row	Pattern Setting	Feeder 1
14	Knit	MC 1
2	Tuck	A
6	Tuck	B
2	Tuck	A
14	Knit	MC1
10	Tuck	G
14	Knit	MC1
4	Tuck	I
2	Tuck	B
4	Tuck	I
14	Knit	MC1
10	Tuck	C
14	Knit	MC1

Row	Pattern Setting	Feeder 1
4	Tuck	F
6	Tuck	B
14	Knit	MC2
10	Tuck	I
14	Knit	MC 2
4	Tuck	D
6	Tuck	F
14	Knit	MC2
4	Tuck	G
2	Tuck	I
4	Tuck	G
14	Knit	MC2
4	Tuck	C
6	Tuck	H
14	Knit	MC2
4	Tuck	G
2	Tuck	B
4	Tuck	G
14	Knit	MC3
6	Tuck	E
4	Tuck	F
14	Knit	MC3
6	Tuck	B
2	Tuck	I
4	Tuck	B
14	Knit	MC3
10	Tuck	E
14	Knit	MC3
10	Tuck	H
14	Knit	MC3
6	Tuck	E
4	Tuck	G
14	Knit	MC4
10	Tuck	D

Cont to work through Cs, changing background MC as required after every 5th circle.

Porthminster Pebbles, close-up showing the textures that can be achieved.

Beach scene variation – having fun.

Method

E wrap cast on 80 sts MC1, RC000, follow patt sequence as required.

Work to about RC800 or until required length reached, ending with 14 rows k, cast off.

The Blue colourway uses the same chart but the colours are changed to include turquoise, yellow, charcoal, pale blue, navy, four different shades of grey, and cream.

Using a background yarn which felts firmly the texture of the pebbles becomes even more pronounced. Some lambswool has the ability to felt firmly at 40°. The pebbles are knitted with a fine non-felting yarn in one colour and are offset with fewer knit rows between. Experiment with various colours and yarns to really get to know and understand the quality of the materials you are using.

Details of a beach scene using tuck stitch and circles in various weights and textures of yarn have been mixed together. The circles represent the rocks and other slip stitch patterns the sea and surf. The scarf has been further embellished by adding copper and brass starfish, limpets and shells for decoration.

Ghirlandia Scarves in Pink, Red and Apricot.

Pink Ghirlandia Scarf.

GHIRLANDIA SCARF

Having been inspired by the Porthminster Pebbles design the decision was made to experiment further by adding colours and breaking up the circles with stripes. Looking at paintings by the artist Jennifer Durrant and the vibrant and exciting way in which she uses colours, I made some sketches and collages. The results of these informed the Ghirlandia series of scarves.

These were a joy to make purely because of the colours and how they worked together. The pink one uses several weights of yarn ranging from 1-ply to 4-ply, cotton, cashmere, wool and silk – in fact, any yarn which was the required colour.

The Pink colourway uses lime, yellow, grey, turquoise, marine blue, bright green, coral, etc. The Red colourway uses maroon, olive, ochre, navy, lilac, purple, pink, yellow, lime, etc. The Apricot colourway uses grey, cherry, lime, pink, pale blue, lilac, pale yellow, cinnamon, etc. The overall effect is very different from the Pebbles design, but the technique is the same.

Further experimentation followed with the Milan range of samples.

Milan Scarves in black and white, apricot and pink.

MILAN SCARF

The circles are bunched together in areas and the colour changes within them. The background and circle colours are swopped halfway through tucking which creates a real energy and contrast in the black and white sample. Experimentation is always invigorating.

Broken Circles Scarf.

BROKEN CIRCLES SCARF

This is a further variation where the circles are worked over eleven stitches and tucked for twelve rows.

Tuck and slip stitch Millefleur Circle Scarves.

Millefleur Circle Scarves in Blue, Pale and Red.

MILLEFLEUR CIRCLE SCARF

Millefleur is the French word for 'a thousand flowers' and is used to describe a background that includes tiny plants and flowers in many tapestries. Hand-blown paperweights are also called millefleur, with their myriad of colours swirling around, and this design was inspired by them.

Method

E wrap cast on using A, RC000, 80 sts. Follow patt sequence working through Cs and rep as required.

At approx RC700, end with 2 k rows and cast off.

Materials

Finished weight 90g.

The design uses various weights of yarn ranging from 2/32s fine 1-ply to 2/28s. The yarn was chosen for its colour and not its weight. However, the resulting effect is one of surface interest as texture, as they weave under and over each other. Use small amounts of an odd number of Cs.

Blue colourway

Cs: A cream, B mid-blue, C denim blue, D navy, E lilac, F turquoise, G sky blue.

Pale colourway

Cs: A cream, B off-white, C beige, D pale grey, E putty, F ecru, G almond.

Red colourway

Cs: A maroon, B bright green, C turquoise, D cream, E red, F denim blue, G yellow.

Measurements

Width 26cm, length 162cm.

Tension

MT 7 24 sts – 43 rows = 10cm.

Machine

Standard gauge electronic or punchcard.

Pattern sequence

Rows	Pattern Setting	Feeder 1
2	Knit	A
8	Slip	B
2	Knit	C
8	Slip	D
2	Knit	E
8	Slip	F
2	Knit	G
8	Slip	A
2	Knit	B
8	Slip	C

Cont in the patt and C sequence.

Punchcard stitch pattern

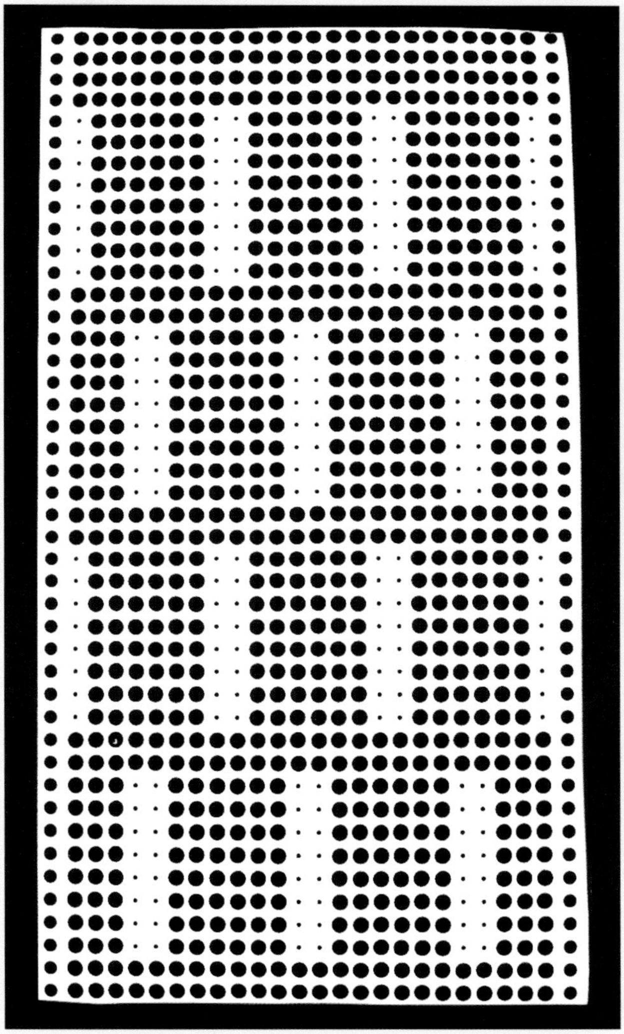

Punchcard stitch pattern for Millefleur Circle Scarves.

Boats Scarves in Red and Blue.

BOATS SCARF

This is a warm, crunchy, textured stitch pattern executed here in Knoll Soft Donegal. It was inspired by brightly coloured boats bobbing about in the water in St Ives harbour.

Method

E wrap cast on C1 80 sts. Follow patt sequence, working through Cs until RC600 or required length reached, ending with 4 k rows, cast off.

Materials
Finished weight 180g.
Knoll Soft Donegal wool.

Red colourway
Cs: O'Byrne 5550 (lime), Brosna 5522 (pink), Healy 5551 (lilac), Roe 5527 (dark blue), Gara 5534 (yellow), Clare 5530 (orange), Killala 5536 (bright green), Abbert 5524 (red), Beltra 5528 (green-blue), Liscannor 5526 (cerise), Dingle 5516 (maroon).

Blue colourway
Cs: Healy 5551 (lilac), Peacock 5564 (turquoise), O'Byrne 5550 (lime), Ballycastle 5502 (khaki), Malone 5548 (pale blue), Beltra 5528 (green-blue), Gara 5534 (yellow), Killala 5536 (bright green), Dariana 5532 (purple), Neagh 5506 (mid-green), Liscannor 5526 (cerise), Rea 5535 (rose pink).

Measurements
Width 31cm, length 130cm.

Tension
Approx MT 8• 29 sts – 44 rows = 10cm.

Machine
Standard gauge electronic or punchcard.

Punchcard stitch pattern
X0000000X0000000X
0000X0000000X0000

Pattern sequence

Row	Pattern Setting	Feeder 1
4	Knit	1
6	Slip	2
8	Slip	3

Rep all 18 rows from beg, working through Cs.

Carry Bag and Shoulder Bag.

Shoulder Bag, attaching binding.

SHOULDER BAG

Method

The stitch pattern is smaller than Boats; the bag uses the same stitch chart and the same pattern colour changes as Luskentyre.

Knit enough fabric to accommodate the size of the bag to include the bag back, bag front and side gusset. The fabric is washed and lightly felted; this will firm the fabric. Steam press.

Knit four lengths in a single colour for the binding around the edges. E wrap cast on 12 sts and knit in st st until length measures 122cm, another 63cm, a third 32cm and the final 12cm.

Materials
Finished weight 150g.
The outer part of the bag is knitted using Jamiesons of Shetland Spindrift wool in oil.
Lining fabric.
Stiffening fabric.
Large button.

Measurements
See schematic.

Tension
Approx MT 7•

Machine
Standard gauge electronic or punchcard.

Finished Shoulder Bag, gusset detail.

Finished Shoulder Bag.

Making up

Cut out 3 pieces required and iron onto stiff backing fabric such as Vilene. Cut out lining fabric; I used Harris tweed. Tack (baste) lining to main pieces, and oversew pieces tog round edges.

Fold 122cm binding in half and sew it to back edge of bag and round flap. Bring it round to front and stitch in place.

Rep with 63cm binding round front edge. Use 32cm binding for side gussets and top front edge. Make strap from fabric or leather (width 3cm, length 130cm) and attach to outside of gussets.

Fold rem 12cm into loop and attach to centre of underside flap. Sew on large button.

Bag Body

A	25cm
B	25cm
C	20cm
D	45cm
E	18cm
F	19.5cm

Bag Gusset

G	7cm
H	65cm

Leather Handle

I	130cm
J	3cm

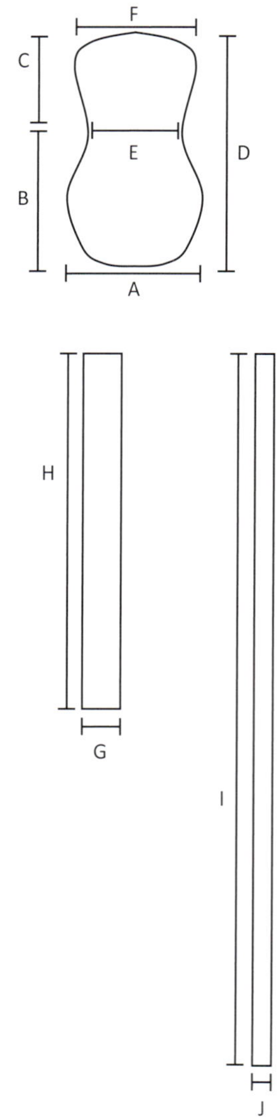

Shoulder Bag schematic.

Boat Carry Bag.

Purple Boat Carry Bag.

CARRY BAG

This is an ideal size, using the same stitch pattern as the Shoulder Bag. It is finished off by leather handles folded in half and attached to the outside.

Materials

Finished weight 250g.
Jamiesons of Shetland Spindrift wool in oil.
Lining fabric.
Large button.
Leather for handles, two pieces 50cm × 3cm.

Measurements

See schematic.

Method

Make 2 side pieces 36cm wide × 36cm long. K 10 rows st st before stitch patt to fold over for neat edge and finish in same way.

Make 1 gusset piece 18cm wide × 102 cm long. Start and finish as before.

Wash, press.

Carry Bag, detail of inside.

Carry Bag, detail of finishing.

Making up

Apply iron-on stiff Vilene fusible interfacing to back of knitted fabric. With right sides facing, pin gusset round edges of side pieces and sew bag tog.

Make lining from fabric 2cm smaller than knitted bag, place it inside (wrong sides tog) and sew round top edge of bag.

Attach handles to outside of bag.

Make loop out of leather and attach to one side of bag at upper edge in centre. Sew on large button on opposite side.

Bag Body

A	34cm
B	35cm

Bag Gusset

C	18cm
D	104cm

Bag Handle

E	50cm
F	3.5cm

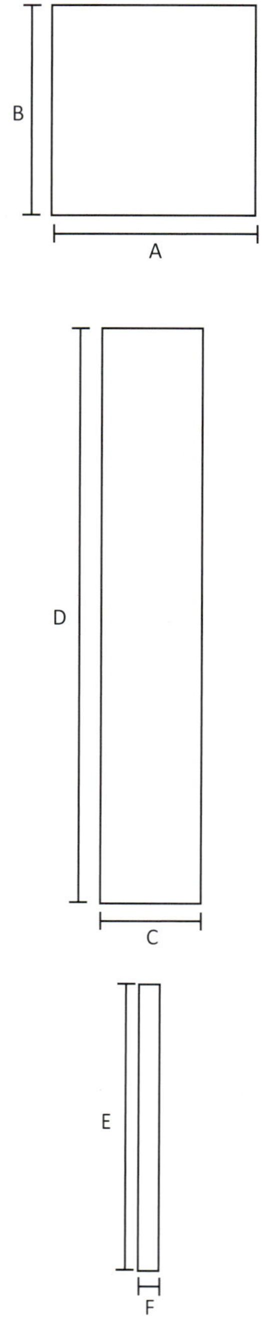

Carry Bag schematic.

Large Picnic Bag.

Large Picnic Bag, detail.

PICNIC BAG

Method

Make 2 side pieces 61cm wide × 39cm long.
Make 1 gusset piece 36cm wide × 130cm long.
Either follow instructions for Carry Bag or add binding round edge by working 2 lengths each 12 sts wide × 130cm long.

Making up
Follow instructions for Shoulder Bag.

Large Picnic Bag with lining material.

Bag Body

A	61cm
B	39cm

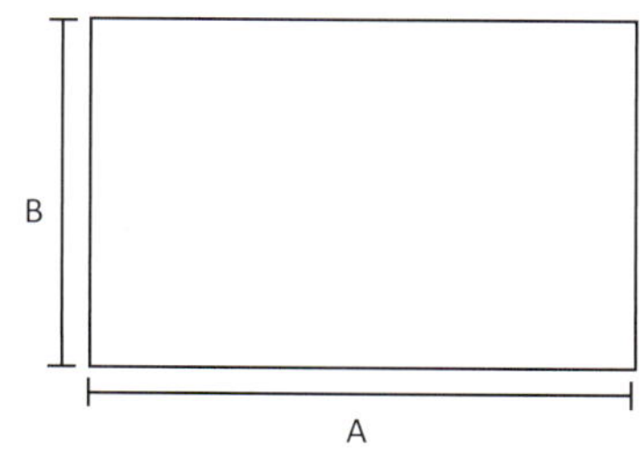

Bag Gusset

C	36cm
D	130cm

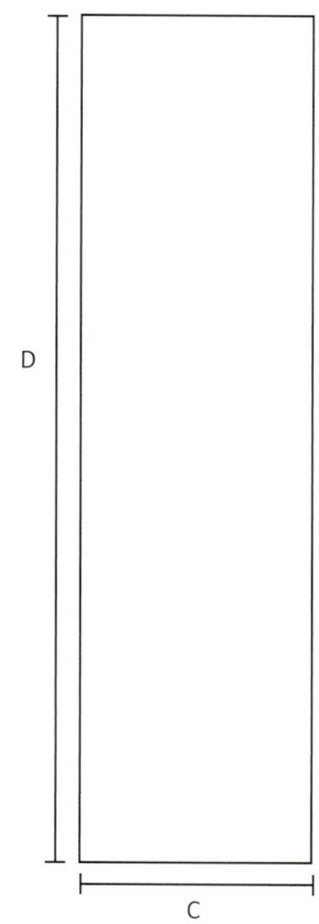

Large Picnic Bag schematic.

CHAPTER 7

FAIR ISLE

Norwegian refugees coming to the UK during the Second World War brought their influence to bear, and their stitch patterns worked well with the traditional Shetland patterns, so it is now very difficult to distinguish the origins of particular methods. The traditional yoked sweater and cardigan shape was also integrated and these continue to be some of the most intricate and beautiful knitwear in the world. To obtain a truly authentic look author Kathleen Kinder suggests brushing the finished article with a teasel or toothbrush.

Scandinavian colours are usually bright with white, while Shetland colours are mixed with several shades incorporated into the one thread to reflect the heathery muted shades of a misty sea and damp hilly landscape.

Jamiesons of Shetland produce a wonderful range of genuine Shetland wool which can be bought in its oiled state: this means it is not only cheaper per kilo but is also easier to run through the machine.

Fair Isle Collars in Bright, Brown, Green and Blue.

TRADITIONAL PATTERN COLLAR

Each collar has fourteen different patterns within it; some are intricate broad bands while others are simpler five-row bands which add to the field of colour.

Method

WY cast on 130 sts.
Follow chart, working through each stitch patt in turn:
A, B, C, D, E, F, G, H, I, J, K, L, M, N, M.
When sequence completed, run off onto WY.

Making up
With right sides facing inwards, sew down long seam. Turn right side out and graft short seams tog to make circle.

Materials
Finished weight 110g.
Jamiesons of Shetland Spindrift wool in oil.

Blue colourway
Cs: Navy 727, Jupiter 633, Heron 315, Granite 122, Aqua 929, White 104, Splash 757, Loganberry 1290, Jade 787, Salmon 301, Mustard 425, Clyde Blue 168.

Brown colourway
Cs: Grouse 235, Sunset 186, Thistledown 237, White 104, Daffodil 390, Havana 248, Pumpkin 470, Moorgrass 286, Cashew 342, Paprika 261, Aqua 929, Clyde Blue 168, Madder 587, Bracken 231, Heron 315.

Green colourway
Cs: Thyme 226, Havana 248, Aqua 929, Sunset 186, Peat 198, Pumpkin 470, Jade 787, Moorgrass 286, Mustard 425, Lime 780, Bracken 231, Paprika 261, Fern 249, Emerald 792, Woodgreen 318.

Bright colourway
Cs: Raspberry 1260, Splash 757, Madder 587, Lime 780, Daffodil 390, Loganberry 1290, Jade 787, Navy 727, Anemone 616, Pumpkin 470, Emerald 792.

Dark colourway (not shown)
Cs: Navy 727, Pumpkin 470, Havana 248, Madder 587, Daffodil 390, Sand 183, Lime 780, Spice 526, Port Wine 293, Loganberry 1290, Rosewood 236, Clyde Blue 168, Jade 787, Granite 122, Splash 757, Salmon 301, White 104, Heron 315, Sunset 186.

Measurements
Width 20cm, length 33cm.

Tension
MT 8• 29 sts – 43 rows = 10cm.

Machine
Standard gauge electronic or punchcard.

Pattern sequences
Blue colourway

Row	Stitch Pattern	Pattern Setting	Feeder 1	Feeder 1
2	A	Knit	Navy	
3	A	Fair Isle	Navy	Jupiter
1	A	Fair Isle	Heron	Granite
1	A	Knit	Aqua	
3	A	Fair Isle	Aqua	White
1	A	Fair Isle	Aqua	Jupiter
3	A	Fair Isle	Aqua	White
1	A	Knit	Aqua	
1	A	Fair Isle	Heron	Granite
3	A	Fair Isle	Navy	Jupiter
2	A	Knit	Navy	
2	B	Knit	Granite	
3	B	Fair Isle	Granite	Splash
2	B	Knit	Granite	
1	C	Fair Isle	Granite	Navy

Row	Stitch Pattern	Pattern Setting	Feeder 1	Feeder 1
1	C	Fair Isle	Loganberry	Navy
3	C	Fair Isle	Loganberry	Sapphire
3	C	Fair Isle	Loganberry	Aqua
3	C	Fair Isle	Loganberry	Sapphire
1	C	Fair Isle	Loganberry	Navy
1	C	Fair Isle	White	Navy
2	D	Knit	White	
2	D	Fair Isle	White	Jade
1	D	Fair Isle	White	Splash
2	D	Fair Isle	White	Jade
2	D	Knit	White	
1	E	Fair Isle	White	Heron
2	E	Fair Isle	Aqua	Heron
3	E	Fair Isle	Aqua	Salmon
1	E	Fair Isle	Sapphire	Salmon
2	E	Fair Isle	Sapphire	Granite
1	E	Fair Isle	White	Heron
2	E	Fair Isle	Sapphire	Granite
1	E	Fair Isle	Sapphire	Salmon
3	E	Fair Isle	Aqua	Salmon
2	E	Fair Isle	Aqua	Heron
1	E	Fair Isle	Navy	Heron
2	F	Knit	Navy	
1	F	Fair Isle	Navy	Mustard
5	F	Fair Isle	Navy	Loganberry
1	F	Fair Isle	Navy	Mustard
2	F	Fair Isle	Navy	
1	G	Fair Isle	Navy	Jupiter
1	G	Knit	Jupiter	
2	G	Fair Isle	Jupiter	Splash
2	G	Fair Isle	White	Sapphire
5	G	Fair Isle	White	Aqua
2	G	Fair Isle	White	Sapphire
2	G	Fair Isle	Jupiter	Splash
1	G	Knit	Jupiter	
1	G	Fair Isle	Jupiter	Jade
2	H	Knit	Jade	
3	H	Fair Isle	Jade	Loganberry
2	H	Knit	Jade	
2	I	Knit	Heron	
4	I	Fair Isle	Heron	Navy
4	I	Fair Isle	Granite	Sapphire
4	I	Fair Isle	White	Clyde Blue
2	I	Fair Isle	Salmon	Aqua
4	I	Fair Isle	White	Clyde Blue
4	I	Fair Isle	Granite	Sapphire

Row	Stitch Pattern	Pattern Setting	Feeder 1	Feeder 1
4	I	Fair Isle	Heron	Navy
2	I	Knit	Heron	
2	J	Knit	Loganberry	
3	J	Fair Isle	Loganberry	Sapphire
3	J	Fair Isle	Jupiter	Aqua
3	J	Fair Isle	Heron	Splash
3	J	Fair Isle	Granite	Salmon
2	J	Knit	Granite	
2	K	Knit	Granite	
3	K	Fair Isle	Granite	Jade
3	K	Fair Isle	Jupiter	Splash
1	K	Fair Isle	Mustard	Navy
3	K	Fair Isle	Jupiter	Splash
3	K	Fair Isle	Granite	Jade
2	K	Knit	Granite	
2	L	Knit	White	
2	L	Fair Isle	White	Loganberry
1	L	Fair Isle	White	Mustard
2	L	Fair Isle	White	Loganberry
1	L	Knit	White	
1	L	Knit	Aqua	
3	L	Fair Isle	Aqua	Mustard
1	L	Fair Isle	Heron	Salmon
3	L	Fair Isle	Aqua	Mustard
1	L	Knit	Aqua	
1	L	Knit	White	
2	L	Fair Isle	White	Loganberry
1	L	Fair Isle	White	Mustard
2	L	Fair Isle	White	Loganberry
1	L	Knit	White	
1	M	Knit	Sapphire	
2	M	Fair Isle	Sapphire	Salmon
2	M	Fair Isle	Sapphire	Loganberry
2	M	Fair Isle	Sapphire	Salmon
1	M	Knit	Sapphire	
1	N	Knit	Sapphire	
4	N	Fair Isle	Sapphire	Granite
4	N	Fair Isle	Splash	Aqua
4	N	Fair Isle	White	Navy
1	N	Fair Isle	Salmon	Mustard
4	N	Fair Isle	White	Navy
4	N	Fair Isle	Splash	Aqua
4	N	Fair Isle	Sapphire	Granite
1	N	Knit	Sapphire	

Rep stitch patt M.

Brown colourway

Rows	Stitch Pattern	Pattern Setting	Feeder 1	Feeder 2
2	A	Knit	Grouse	
3	A	Fair Isle	Grouse	Sunset
1	A	Fair Isle	Thistledown	White
1	A	Knit	Daffodil	
3	A	Fair Isle	Daffodil	Havana
1	A	Fair Isle	Daffodil	Pumpkin
3	A	Fair Isle	Daffodil	Havana
1	A	Knit	Daffodil	
1	A	Fair Isle	Thistledown	White
3	A	Fair Isle	Grouse	Sunset
2	A	Knit	Grouse	
2	B	Fair Isle	Moorgrass	
3	B	Fair Isle	Moorgrass	Cashew
2	B	Knit	Moorgrass	
1	C	Fair Isle	Moorgrass	Havana
1	C	Fair Isle	Pumpkin	Havana
3	C	Fair Isle	Pumpkin	Cashew
3	C	Fair Isle	Paprika	White
3	C	Fair Isle	Pumpkin	Cashew
1	C	Fair Isle	Pumpkin	Havana
1	C	Fair Isle	Cashew	Havana
2	D	Knit	Cashew	
2	D	Fair Isle	Cashew	Moorgrass
1	D	Fair Isle	Cashew	Daffodil
2	D	Fair Isle	Cashew	Moorgrass
2	D	Knit	Cashew	
1	E	Fair Isle	Cashew	Aqua
2	E	Fair Isle	Pumpkin	Aqua
3	E	Fair Isle	Pumpkin	Havana
1	E	Fair Isle	Daffodil	Havana
2	E	Fair Isle	Daffodil	Clyde Blue
1	E	Fair isle	White	Aqua
2	E	Fair isle	Daffodil	Clyde Blue
1	E	Fair Isle	Daffodil	Havana
3	E	Fair Isle	Pumpkin	Havana
2	E	Fair Isle	Pumpkin	Aqua
1	E	Fair Isle	Thistledown	Aqua

Rows	Stitch Pattern	Pattern Setting	Feeder 1	Feeder 2
2	F	Knit	Thistledown	
1	F	Fair Isle	Thistledown	Sunset
5	F	Fair Isle	Thistledown	Navy
1	F	Fair Isle	Thistledown	Sunset
2	F	Knit	Thistledown	
1	G	Fair Isle	Thistledown	Madder
1	G	Knit	Madder	
2	G	Fair Isle	Madder	Sunset
2	G	Fair Isle	White	Bracken
5	G	Fair Isle	White	Paprika
2	G	Fair Isle	White	Bracken
2	G	Fair Isle	Madder	Sunset
1	G	Knit	Madder	
1	G	Fair Isle	Madder	Havana
2	H	Knit	Havana	
3	H	Fair Isle	Havana	White
2	H	Knit	Havana	
2	I	Knit	Havana	
4	I	Fair Isle	Havana	Daffodil
4	I	Fair Isle	Thistledown	Pumpkin
4	I	Fair Isle	Cashew	Sunset
2	I	Fair Isle	White	Madder
4	I	Fair Isle	Cashew	Sunset
4	I	Fair Isle	Thistledown	Pumpkin
4	I	Fair Isle	Havana	Daffodil
2	I	Knit	Havana	
2	J	Knit	Heron	
3	J	Fair Isle	Heron	Sunset
3	J	Fair Isle	Bracken	Aqua
3	J	Fair Isle	Cashew	Paprika
3	J	Fair Isle	Thistledown	Clyde Blue
2	J	Knit	Thistledown	
2	K	Knit	Havana	
3	K	Fair Isle	Havana	Bracken
3	K	Fair Isle	Heron	Bracken
1	K	Fair Isle	White	Pumpkin
3	K	Fair Isle	Heron	Bracken
3	K	Fair Isle	Havana	Bracken
2	K	Knit	Havana	

Rows	Stitch Pattern	Pattern Setting	Feeder 1	Feeder 2
2	L	Knit	Pumpkin	
2	L	Fair Isle	Pumpkin	Aqua
1	L	Fair Isle	Pumpkin	Heron
2	L	Fair Isle	Pumpkin	Aqua
1	L	Knit	Pumpkin	
1	L	Knit	Daffodil	
3	L	Fair Isle	Daffodil	Clyde Blue
1	L	Fair Isle	Madder	Thistledown
3	L	Fair Isle	Daffodil	Clyde Blue
1	L	Knit	Daffodil	
1	L	Knit	Pumpkin	
2	L	Fair Isle	Pumpkin	Aqua
1	L	Fair Isle	Pumpkin	Heron
2	L	Fair Isle	Pumpkin	Aqua
2	L	Knit	Pumpkin	
2	M	Knit	Havana	
2	M	Fair Isle	Havana	Thistledown
2	M	Fair Isle	Havana	White
2	M	Fair Isle	Havana	Thistledown
2	M	Knit	Havana	
4	N	Fair Isle	Peat	Sunset
4	N	Fair Isle	Thistledown	Paprika
4	N	Fair Isle	Madder	White
1	N	Fair Isle	Daffodil	Pumpkin
4	N	Fair Isle	Madder	White
4	N	Fair Isle	Thistledown	Paprika
4	N	Fair Isle	Peat	Sunset

Rep stitch patt M.

Green colourway

Row	Stitch Pattern	Pattern Setting	Feeder 1	Feeder 2
2	A	Knit	Thyme	
3	A	Fair Isle	Thyme	Havana
1	A	Fair Isle	Aqua	Sunset
1	A	Knit	Peat	
3	A	Fair Isle	Peat	Pumpkin
1	A	Fair Isle	Peat	Jade
3	A	Fair Isle	Peat	Pumpkin
1	A	Knit	Peat	
1	A	Fair Isle	Aqua	Sunset
3	A	Fair Isle	Thyme	Havana
2	A	Knit	Thyme	
2	B	Knit	Moorgrass	
3	B	Fair Isle	Moorgrass	Mustard
2	B	Knit	Moorgrass	
1	C	Fair Isle	Moorgrass	Lime
1	C	Fair Isle	Bracken	Lime
3	C	Fair Isle	Bracken	Aqua
3	C	Fair Isle	Fern	Lime
3	C	Fair Isle	Bracken	Aqua
1	C	Fair Isle	Bracken	Lime
1	C	Fair Isle	Paprika	Lime
2	D	Knit	Paprika	
2	D	Fair Isle	Paprika	Peat
1	D	Fair Isle	Paprika	Mustard
2	D	Fair Isle	Paprika	Peat
2	D	Knit	Paprika	
1	E	Fair Isle	Paprika	Emerald
2	E	Fair Isle	Pumpkin	Emerald
3	E	Fair Isle	Pumpkin	Aqua
1	E	Fair Isle	Thyme	Aqua
2	E	Fair Isle	Thyme	Mustard
1	E	Fair Isle	Lime	Peat
2	E	Fair Isle	Thyme	Mustard
1	E	Fair Isle	Thyme	Aqua
3	E	Fair Isle	Pumpkin	Aqua
2	E	Fair Isle	Pumpkin	Emerald
1	E	Fair Isle	Fern	Emerald

Row	Stitch Pattern	Pattern Setting	Feeder 1	Feeder 2
2	F	Knit	Fern	
1	F	Fair Isle	Fern	Sunset
5	F	Fair Isle	Fern	Bracken
1	F	Fair Isle	Fern	Sunset
2	F	Knit	Fern	
1	G	Fair Isle	Fern	Havana
1	G	Knit	Havana	
2	G	Fair Isle	Havana	Lime
2	G	Fair Isle	Sunset	Emerald
5	G	Fair Isle	Paprika	Emerald
2	G	Fair Isle	Sunset	Emerald
2	G	Fair Isle	Havana	Lime
1	G	Knit	Havana	
1	G	Fair Isle	Havana	Thyme
2	H	Knit	Thyme	
3	H	Fair Isle	Thyme	Pumpkin
2	H	Knit	Thyme	
2	I	Knit	Woodgreen	
4	I	Fair Isle	Woodgreen	Fern
4	I	Fair Isle	Bracken	Aqua
4	I	Fair Isle	Paprika	Jade
2	I	Fair Isle	Peat	Lime
4	I	Fair Isle	Paprika	Jade
4	I	Fair Isle	Bracken	Aqua
4	I	Fair Isle	Woodgreen	Fern
2	I	Knit	Woodgreen	
2	J	Knit	Havana	
3	J	Fair Isle	Havana	Lime
3	J	Fair Isle	Woodgreen	Sunset
3	J	Fair Isle	Aqua	Paprika
3	J	Fair Isle	Peat	Thyme
2	J	Knit	Peat	
2	K	Knit	Bracken	
3	K	Fair Isle	Bracken	Mustard
3	K	Fair Isle	Fern	Paprika
1	K	Fair Isle	Lime	Pumpkin
3	K	Fair Isle	Fern	Paprika
3	K	Fair Isle	Bracken	Mustard
2	K	Knit	Bracken	

Row	Stitch Pattern	Pattern Setting	Feeder 1	Feeder 2
2	L	Knit	Peat	
2	L	Fair Isle	Peat	Woodgreen
1	L	Fair Isle	Peat	Paprika
2	L	Fair Isle	Peat	Woodgreen
1	L	Knit	Peat	
1	L	Knit	Aqua	
3	L	Fair Isle	Aqua	Fern
1	L	Fair Isle	Lime	Sunset
3	L	Fair Isle	Aqua	Fern
1	L	Knit	Aqua	
1	L	Knit	Peat	
2	L	Fair Isle	Peat	Woodgreen
1	L	Fair Isle	Peat	Paprika
2	L	Fair Isle	Peat	Woodgreen
1	L	Knit	Peat	
2	M	Knit	Woodgreen	
2	M	Fair Isle	Woodgreen	Lime
2	M	Fair Isle	Woodgreen	Bracken
2	M	Fair Isle	Woodgreen	Lime
2	M	Knit	Woodgreen	
4	N	Fair Isle	Woodgreen	Sunset
4	N	Fair Isle	Fern	Paprika
4	N	Fair Isle	Emerald	Pumpkin
1	N	Fair Isle	Lime	Peat
4	N	Fair Isle	Emerald	Pumpkin
4	N	Fair Isle	Fern	Paprika
4	N	Fair Isle	Woodgreen	Sunset
2	N	Knit	Woodgreen	
2	M	Fair Isle	Woodgreen	Lime
2	M	Fair Isle	Woodgreen	Bracken
2	M	Fair Isle	Woodgreen	Lime
2	N	Knit	Woodgreen	

Bright colourway

Row	Stitch Pattern	Pattern Setting	Feeder 1	Feeder 2
2	A	Knit	Raspberry	
3	A	Fair Isle	Raspberry	Splash
1	A	Fair Isle	Madder	Lime
1	A	Knit	Daffodil	
3	A	Fair Isle	Daffodil	Loganberry
1	A	Fair Isle	Daffodil	Jade
3	A	Fair Isle	Daffodil	Loganberry
1	A	Knit	Daffodil	
1	A	Fair Isle	Madder	Lime
3	A	Fair Isle	Raspberry	Splash
2	A	Knit	Raspberry	
2	B	Knit	Navy	
3	B	Fair Isle	Navy	Lime
3	B	Knit	Navy	
1	C	Fair Isle	Navy	Madder
1	C	Fair Isle	Anemone	Madder
3	C	Fair Isle	Anemone	Lime
3	C	Fair Isle	Loganberry	Jade
3	C	Fair Isle	Anemone	Lime
1	C	Fair Isle	Anemone	Madder
1	C	Fair Isle	Splash	Madder
2	C	Knit	Splash	
2	D	Fair Isle	Splash	Pumpkin
1	D	Fair Isle	Splash	Daffodil
2	D	Fair Isle	Splash	Pumpkin
2	D	Knit	Splash	
1	E	Fair Isle	Splash	Lime
2	E	Fair Isle	Raspberry	Lime
3	E	Fair Isle	Raspberry	Anemone
1	E	Fair Isle	Daffodil	Anemone
2	E	Fair Isle	Daffodil	Splash
1	E	Fair Isle	Loganberry	Lime
2	E	Fair Isle	Daffodil	Splash
1	E	Fair Isle	Daffodil	Anemone
3	E	Fair Isle	Raspberry	Anemone
2	E	Fair Isle	Raspberry	Lime

Row	Stitch Pattern	Pattern Setting	Feeder 1	Feeder 2
1	E	Fair Isle	Emerald	Lime
2	F	Knit	Emerald	
1	F	Fair Isle	Emerald	Loganberry
5	F	Fair Isle	Emerald	Pumpkin
1	F	Fair Isle	Emerald	Loganberry
2	F	Knit	Emerald	
1	G	Fair Isle	Emerald	Madder
1	G	Knit	Madder	
2	G	Fair Isle	Madder	Anemone
2	G	Fair Isle	Loganberry	Jade
5	G	Fair Isle	Loganberry	Splash
2	G	Fair Isle	Loganberry	Jade
2	G	Fair Isle	Madder	Anemone
1	G	Knit	Madder	
1	G	Fair Isle	Madder	Navy
2	H	Knit	Navy	
3	H	Fair Isle	Navy	Daffodil
2	H	Knit	Navy	
2	I	Knit	Navy	
4	I	Fair Isle	Navy	Loganberry
4	I	Fair Isle	Navy	Raspberry
4	I	Fair Isle	Navy	Anemone
2	I	Fair Isle	Navy	Lime
4	I	Fair Isle	Navy	Anemone
4	I	Fair Isle	Navy	Raspberry
4	I	Fair Isle	Navy	Loganberry
2	I	Knit	Navy	
2	J	Knit	Emerald	
3	J	Fair Isle	Emerald	Madder
3	J	Fair Isle	Pumpkin	Anemone
3	J	Fair Isle	Daffodil	Lime
3	J	Fair Isle	Raspberry	Splash
2	J	Knit	Raspberry	
2	K	Knit	Daffodil	
3	K	Fair Isle	Daffodil	Lime
3	K	Fair Isle	Pumpkin	Emerald
1	K	Fair Isle	Madder	Anemone
3	K	Fair Isle	Pumpkin	Emerald
3	K	Fair Isle	Daffodil	Lime

Row	Stitch Pattern	Pattern Setting	Feeder 1	Feeder 2
2	K	Knit	Daffodil	
2	L	Knit	Splash	
2	L	Fair Isle	Splash	Navy
1	L	Fair Isle	Splash	Madder
2	L	Fair Isle	Splash	Navy
1	L	Knit	Splash	
1	L	Knit	Jade	
3	L	Fair Isle	Jade	Raspberry
1	L	Fair Isle	Navy	Madder
3	L	Fair Isle	Jade	Raspberry
1	L	Knit	Jade	
1	L	Knit	Splash	
2	L	Fair Isle	Splash	Navy
1	L	Fair Isle	Splash	Madder
2	L	Fair Isle	Splash	Navy
2	L	Knit	Splash	
2	M	Knit	Loganberry	
2	M	Fair Isle	Loganberry	Anemone
2	M	Fair Isle	Loganberry	Raspberry
2	M	Fair Isle	Loganberry	Anemone
2	M	Knit	Loganberry	
4	N	Fair Isle	Loganberry	Jade
4	N	Fair Isle	Madder	Splash
4	N	Fair Isle	Raspberry	Lime
1	N	Fair Isle	Daffodil	Pumpkin
4	N	Fair Isle	Raspberry	Lime
4	N	Fair Isle	Madder	Splash
4	N	Fair Isle	Loganberry	Jade

Rep stitch patt M.

Dark colourway

Row	Stitch Pattern	Pattern Setting	Feeder 1	Feeder 2
2	A	Knit	Navy	
3	A	Fair Isle	Navy	Sand
1	A	Fair Isle	Daffodil	Pumpkin
1	A	Knit	Havana	
3	A	Fair Isle	Havana	Lime
1	A	Fair Isle	Havana	Madder
3	A	Fair Isle	Havana	Lime
1	A	Knit	Havana	
1	A	Fair Isle	Daffodil	Pumpkin
3	A	Fair Isle	Navy	Sand
2	A	Knit	Navy	
2	B	Knit	Port Wine	
3	B	Fair Isle	Port Wine	Spice
2	B	Knit	Port Wine	
1	C	Fair Isle	Port Wine	Madder
1	C	Fair Isle	Havana	Madder
3	C	Fair Isle	Havana	Daffodil
3	C	Fair Isle	Loganberry	Lime
3	C	Fair Isle	Havana	Daffodil
1	C	Fair Isle	Havana	Madder
1	C	Fair Isle	Rosewood	Madder
2	C	Knit	Rosewood	
2	D	Fair Isle	Rosewood	Clyde Blue
1	D	Fair Isle	Rosewood	Jade
2	D	Fair Isle	Rosewood	Clyde Blue
2	D	Knit	Rosewood	
1	E	Fair Isle	Rosewood	Granite
2	E	Fair Isle	Pumpkin	Granite
3	E	Fair Isle	Pumpkin	Clyde Blue
1	E	Fair Isle	Daffodil	Clyde Blue
2	E	Fair Isle	Daffodil	Splash
1	E	Fair Isle	Salmon	Lime
2	E	Fair Isle	Daffodil	Splash
1	E	Fair Isle	Daffodil	Clyde Blue
3	E	Fair Isle	Pumpkin	Clyde Blue
2	E	Fair Isle	Pumpkin	Granite
1	E	Fair Isle	Rosewood	Granite

Row	Stitch Pattern	Pattern Setting	Feeder 1	Feeder 2
2	F	Knit	Rosewood	
1	F	Fair Isle	Rosewood	Salmon
5	F	Fair Isle	Rosewood	White
1	F	Fair Isle	Rosewood	Salmon
2	F	Knit	Rosewood	
1	G	Fair Isle	Rosewood	Madder
1	G	Knit	Madder	
2	G	Fair Isle	Madder	Lime
2	G	Fair Isle	Loganberry	Jade
5	G	Fair Isle	Loganberry	Splash
2	G	Fair Isle	Loganberry	Jade
2	G	Fair Isle	Madder	Lime
1	G	Knit	Madder	
1	G	Fair Isle	Rosewood	Madder
2	H	Knit	Rosewood	
3	H	Fair Isle	Rosewood	Jade
2	H	Knit	Rosewood	
2	I	Knit	Heron	
4	I	Fair Isle	Heron	Sunset
4	I	Fair Isle	Granite	Salmon
4	I	Fair Isle	Sand	Madder
2	I	Fair Isle	White	Port Wine
4	I	Fair Isle	Sand	Madder
4	I	Fair Isle	Granite	Salmon
4	I	Fair Isle	Heron	Sunset
2	I	Knit	Heron	
2	J	Knit	Rosewood	
3	J	Fair Isle	Rosewood	Jade
3	J	Fair Isle	Havana	Daffodil
3	J	Fair Isle	Navy	Lime
3	J	Fair Isle	Port Wine	Splash
2	J	Knit	Port Wine	
2	K	Knit	Madder	
3	K	Fair Isle	Madder	Lime
3	K	Fair Isle	Loganberry	Jade
1	K	Fair Isle	White	Salmon
3	K	Fair Isle	Loganberry	Jade
3	K	Fair Isle	Madder	Lime
2	K	Knit	Madder	

Row	Stitch Pattern	Pattern Setting	Feeder 1	Feeder 2
2	L	Knit	Havana	
2	L	Fair Isle	Havana	Daffodil
1	L	Fair Isle	Havana	Pumpkin
2	L	Fair Isle	Havana	Daffodil
1	L	Knit	Havana	
1	L	Knit	Splash	
3	L	Fair Isle	Splash	Pumpkin
1	L	Fair Isle	Daffodil	Lime
3	L	Fair Isle	Splash	Pumpkin
1	L	Knit	Splash	
1	L	Knit	Havana	
2	L	Fair Isle	Havana	Daffodil
1	L	Fair Isle	Havana	Pumpkin
2	L	Fair Isle	Havana	Daffodil
2	L	Knit	Havana	
1	M	Knit	Rosewood	
2	M	Fair Isle	Rosewood	Splash
2	M	Fair Isle	Rosewood	Lime
2	M	Fair Isle	Rosewood	Splash
1	M	Knit	Rosewood	
1	N	Knit	Rosewood	
4	N	Fair Isle	Rosewood	Jade
4	N	Fair Isle	Madder	Splash
4	N	Fair Isle	Port Wine	Daffodil
1	N	Fair Isle	Lime	White
4	N	Fair Isle	Port Wine	Daffodil
4	N	Fair Isle	Madder	Splash
4	N	Fair Isle	Rosewood	Jade
1	N	Knit	Rosewood	

Rep stitch patt M.

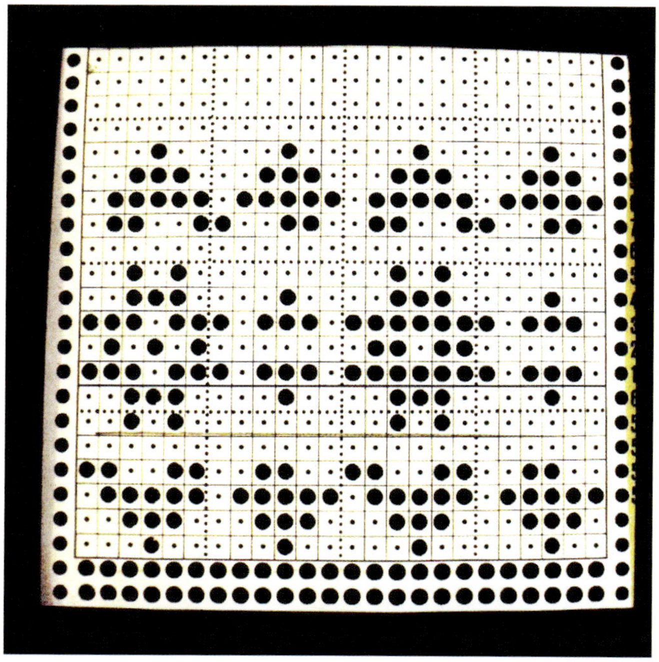

Punchcard stitch pattern A.

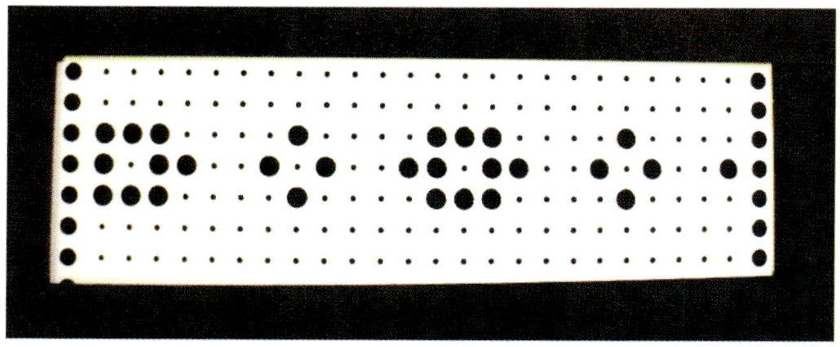

Punchcard stitch pattern B.

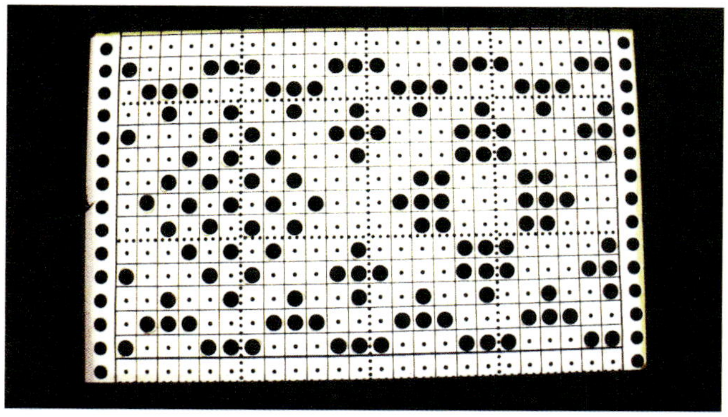

Punchcard stitch pattern C.

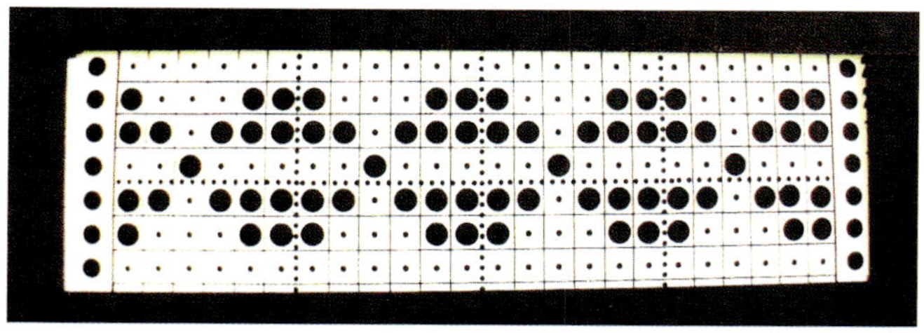

Punchcard stitch pattern D.

Stitch pattern A in Bright, Brown, Green and Blue.

Stitch pattern B, C and D in Bright.

Stitch pattern B, C and D in Brown.

Stitch pattern B, C and D in Green.

Stitch pattern B, C and D in Blue.

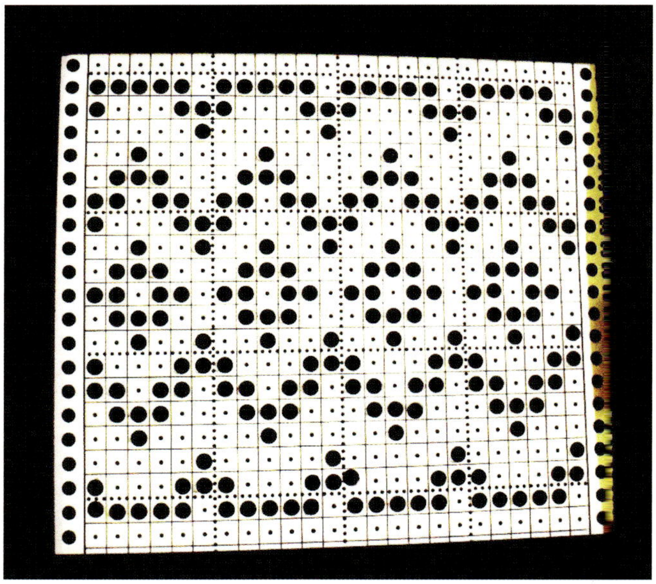

Punchcard stitch pattern E.

Stitch pattern E in Bright.

Stitch pattern E in Brown.

Stitch pattern E in Green.

Stitch pattern E in Blue.

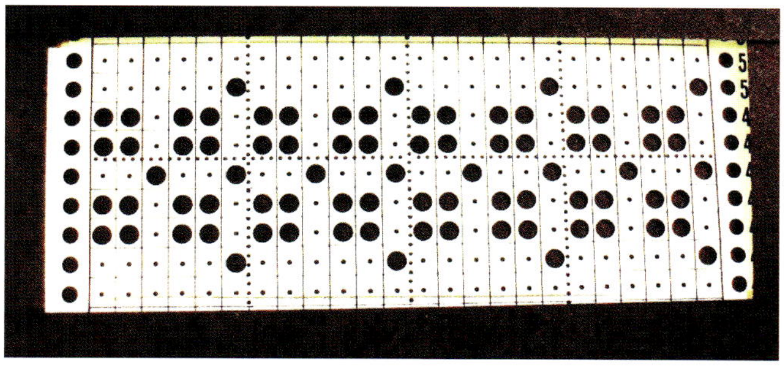

Punchcard stitch pattern F.

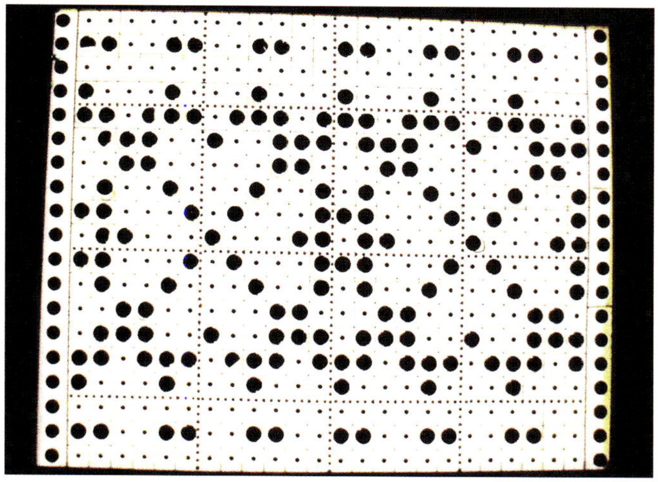

Punchcard stitch pattern G.

Stitch pattern F and G in Bright.

Stitch pattern F and G in Brown.

Stitch pattern F and G in Green.

Stitch pattern F and G in Blue.

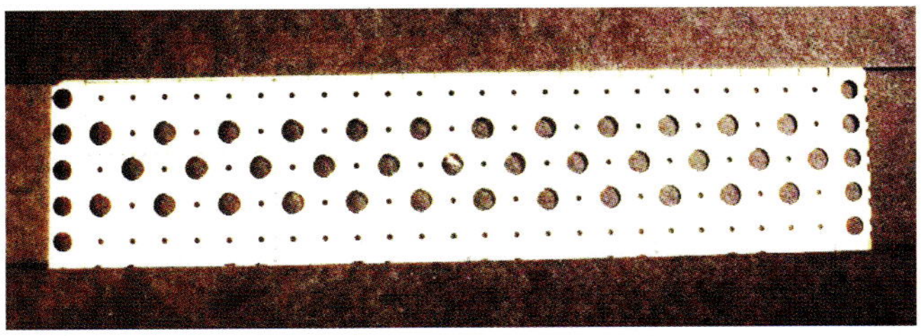

Punchcard stitch pattern H.

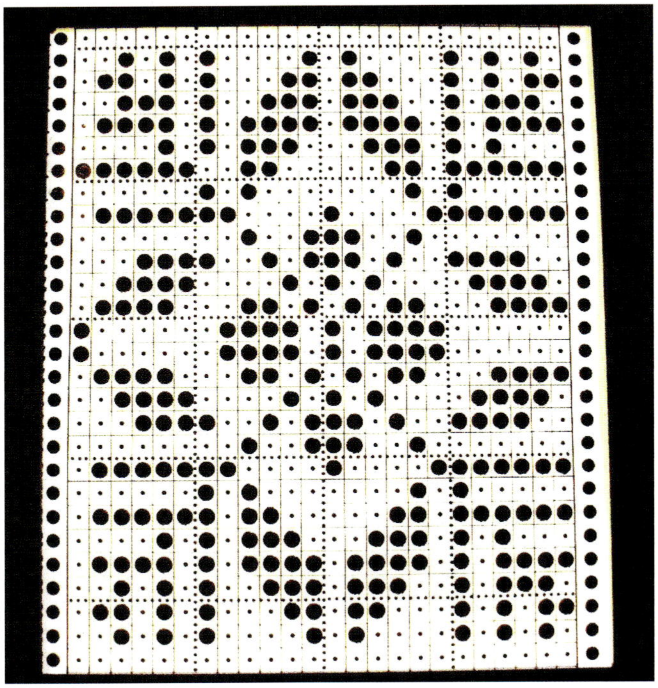

Punchcard stitch pattern I.

Stitch pattern H and I in Bright.

Stitch pattern H and I in Brown.

Stitch pattern H and I in Green.

Stitch pattern H and I in Blue.

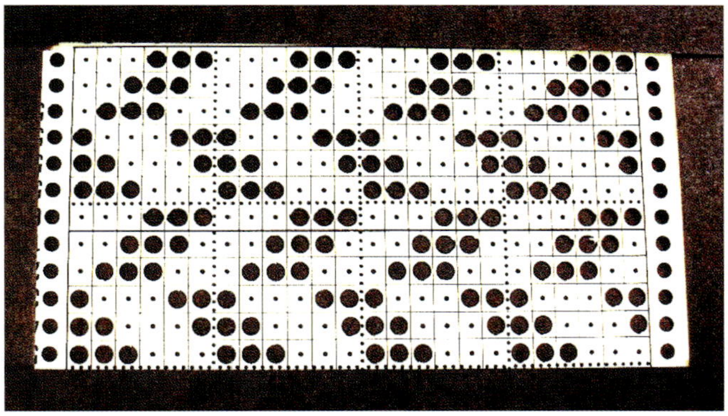

Punchcard stitch pattern J.

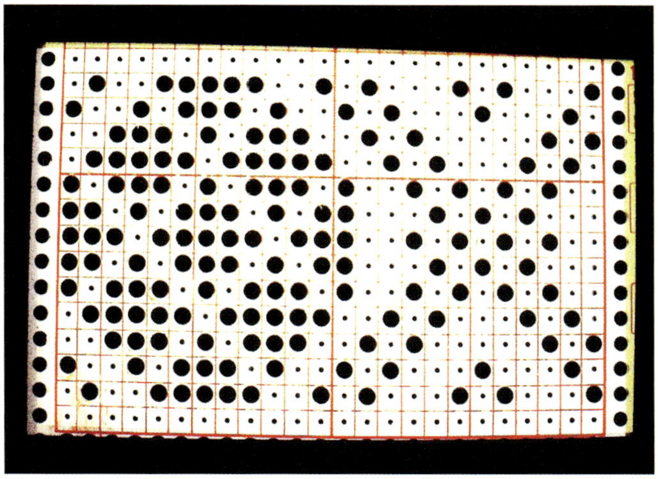

Punchcard stitch pattern K.

Stitch pattern J and K in Bright.

Stitch pattern J and K in Brown.

Stitch pattern J and K in Green.

Stitch pattern J and K in Blue.

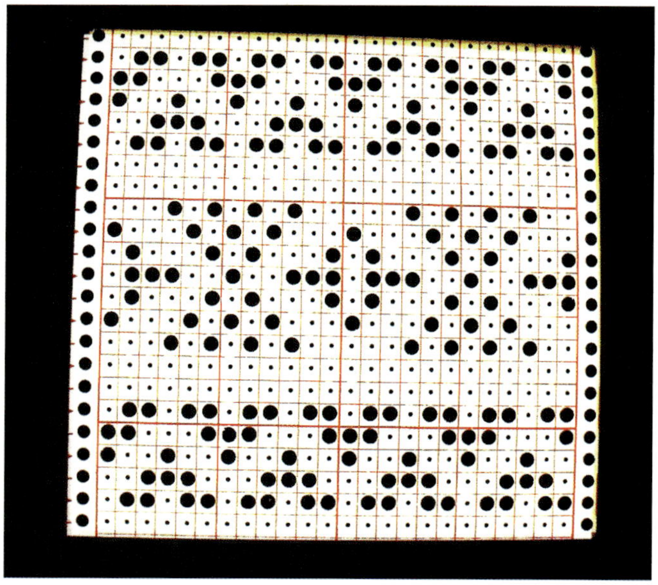

Punchcard stitch pattern L.

Stitch pattern L in Bright.

Stitch pattern L in Brown.

Stitch pattern L in Green.

Stitch pattern L in Blue.

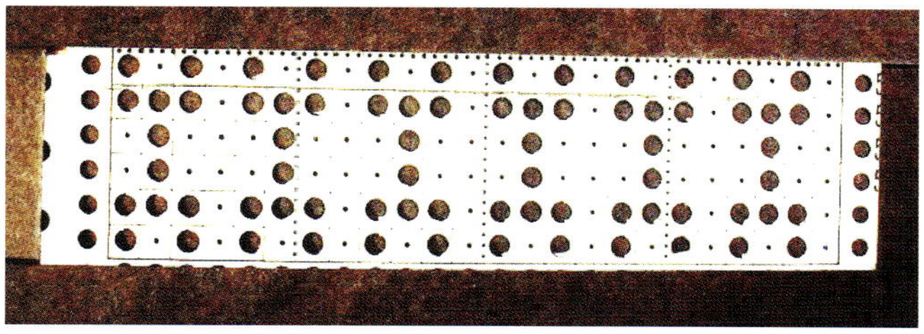

Punchcard stitch pattern M.

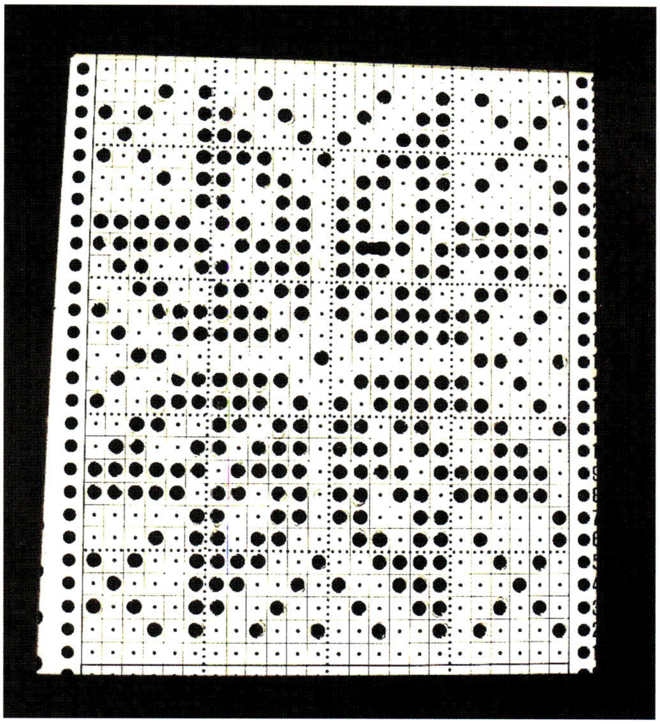

Punchcard stitch pattern N.

Stitch pattern M, N and M in Bright.

Stitch pattern M, N and M in Brown.

Stitch pattern M, N and M in Green.

Stitch pattern M, N and M in Blue.

Fair Isle Scarf in dark and multi colourways.

Materials
Finished weight 320g.

Measurements
Width 20cm, length 166 cm.

Tension
MT 8• 29 sts – 36 rows = 10 cm.

Machine
Standard gauge electronic or punchcard.

TRADITIONAL PATTERN SCARF

The scarf is three times the length of the collar, so work through the length of any chart three times.

The image shows some of the stitch patterns are placed with different stitch patterns and varying colours when the pattern is repeated. It is a great way to play with colour and patterns and be inventive.

Method

Follow instructions for collar, but work through patt sequence 3 times.

Making up
As for Fair Isle Collar but graft ends tog.

Materials

Finished weight 350g.

Jamiesons of Shetland 2/21s wool in oil on cone.

Bright colourway

Cs: this uses Cs similar to the bright coloured collar. The top block uses Heron 315 and Blueberry 295.

Sea Blue colourway

Cs: this uses Cs similar to the blue collar and the top block is knitted with Granite 122 and Aqua 929.

8 buttons plus 1 spare.

Measurements

Chest 98cm, length to shoulder 59cm, sleeve length 44cm.

Tension

MT 8• 30 sts – 36 rows = 10cm.

Machine

Standard gauge electronic or punchcard.

Skye punchcard stitch pattern

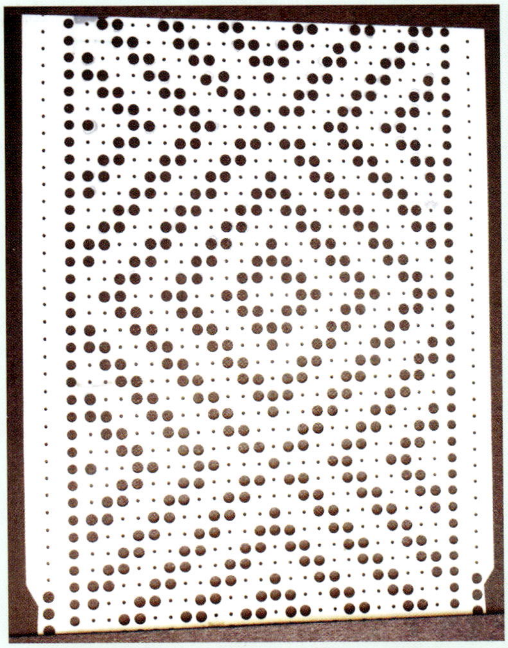

Punchcard stitch pattern for Stonybreck Cardigan.

Fronts and back

Use the punchcard stitch patterns from the collar starting at L, B, E, F, K, G, H and then use the Skye stitch pattern from the armhole to the top of the shoulder.

Sleeves

Work through the following stitch patterns: A, D, E, F, C, B, K, J, L, D, H.

STONYBRECK CARDIGAN

The cardigans are made up of a combination of the previous traditional Fair Isle patterns. These can be swapped around and any colour combinations mixed together. The top two-colour block is knitted using the Skye stitch pattern, but obviously you can continue the Fair Isle stripes up to the shoulder.

Stonybreck Cardigans in Sea Blue and Dark.

Stonybreck Sea Blue Cardigan.

Stonybreck Dark cardigan.

Method

Back

With WY cast on 73 sts, change to any C, k 20 rows for hem and start to follow FI stitch patt sequence and colourway of choice.

RC000, after 20 rows pick up hem sts and cont to knit.

Complete stitch patts L, B, E, F, K, G, H.

Place marker at each side. RC103 change to Skye stitch patt and cont until RC204.

Shape shoulder place into HP 5 Ns at beg of each row until 40 sts remain.

Run off onto WY.

Front

With WY cast on 73 sts and work as for back up to RC103.

Front shaping dec 1 st at front edge every 4th row until 20 sts have been dec. Cont to RC204 and shape shoulder to match back.

Pick up shoulder sts from back and unravel WY, knit 1 row MT10 and latch off.

Rep for second front.

Fair Isle Cardigan schematic.

A	49cm
B	26cm
C	60cm
D	30cm
E	17.5cm

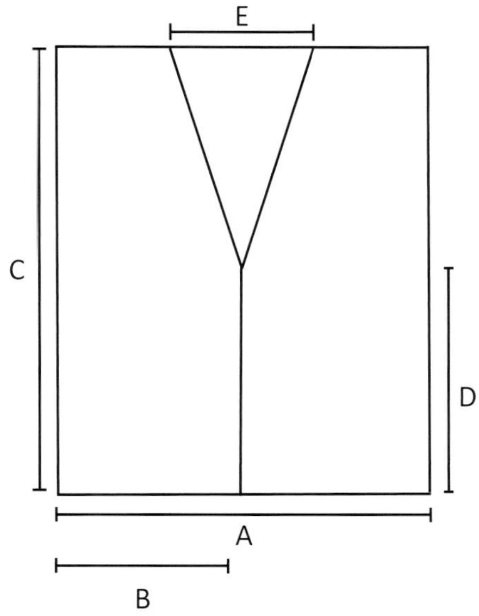

F	20cm
G	44cm
H	52cm

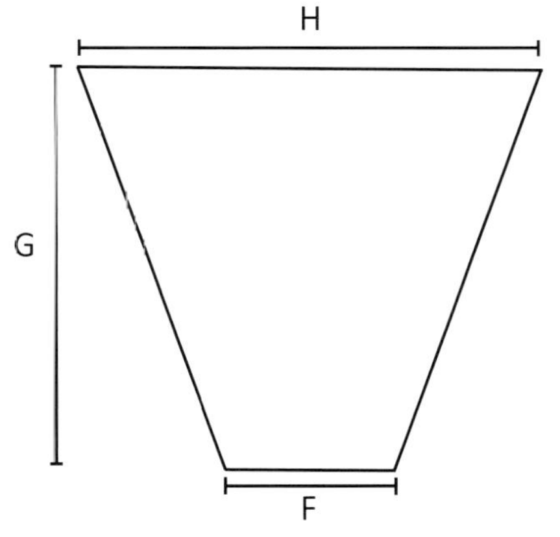

Sleeves

With right side of front and back facing, pick up 140 sts from armhole marker to marker.

K 2 rows. Start to follow punchcard stitch patts and patt sequence J, D, dec 1st at each end of every 3rd row until 70 sts remain. At same time cont to work stitch patts L, J, K, B, C, F, E, D, A.

K 20 rows any C and latch off.

Button bands

With WY cast on 20 sts for back neck and 145 sts for R front.

K 2 rows, k 6 rows FI using J stitch patt, placing 8 buttonholes evenly down front. K 2 rows.

Change to any C and k 10 rows.

Pick up sts and unravel WY. K 1 row and then pick up 20 sts from back neck and 145 sts down front edge. K 1 row, MT+2 k 1 row and latch off.

With WY cast 145 sts for rem front and rep.

Making up

Sew sleeve seams. Sew down side seams of cardigan and sew on buttons.

Sunflower Shawl Collar Jacket.

Sunflower Jacket, pocket detail.

Sunflower Jacket, detail.

SUNFLOWER SHAWL COLLAR JACKET

Method

Back

E wrap cast on MC, MT–2, k 22 rows.

MT+2, k 1 row. Insert punchcard and lock, k 1 row.

RC000, release punchcard and follow patt chart.

K to RC86, inc 1 st at each end of every 10th row until 182 sts.

K to RC174.

Shape armholes

Cast off 14 sts at beg of next 2 rows. Cont in patt sequence to RC256.

Place onto WY.

Pocket linings

Make two. E wrap cast on MC 40 sts and k 68 rows. Knit onto WY.

Left front

E wrap cast on MC 75 sts (Ns 83 to 9 at L).

MT–2, knit 22 rows, COR. Cast on 32 sts at R using MC. TD + 2, k 1 row. Insert punchcard and lock on first row. 107 sts.

MT k 1 row, RC000, release punchcard and work in patt RC70.

Placing pocket

Place onto WY sts from Ns 63–24 at L. On wrong side of pocket lining facing pick up sts from last row of pocket lining in MC 63–24.

Cont in patt RC86 inc 1 st at left on next and every foll 10th row until 114 sts. RC147.

Inc 1 st at R and every foll alt row until 119 sts. RC156.

Inc 1 st on L of next row.

Inc 1 st on R on next and every foll alt row until 129 sts.

K 1 row RC175.

Shape armhole

Cast off 14 sts at beg of next row, inc 1 st at end of next row. 124 sts.

Inc 1 st at R and every foll alt row until 154 sts. K 1 row. RC257.

Materials
Finished weight 550g.
Jamiesons of Shetland Spindrift wool in oil.
MC: 250g Daffodil 390.
Cs: 60g each of Fern 249 and Lime 780; 70g Peat 198; 90g each of Port Wine 293 and Sapphire 676; 65g Havana 248; 130g Burnt Ochre 423 and Tan Green 241; 50g White 104, plus a small amount of Madder 587.

Measurements
This sample garment: chest 110cm, length to shoulder 72cm, sleeve seam 54cm.

Tension
MT 8• 33 sts – 36 rows = 10cm.

Machine
Standard gauge electronic or punchcard.

Punchcard stitch pattern
Use the M and N punchcard stitch patterns shown in the previous Fair Isle collar pages.

Pattern sequence

Rows	Stitch Pattern	Pattern Setting	Feeder 1	Feeder 2
*2	M	Knit	Daffodil	
2	M	Fair Isle	Daffodil	Fern
2	M	Fair Isle	Daffodil	Lime
2	M	Fair isle	Daffodil	Fern
2	M	Knit	Daffodil	
3	N	Fair Isle	Daffodil	Havana
3	N	Fair Isle	Burnt Ochre	Peat
3	N	Fair Isle	White	Port Wine
3	N	Fair Isle	Tan Green	Sapphire
1	N	Fair Isle	Tan Green	Madder
3	N	Fair Isle	Tan Green	Sapphire
3	N	Fair Isle	White	Port Wine
3	N	Fair Isle	Burnt Ochre	Peat
3	N	Fair Isle	Daffodil	Havana

Rep from *.

Shape shoulder
COL, at beg of next row run 54 sts off onto WY.

Collar
Cont in patt sequence over rem 100 sts RC290. Cast off.

Right front
Work as for L front, reversing shaping, and work in buttonholes on rows evenly placed at end of each M stitch patt, but note top button is a sewn loop.

Sleeves
E wrap cast on MC 80 sts. TD2, k 22 rows COR.
MT+2, k 1 row. Insert punchcard and lock.
MT, k 1 row, release punchcard RC000.
Follow stitch patt sequence, inc 1 st each of every 6th row until 160 sts.
Cont to RC175. Cast off.

Pocket tops
Using punchcard stitch patt M, make a 40 sts pocket top and pick up sts from WY at pocket edge. K 1 row MT10 and latch off.

Making up
Join shoulders, pick up 54 sts from front and back. K 1 row MT+1 and latch off.

Set in sleeves, join side and sleeve seams. Join collar seam at centre back. Fold lower edge and cuff facing, sew into place, also collar and front facing, Fold in half the 32 sts cast on to wrong side and sew into place. Neaten buttonholes as you go. Make a loop in MC for final top buttonhole and use larger contrasting button. Sew down pocket tops and side seam to linings.

Inspirations for the Sunflower Jacket.

Sunflower Jacket.

A	71cm
B	48cm
C	28cm
D	47cm
E	56cm
F	68cm
G	18cm

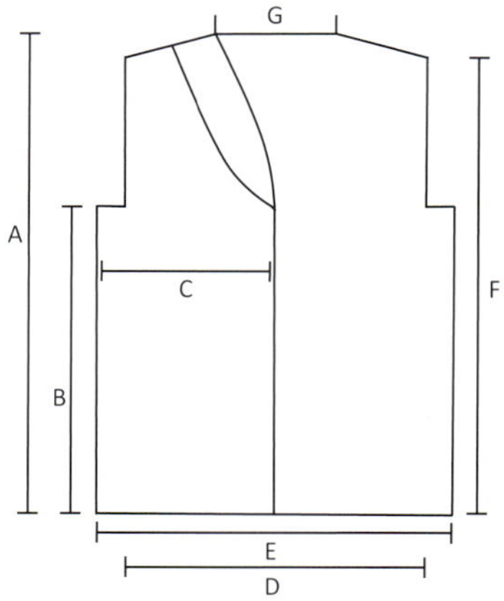

H	27cm
I	52cm
J	43cm

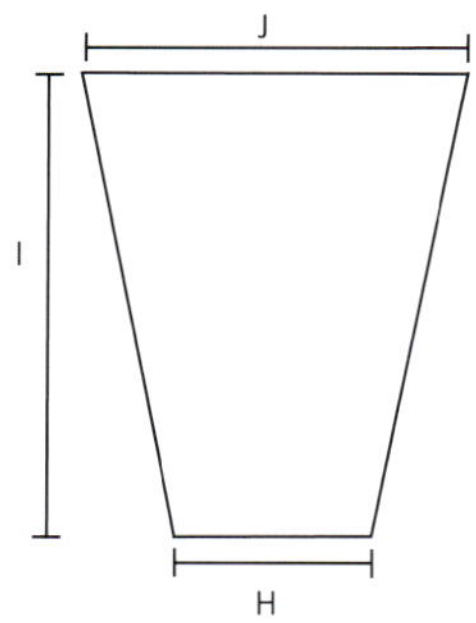

Sunflower Shawl Collar Jacket schematic.

SKYE SCARF AND TURNING TIDE SCARF

Skye Scarf

Following on from the designs incorporating traditional Fair Isle patterns I continued to experiment with both Shetland and Donegal wool, building on their ability to felt in a hot wash, and mixing the wool with a non-felting yarn to create a delicate textured fabric. The floats at the back of the Fair Isle design are small so the scarves do not require folding over, and the pattern on the wrong side after felting is also attractive.

The Skye Scarf uses an all-over diamond-shape stitch pattern. Glorious colour combinations can be used in all the felted scarves in this section. Donegal Soft wool was used in most of them as the felting yarn and similar colours in a non-felting yarn. It is also a versatile pattern and can used on a larger scale for a blanket.

Pale colourway

Cs: Donegal Soft wool in the following: Annalee 5504 (pale blue), Duffy 5537 (pale beige), Swilly 5507 (cream), Bann 5505 (pale green), Eske 5529 (stone) – all very pale cream and beige tones. The non-felting Cs are lilac, grey, cream, blue and pale green.

Bright colourway

Cs: Donegal Soft wool in the following: Clare 5530 (orange), Roe 5527 (dark blue), Gara 5534 (yellow), Dariana 5532 (purple), Killala 5536 (bright green), Brosna 5522 (pink), Liscannor 5526 (cerise). The non-felting Cs are purple, white, red, bright pink and rust.

Dark colourway

Cs: Donegal Soft wool in the following: Bantry 5531 (elderberry), Beltra 5528 (green-blue), Sheelin 5520 (black), Dingle 5516 (blackberry), Ballycastle 5502 (dark green). The non-felting Cs are rust, olive, maroon, amethyst and green.

Skye Scarf in Red.

Skye Scarves in Pale, Bright and Dark placed on a large throw.

Turning Tide Scarves in felted Donegal wool.

Materials
Finished weight 170g.
See above for colourways.

Measurements
Width 19cm, length 166cm.

Tension
MT 8• 42 sts – 34 rows = 10 cm over stitch pattern and after felting.

Machine
Standard gauge electronic or punchcard.

Punchcard stitch pattern
Use either the Skye stitch pattern or the Herringbone stitch pattern.

Turning Tide Scarf

These are knitted using the Herringbone stitch pattern. Every colour combination works well in this design.

The photo of the Turning Tide scarves in felted Donegal wool shows seven different colourways: every shade of green; yellow and cream; every autumnal shade; pared-back soft subtle colours; every bright colour available; various shades of blue; and shades of grey highlighted with black and cream.

Method for both scarves

E wrap cast on with three strands of Donegal Soft wool.
K 1 row.
Use the thicker Donegal Soft wool in feeder 1 and the fine yarn in feeder 2.
K 2 rows single thread and start FI patt, changing Cs every 20 rows. RC000.
Cont for approx RC660 rows or required length.
K 1 row using ends of 3 threads, MT10 and latch off.
Machine wash at 40° wash, 800 spin speed.

SANQUHAR SCARF

Sanquhar is a town in Dumfriesshire, on the west side of Scotland about sixty miles from Carlisle. The eponymous pattern is based around a square or diamond and is usually found knitted with two colours. The shape of these designs lends itself to machine knitting.

The names of the stitch patterns and their variations are delightful – Shepherds Plaid, Midge and Fly, and Prince of Wales. They can be used as small separate designs, and when repeated over a larger area another pattern becomes visible. They do also have some similarity with some of the traditional patterns worked in Cumberland and there is something very attractive about their simplicity, and when worked in two colours they can be striking and instantly recognizable. The stitch pattern I have used is a traditional one but with various colours added.

This stitch pattern is usually worked in two colours throughout, and is a distinctive, dramatic and eye-catching pattern which has been used for many years. It is well worth looking at further patterns based on this principle as there are many and they lend themselves to machine knitting, with small floats and intricate colour changes.

It is based on squares and has small floats on the wrong side so is ideal for this form of scarf.

Punchcard stitch pattern

The colours of the ones made here change with every square so knit 1 row MC, then 9 rows Fair Isle MC and C patt setting F, knit 1 row MC. Change to another colour and so on. The colours chosen are similar to the scarves above, as are the general making instructions. It is worth noting that when washed the edges are wavy as there is less of the MC felting, apart from the two knit rows between the squares. This makes for an interesting edge.

Sanquhar Scarves in cream, bright and dark shades in lightly felted Donegal wool and silk.

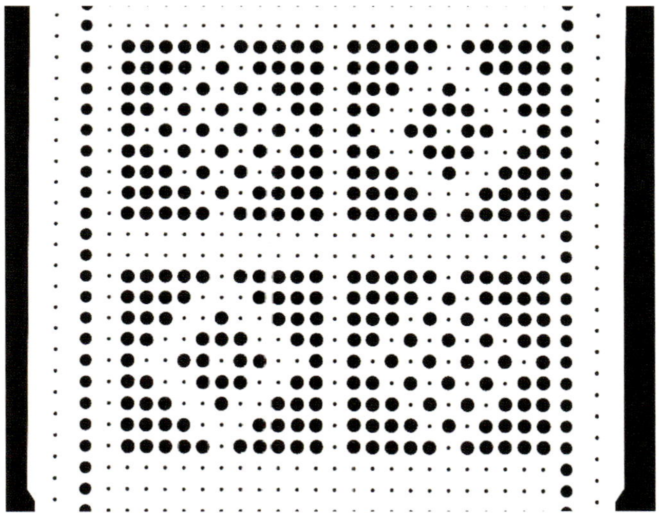

Punchcard stitch pattern for Sanquhar Scarf.

Skye Throw.

Skye Throw, detail.

Materials
Finished weight 900g.
MCs: Knoll Soft Donegal wool in various shades used in feeder 1.
Cs: contrasting C2, C3 non-felting yarn in various shades in feeder 2.

Measurements
Width 198cm, length 124cm.

Tension
MT 7• 41 sts – 35 rows = 10cm.

Machine
Standard gauge electronic or punchcard.

Punchcard stitch pattern
Use the Skye pattern as above.

SKYE THROW

The Skye throw has been knitted in strips and sewn together to make a large patchwork of jewel colours. Donegal wool and a contrast fine non-felting yarn have been used to create a textured surface.

Method

Using MC E wrap cast on 76 sts and k 2 rows.
RC000. Start FI patt and work 60 rows, change Cs and work further 60 rows.
Rep FI blocks until there are 7 in total. RC420, k 2 rows, cast off.
Using different set of Cs make further seven strips, so you have eight in total. Sew strips tog.
Machine wash at 40°, 800 spin speed, to felt.

Scarves with Houndstooth variations.

Dogstooth samples.

HOUNDSTOOTH, DOGSTOOTH AND PUPPYTOOTH SCARVES

Also known as Shepherd's Check, this staple pattern is never out of fashion. The original two-colour pattern resembles a dog's tooth, and such fabric was worn by shepherds as an outer layer. Examples have been traced to the Scottish Lowlands in the nineteenth century, but it really came into its own in the 1930s, since when it has been used extensively in weaving and printed fabrics.

It was adopted by the upper classes as a symbol of status and style; Christian Dior used it in his 1948 haute couture collection and it was considered by some as the Dior fashion house trademark. In 1959, Roger Vivier designed pointed court shoes for Dior using a smaller-scale pattern, which became known as Puppytooth. Six years later it was enlarged to Dogstooth size and a stunning two-colour black and turquoise A-line coat was shown.

The two-colour pattern resembles a woodcut with its deceptively simple shape, and it is a versatile pattern which can be adapted to suit many different textiles. Many designers have played with the colours and scale of the pattern which has meant that it is always in fashion. This versatility is shown by changing the background colours to bright rainbow colours, for example.

Dogstooth Rainbow Scarf

The rainbow has been used many, many times and countless children sing about the colours. Endless books have been written about the meaning of various colours and this changes across cultures, yet it has always been a symbol of hope. In the book of Genesis it appears as proof of a covenant between God and all living creatures. References can also be found in historical documents in China, Egypt and native America, always as a symbol of hope.

The designer Gilbert Baker used it to great effect in 1978 when he was asked for a design for the Gay Pride flag, which has become a potent symbol for most people of tolerance, equality and joy. Baker gave meaning to each of the colours he used. The original design had eight stripes: hot pink for sexuality, red for life, orange for healing, yellow for sunlight, green for nature, turquoise for art, indigo for serenity and harmony, and violet for spirit. However, during manufacture this was honed down to six; hot pink was discarded and the indigo and turquoise mixed together.

How many colours make up a rainbow design is somewhat arbitrary: the children's rhyme has seven, the Gay Pride flag six. It is a spectrum, a colour circle, but it is such a universal motif that it is recognized around the world and across cultures.

It is possible to pick up any colour you like and work with it, so that a whole new exciting world of understanding and exploration opens up and enriches your work. In the changing times in which we live, politics of all kinds are reflected in our choices and therefore in our routes through our practice and discipline.

Dogstooth Rainbow Scarves in navy, turquoise and black.

Materials
Finished weight 210g.
Various Cs in 2/20s 2-ply yarn.

Measurements
Width 14cm after folding, length 180cm.

Tension
MT 8• 30 sts – 32 rows = 10 cm.

Machine
Standard gauge electronic or punchcard.

Using a traditional design of Dogstooth and a rainbow background seemed a way forward with this design. Playing with the scale of the shape was an interesting exercise, with the small Puppytooth morphing into the larger Dogstooth. This was done by changing the pattern stitch card and, after several rows, repeating each row twice using the elongation button on the machine to make the Houndstooth pattern. The initial symbol or shape remains the same colour and the background colours recur and react in a different way which keeps the eye moving and makes for an interesting design.

Notice that in the turquoise colourway, the vibrant background colour remains the same but the motif changes colour and works its way through the rainbow spectrum.

Method

Basic shape

E wrap cast on 110 sts and work Dogstooth patt in FI, changing background C every 10 rows. The finished fabric is folded over and sewn down.

Using a mix of some tweedy marled yarn can create a more country rugged look. With minor colour changes each scarf changes considerably.

This version of the scarf is larger and the finished weight is 400g; the yarn used is 2/14s 3-ply and felted. The floats on the wrong side of the yarn could create a problem as they are too long, so experiment with small sample swatches on 40° wash and ascertain which lightly matts to anchor the fibres together.

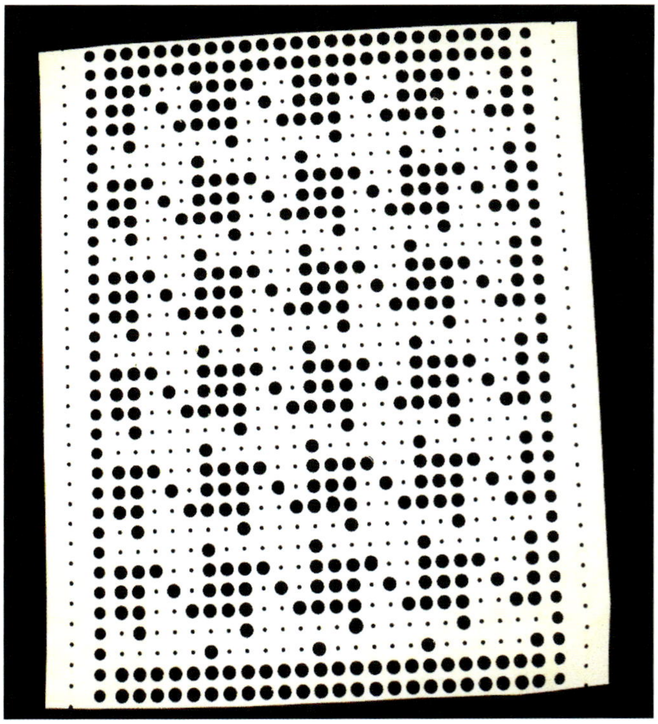

Punchcard stitch pattern for Puppytooth.

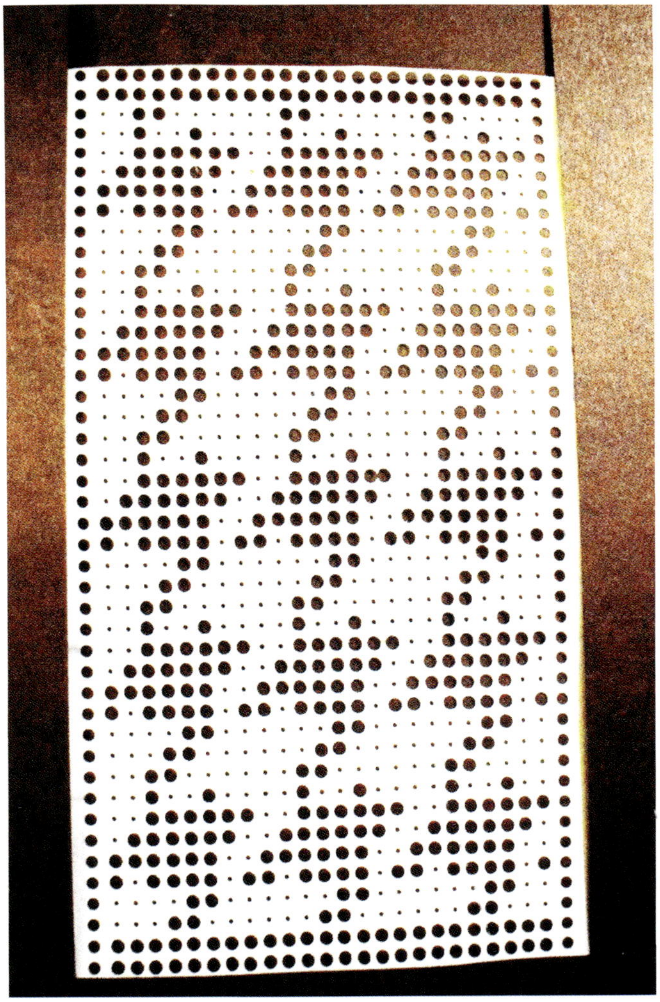

Punchcard stitch pattern for Dogstooth, elongated by repeating each row twice to make Houndstooth.

Houndstooth tweedy scarves in yellow, red and blue.

Dogstooth samples before and after felting.

Method variation

E wrap cast on 110 sts MT8•
Using Puppytooth stitch patt, rep motif 5 times.
Change to Dogstooth patt, rep motif 12 times.
Change to Houndstooth patt, elongate or rep each row twice, repeating motif 22 times.
Rep Dogstooth motif 12 times.
Rep Puppytooth motif 5 times.
Change background C every time a motif is started. Cast off.
Decide if you want a felted finish, and if so, place in a washing machine.

Animal Print Scarf in beige, coral and grey.

ANIMAL PRINT SCARF

Each of the colourways has its own identity and it's a matter of collecting all the colours together within the colour palette chosen and working through them. The mottled shapes remain the same colour throughout.

Method

E wrap cast on MC 110 sts and work in F throughout. The MC is in feeder 2 and the other Cs change every 10, 12, 16 and 20 rows.
Rep until required length reached. Cast off.

Materials
Finished weight 230g.
Yarn used is combination of wool 2/20s 2-ply and 2/14s 3-ply, some of which felt more densely than others.

Tension
MT 8• 37 sts – 36rows = 10cm.

Measurements
Width 26.5cm, length 162cm.

Machine
Standard gauge electronic or punchcard.

Punchcard stitch pattern
The original stitch pattern had too many large floats so extra stitches were added to create a busier pattern but smaller floats.

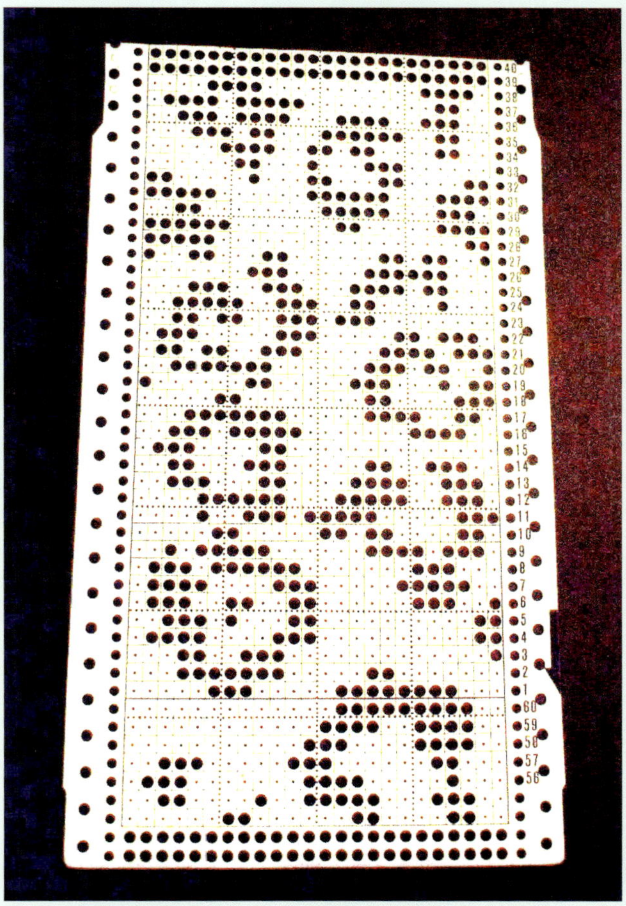

Original Animal Print stitch chart producing long floats.

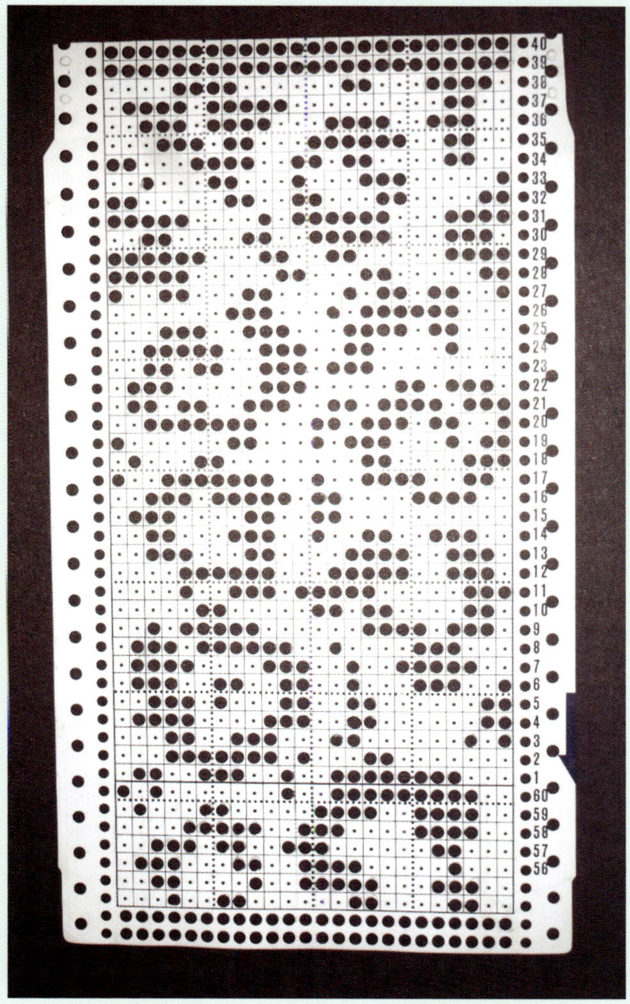

Animal Print stitch chart after changes to remove long floats.

Checks and Balances Scarves, detail of Bright and Yellow colourways.

Checks and Balances in Blue, Yellow and Bright.

CHECKS AND BALANCES SCARF

Stitch patterns do not need to be complicated, as using a basic pattern and changing colours can create some exciting results. All the Checks and Balances Scarves use only six colours and these are moved up and down the scarf. The yarn required to knit this design will need to be susceptible to felting on a hot wash. It is this factor which changes the flat loose design to dense ridges and a gloriously bumpy texture.

The colour choice of the Red and Blue versions was based on colours used by the Bauhaus movement. Having looked at many beautiful Bauhaus textiles, mainly woven, the colours they used proved to be the inspiration for these designs. Making notes on the wide palette used by the Bauhaus, and which worked well together, was a great exercise – yellow, olive green, white, black, grey and turquoise; yellow, white, blue, lilac; and finally, yellow, purple, green, white and grey.

Materials

Finished weight 250g.

Approximate weights per colour are A 35g, B 30g, C 90g, D 50g, E 25g, F 20g.

Blue colourway

Cs: A cream, B navy, C grey, D pale blue, E orange, F yellow.

Yellow colourway

Cs: A red, B black, C yellow, D grey, E cream, F brown.

Bright colourway

Cs: A lilac, B green, C blue, D pink, E yellow, F coral.

Measurements

Width 24cm, length 180cm.

Tension

MT 8• 48 sts – 36 rows = 10cm after felting.

Machine

Standard gauge electronic or punchcard.

Punchcard stitch pattern

XXXX0000XXXX0000XXXX0000

FI patt selector used throughout.

Pattern sequence

Feeder 1	Feeder 2
A	B
C	D
C	A
D	E
B	D
D	C
C	F
A	D
D	C
C	B
C	B
E	D
D	A
F	C
A	D
E	B
C	A
A	D
D	C
C	F

Rep C sequence until 828 rows knitted or required length reached.

Method

E wrap cast on using A, k 2 rows.

Start to follow patt sequence in chart and k 12 rows for each set of Cs.

K 2 rows in required C and cast off.

Machine wash at 40°, 800 spin speed, to felt.

Kelp Scarves in Gold, Blue and Brown.

KELP SCARF

The story of this pattern is a perfect illustration of taking a calculated risk. The stitch pattern started off with the intention of making a textured scarf suggesting tree bark. Sketches were made and the pattern drawn out. It was to be firmly felted so I was not too worried about long floats. However, when samples were made, they were not satisfactory and the colours just didn't work. So the idea was shelved for many months. When the decision was made to revisit it, the brown version was knitted; the card was rolled back and turned back to front and the result was interesting but it didn't look like the bark I had in mind. I had been working on a seaweed design which was proving troublesome, and it occurred to me that the bark design strongly resembled kelp floating in the sea. After that, the colours reflected this change of inspiration and a totally different design came about.

It always pays to keep an open mind, and revisiting ideas after a break clears the mind, so nothing is ever wasted.

Method

E wrap cast on 100 sts MC k 2 rows, RC000 start FI patt, working through Cs. Change at random after 18, 16, 20 rows or whenever you like.

Roll back stitch patt, turn it upside down and back to front at random intervals. Cont until RC600, k 2 rows MC and cast off.

Machine wash at 40°, 800 spin speed, to felt. Firm steam press.

Materials

Finished weight 210g.
Yarns ranging from MC 2/14s 3-ply to C 2/20s 2-ply.

Brown colourway
MC: dark brown.
Cs: C1, C2, C3, etc., in pale blue, green, lime, purple, bright blue, mid-blue.

Blue colourway
MC: denim blue.
Cs: C1, C2, C3, etc., in four varying shades of blue, two shades of green.

Gold colourway
MCs: ochre, gold, yellow.
Cs: C1, C2, C3, etc., in lime, turquoise, pale blue, bright blue, purple.
The MC and the C change after random rows but do not change both colours at the same time.

Measurements

Width 24cm, length 156cm.

Tension

MT 8 34 sts – 28 rows = 10cm after felting.

Machine

Standard gauge electronic or punchcard.

Punchcard stitch pattern

Punchcard stitch pattern for Kelp Scarf.

Play on Water in Cream, Blue and Grey.

Play on Water, Grey detail.

PLAY ON WATER SCARF

Play on Water was a spontaneous design, drawing straight onto a punchcard with no preliminary sketches. The aim was to capture the rushing, swirling and falling of water. The spirals in particular give a sense of movement, and the intricate nature of the stitch pattern creates an overall intensity.

Method

E wrap cast on MC 110 sts, k 2 rows.
RC000 start punchcard stitch patt, changing C every 10, 12, 16, 20 rows.
Rep to RC640 rows. Cast off.
Machine wash at 40°, 800 spin speed, to felt.

Materials

Finished weight 200g.

Cream colourway

MC: Knoll Soft Donegal wool 100g Swilly 5507.

Cs: C1, C2, C3, C4 in various weights: pale blue, pale green, lilac, pale grey, pale pink.

Blue colourway

MC: Knoll Soft Donegal wool 100g Silver Mist 5580.

Cs: C 1, C2, C3, C4 in various weights: dark green, purple, turquoise, pale green, two shades of blue.

Grey colourway

MC: Knoll Soft Donegal wool 100g Silver Mist 5580.

Cs: C1, C2, C3, C4 are varied yarns ranging in weight from 2/34s fine 1-ply to 2/10s 4-ply. For the grey colours use cream, white, pale grey, beige.

Measurements

Width 21cm, length 152cm.

Tension

MT 8 40 sts – 30 rows = 10cm after felting.

Machine

Standard gauge electronic or punchcard.

Punchcard stitch pattern

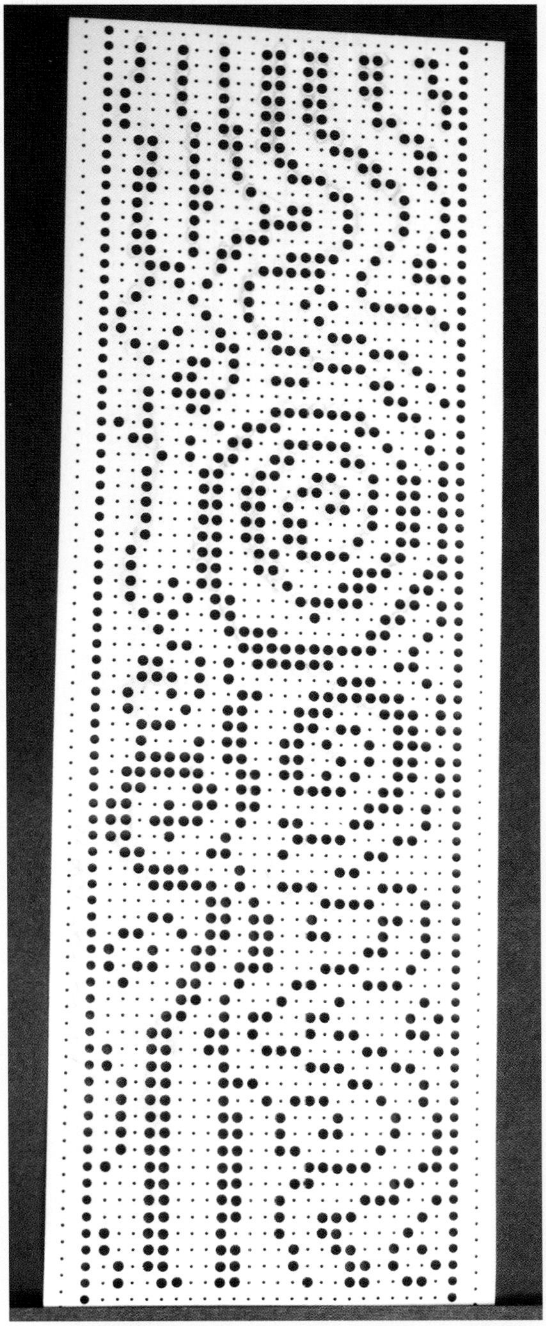

Punchcard stitch pattern for Play on Water Scarf.

Fretwork Scarves in Bright, Brown/Gold and Black/Cream.

FRETWORK SCARF

Fretwork is a geometric decorative design with intricate shapes which is based on the Greek key pattern, where the background is solid to enable the pattern to show up. The stitch pattern is based on intricate squares which change and move around, with a definite pinstripe through the design.

The design is relatively simple and this characteristic can be hard to achieve. Many ideas were thrown into the melting pot and, through a certain amount of trial and error and distillation, the design was honed down to the bare elements. Using only two colours may appear simple but any stitch out of place or pattern blip will stand out like a sore thumb. Designs like this one are often the most difficult to achieve as there is nowhere to hide, no multiple colours to distract the eye, or felting techniques to cover up a dodgy stitch. In some cases less is more, but do not underestimate the process to get there; it will have taken time and experimentation, and facing challenges in deciding what to discard and pare down. The basic design is a formal pattern which random colour changing does not enhance, as the fretwork pattern will simply disappear into the resulting colour chaos.

Two of the samples use two colours: black/cream and dark brown/gold. The stitch design shows up well and is unfussy. The Bright colourway has a bright blue background and three contrasting colours – lime green, yellow and pink – which change every fourteen rows.

Method

E wrap cast on 100 sts MC, k 2 rows.

RC000, k punchcard stitch patt Fretwork FI chart to RC588 or until required length reached, ending with complete square of fretwork. Cast off.

The Bright colourway starts with three 2-row stripes using C1, C2, C3, then MC2 rows. Start with FI patt using MC1 throughout and changing C1, C2, C3 every 14 rows.

Materials

Finished weight 250g.
Yarn 2/20s 2-ply.

Bright colourway
MC: bright blue.
Cs: C1 lime green, C2 yellow, C3 pink.

Brown/Gold colourway
MC: gold.
Cs: C1 brown.

Black/Cream colourway
MC: cream.
Cs: C1 black.

Measurements

Width 25cm, length 176cm.

Tension

MT 8 35 sts – 37 rows = 10cm over Fair Isle pattern.

Machine

Standard gauge electronic or punchcard.

Punchcard stitch pattern

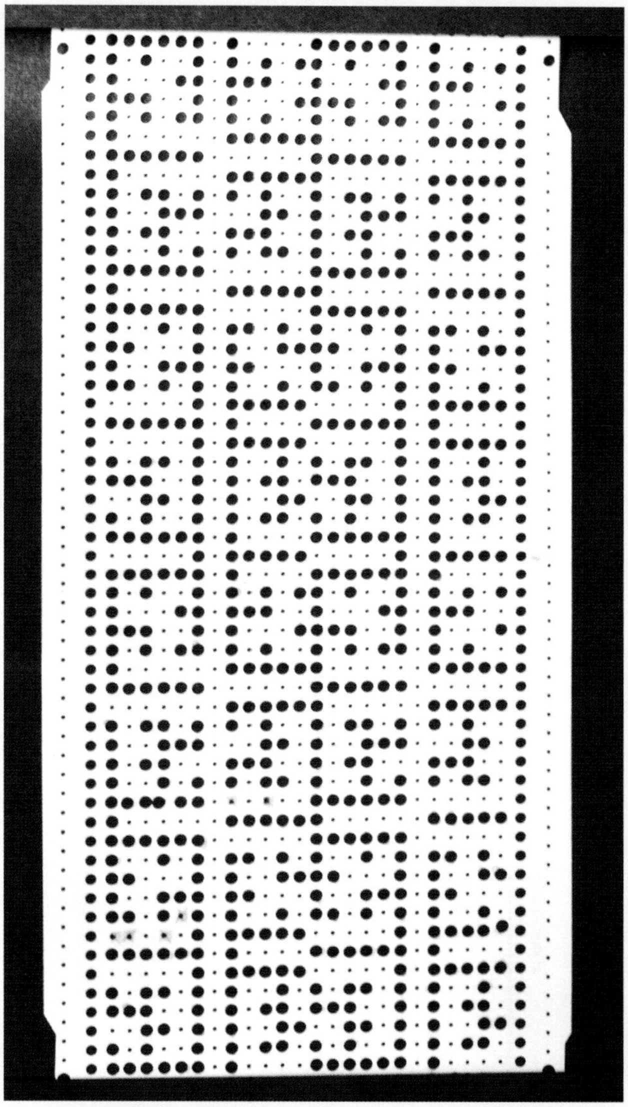

Punchcard stitch pattern for Fretwork Scarf.

Fleeting Scarves in bright colour variations.

Fleeting Scarf in gold.

Materials
Finished weight 200g.

Measurements
Width 25cm, length 160cm.

Tension
MT 7• 38 sts – 30 rows = 10cm over pattern.

Machine
Standard gauge electronic or punchcard.

Punchcard stitch pattern
Use the St Ives punchcard stitch pattern, elongating the diagonal to 20 rows.

FLEETING SCARF

Fair Isle diagonals and rows of stocking stitch make for a busy vibrant fabric. The combination of yarns which felt, densely juxtaposed with those which felt very little, enhances the slightly puckered texture of some of the blocks of colour. It is a great vehicle for using up lots of colours. The numbers of broad stripes between the diagonals varies from three to four and the diagonal stripes from ten rows to twenty rows. It is up to you to decide as you knit.

Method

E wrap cast on 100 sts and work to 550 rows or required length. Cast off.

VENICE SCARF

The very simple stitch pattern of the Venice design is an excellent vehicle for many colourways, all with a different character. The initial idea was based on the striped gondola-anchoring poles which rise out of the water like Christmas candy sticks in Venice. Any colour combination works well with this stitch pattern.

To add to the texture, use two different weight of yarns in feeder 1 and feeder 2. Use different colours together when they are repeated.

Method

E wrap cast on 80 sts using C, k 2 rows.
RC000. Start FI patt, work 10 rows, change Cs, FI 10 rows.
Rep 5 times.
Change Cs, FI 30 rows, rep until RC440.
Rep 10 rows bottom border to RC490.
K 2 rows. Cast off.

Materials
Finished weight 100g.
Variety of Cs in 2/16s 2-ply.

Blue colourway
Cs: C1, C2, C3, etc., in lilac, bright blue, vanilla, pale blue, pink, grey, navy and pale green.

Brown colourway
Cs: C1, C2, C3, etc., in chilli, rust, olive, navy, brown, green and lemon.

Dark colourway
Cs: C1, C2, C3, etc., in maroon, green, brown, navy, purple, wine and rust.

Measurements
Width 25.5cm, length 180cm.

Tension
MT 7• 36 sts – 37 rows = 10cm.

Machine
Standard gauge electronic or punchcard.

Stitch pattern
XOXOXOXOXO

Venice Scarves in bright, pale, blues, pearl, darks, new blue, brown and green.

Venice Scarves in Blue, Dark and Brown colourways.

St Ives Scarves in Sand, Rocks and Sea colourways.

St Ives Sand Scarf on Lambeth beach.

ST IVES SCARF AND ZIGGY SCARF

The zigzag lines in the St Ives design create a restlessness like the waves on the shore, and the colour changes magnify this movement. The patterns left on the sand like large tyre tracks are the colours reflected in the Sand colourway. Use a limited colour palette with at least four shades of grey. The Rocks colourway uses a palette of dark and light brown to emulate the wet rocks, while the Sea version is a beautiful sunny day on the beach looking out across the water.

St Ives Scarf
Method

E wrap cast on 80 sts C, k 2 rows.
RC000 FI patt 10 rows, change Cs, rep 5 times.
FI patt 20 rows, rep to RC450.
Rep 10-row bottom border 5 times to RC500.
K 2 rows, cast off.

Materials
Finished weight 100g.
Variety of Cs in 2/16s 2-ply.

Sand colourway
Cs: C1, C2, C3, C4, etc., in four shades of grey, cream, beige, black, navy.

Rocks colourway
Cs: C1, C2, C3, C4, etc., in several shades of brown ranging from dark to light beige.

Sea colourway
Cs: C1, C2, C3, C4, etc., in navy, purple, dark green, lilac, pale blue, bright blue, cream.

Measurements
Width 25.2 cm, length 180cm.

Tension
MT 7•36 sts – 38 rows = 10cm.

Machine
Standard gauge electronic or punchcard.

Punchcard stitch pattern

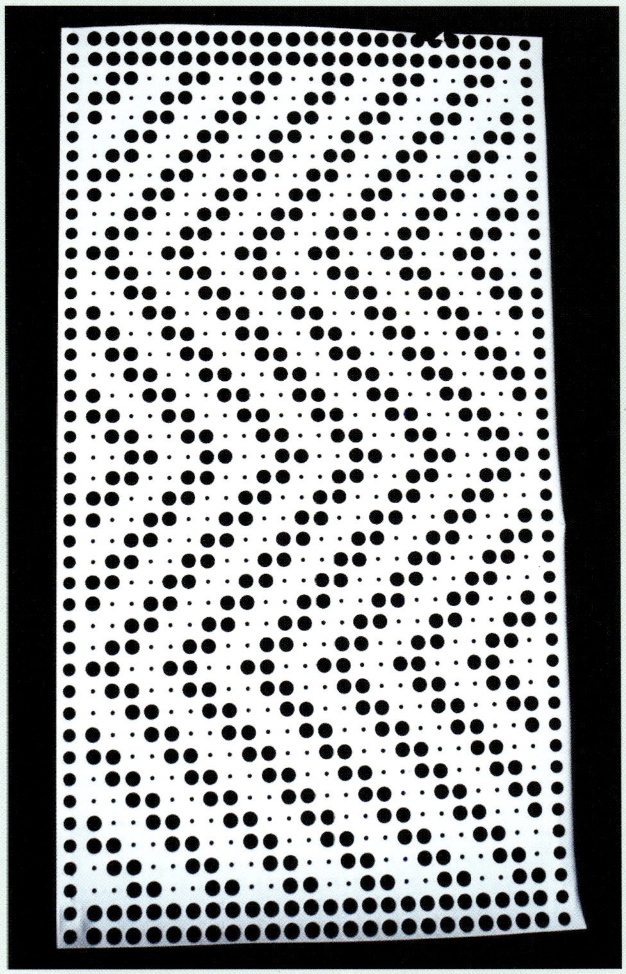

Punchcard stitch pattern for St Ives Scarf.

Ziggy Scarves in Brown/Green, Pale and Bright colourways.

Ziggy Scarf

Adapted from the St Ives design, this now becomes something very different by using vibrant and clashing colours and adding a small wave border.

Method

Wave border

E wrap cast on 80 sts using C1, *k 6 rows. Using C2 6 rows sl st*. Rep * to * five times changing Cs each k and sl st rows.

Change to St Ives punchcard stitch pattern TD Fl. Cont to patt, changing Cs every 20 rows.

When required length completed, approx 450 rows, rep Wave patt border and cast off.

Materials

Finished weight 100g.

Variety of Cs in 2/16s 2-ply.

Brown/Green colourway

Cs: magnified bright autumnal Cs such as rust, lime green, orange, dark brown, yellow, beige and ochre.

Pale colourway

Cs: beige, lilac, pale blue, grey, pale green, pink, cream, white and stone.

Bright colourway

Cs: more vibrant Cs such as red, bright blue, purple, lilac, navy, green, ochre, bright pink and orange.

Measurements

Width 25.2 cm, length 180cm.

Tension

MT 7• 36 sts – 38 rows = 10cm.

Machine

Standard gauge electronic or punchcard.

Punchcard stitch pattern: Wave border

0X0X0X0X0X0X

St Ives and Herringbone Jackets.

St Ives Jacket, detail.

ST IVES JACKET (HERRINGBONE TWEED JACKET/VENICE JACKET)

The Herringbone, St Ives and Venice stitch patterns all suit this style. It produces a dropped shoulder jacket with a loose drape look – a versatile pattern which I have used many times. The Herringbone pattern has similarities to the St Ives jacket but the V shape is wider and less pronounced. The pattern is written out in full.

Materials
Finished weight 260g.
Cs: various shades, C1, C2, C3, etc.
3 buttons plus 1 spare.

Measurements
The sizing is flexible. This sample garment, excluding borders: chest 123.5cm, length to shoulder 48cm, sleeve seam 36cm.

Tension
MT 7 32 sts – 34 rows = 10cm.

Machine
Standard gauge electronic or punchcard.

Punchcard stitch pattern
Use Venice, St Ives or Herringbone.

Method

Main body

Push 174 Ns at centre of machine to WP. Insert card and lock on row.

Using MT and WY, cast on and knit a few rows ending with COL.

Using nylon cord, k 1 row. COR.

Using C1, cast on by hand. RC000. Do not release card. (Electronic: release card to memorize row, then lock.)

Cont in FI with C1 in feeder 1 and C2 in feeder 2, k 10 rows*.

Change to different Cs in both feeders. K 10 rows*.

Rep * to * 6 more times. RC80. Set RC000.

Shape collar

Cast off 20 sts at R edge. 154 sts rem. ** Change to different Cs in both feeders. K 30 rows **.

Rep ** to ** twice more. RC90.

Herringbone Jacket, detail.

Shape armhole

Cast off 60 sts at R edge, leaving empty Ns in WP. Cast on over these 60 Ns. Rep ** to ** 3 more times. Place marker at R edge.

Rep ** to ** twice more. Place marker at R edge.

Rep ** to ** 3 more times. RC330.

Shape armhole

Cast off 60 sts at R edge, leaving empty Ns in WP. Cast on over these 60 Ns. Rep ** to ** 3 more times. RC420. Set RC000.

Shape collar

Cast on 20 sts at R edge. 174 sts. Rep * to * 3 more times.

Counting from L edge, transfer sts 72, 82, 92 onto adjacent Ns. Leave empty Ns in WP.

Rep * to * once more.

Make buttonholes over same Ns as before.

Rep * to * 4 more times. RC80. Cast off.

Sleeves

Push 72 Ns at centre of machine to WP. Insert card and lock on row.

Using MT and WY, cast on and k a few rows ending with COL.

Using nylon cord, k 1 row. COR.

Using I end of two different Cs tog, cast on by hand. Set RC000. Do not release the card. (Electronic: release card to memorize row and then lock.)

Inc 1 st at each end of every 4th row and, at same time, cont in FI patt with C1 in feeder 1 and C2 in feeder 2, k 10 rows.*

Change to different Cs in both feeders. K 10 rows*.

Rep * to * 6 more times, 112sts. RC80.

Change Cs in both feeders and cont to inc on every foll 4th row until there are 120 sts.

K 24 rows. RC120.

Making up

Join shoulder seams and sleeve seams. Set in sleeves. Join centre back of collar and sew into position, stretching to fit. Fold collar in half and catch down loosely. Matching pairs of buttonholes, fold front bands to inside and catch down loosely. Neaten lower ends of bands. Sew on buttons.

Venice Jacket with Herringbone Scarf.

A	54.25cm
B	48cm
C	18.75cm
D	23.5cm
E	123.5cm
F	17.5cm

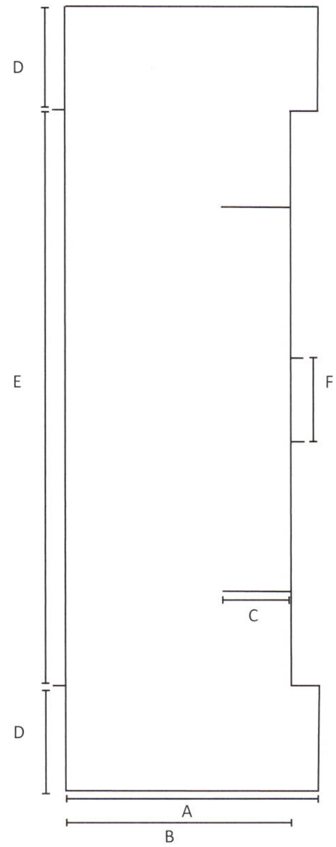

G	22.5cm
H	35cm
I	37.5cm

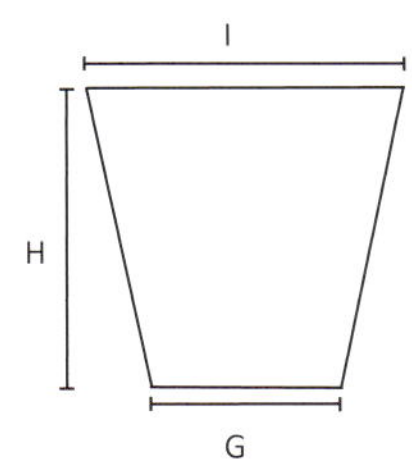

St Ives Jacket schematic.

Ancient herringbone stonework at St Mary's Church, Edvin Loach, near Bromyard in Herefordshire.

HERRINGBONE SCARF

This is a traditional pattern which has proved very useful, adaptable and fun over the years. It has a basic V-shaped weaving pattern, also known as 'broken twill'. When worked, it has a striking similarity to a chevron pattern; however, the zigzag stripes which travel across the fabric are broken up by alternating the colours in each direction.

The pattern can be traced back to ancient Egyptian jewellery and the earliest fabric examples have been found in ancient Italy. The name 'herringbone' comes from the fact that the finished pattern resembles the bones of a herring fish.

The Romans also used the pattern when building roads, where the interlocking paving design was placed on top of a foundation of smaller stones, which absorbed the compression of the traffic and people, making it stable and long-lasting. The herringbone design has stood the test of time and is still used extensively today in tiling and flooring, notably parquet flooring.

It is an extremely versatile pattern and on a small scale it can look almost solid, but with the use of bolder colours it takes on a more striking effect. It works well for both furnishings and clothing for children and adults.

The samples shown are three colourways: Dawn, Evening and Tweed. The Dawn and Evening colourways express in an abstract way the colours of a clear bright dawn, and a quiet evening with soft muted colours. The Tweed colourway uses the colours of a shred of Harris tweed – it was amazing to discover how many colours a small piece of tweed had within it.

Herringbone Scarves in Dawn, Evening and Tweed.

The pattern can be knitted using similar weight yarn throughout, 2/20s 2-ply, or you could use a thicker 2/14s 3-ply yarn in feeder 1 and a finer yarn in feeder 2. This makes for an interesting textured fabric.

Method

The instructions are the same as for the St Ives Scarf on the previous pages.

Materials
Finished weight 100g.

Dawn colourway
Cs: C1, C2, C3, C4 in maroon, turquoise, amethyst, lilac, cream, bright green, bright blue.

Evening colourway
Cs: C1, C2, C3, C4 in cream, beige, sage green, lilac, pale yellow, light brown.

Tweed colourway
Cs: C1, C2, C3, C4 in beige, olive, green, brown, grey, dark green, dark brown, charcoal, mustard, maroon.

Measurements
Width 25cm, length 180cm.

Tension
MT 7 36 sts – 37 rows = 10cm.

Machine
Standard gauge electronic or punchcard.

Punchcard stitch pattern

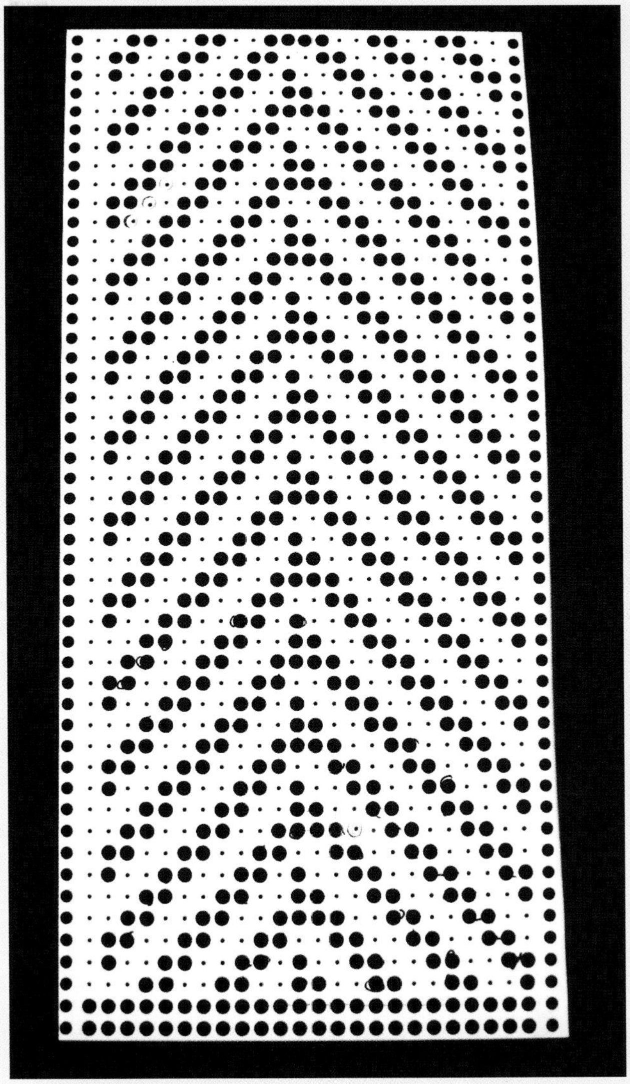

Punchcard stitch pattern for Herringbone Scarf.

Herring Stripe Scarves in Red, Green and Brown.

Variation and added stitches

To make a variation the Herringbone Fair Isle pattern can be mixed with blocks of stripes and a small tuck stitch pattern. Not surprisingly, I have called this Herring Stripe.

Method

Rep 7 times for length of scarf or required length reached.
Cast off.

Materials

Various small amounts of Cs.

Red colourway

Cs: A tomato, B slate grey, C mid-grey, D navy, E maroon, F amethyst, G cherry, H black, I pale blue, J lilac.

Green colourway

Cs: A dark brown, B beige, C camel, D bright green, E pale green, F olive, G dark green, H black, I maroon, J mid-brown.

Brown colourway

Cs: A ochre, B brown, C orange, D dark brown, E pale green, F dark green, G slate grey, H dark orange, I mustard, J beige.

Pattern sequence

Rows	Pattern Setting	Feeder 1	Feeder 2
20	Fair Isle	A	B
2	Knit	C	
4	Fair Isle	D	E
8	Fair Isle	D	F
8	Fair Isle	D	G
2	Knit	H	
4	Tuck	I	
2	Knit	B	
4	Tuck	J	
2	Knit	C	
8	Fair Isle	D	G
8	Fair Isle	D	G
4	Fair Isle	D	E
2	Knit	C	

Rep from beg.

Punchcard stitch pattern

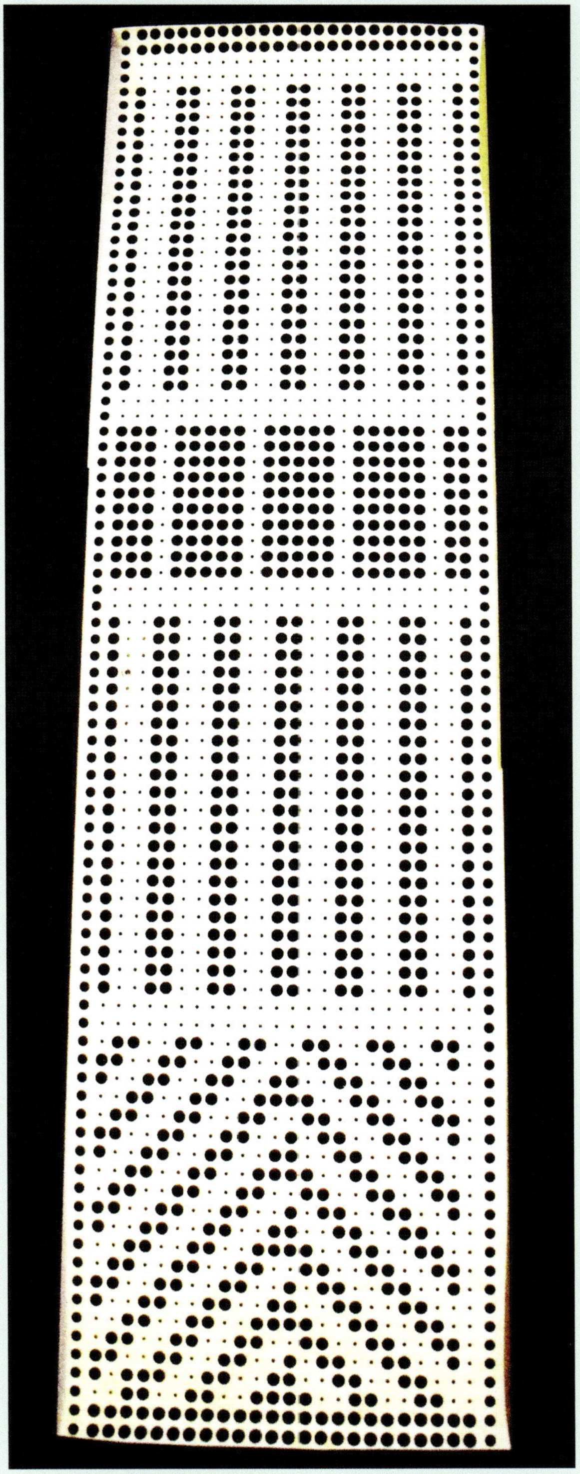

Punchcard stitch pattern for Herring Stripe Scarf.

Sean Scully sculpture at the Yorkshire Sculpture Park near Wakefield.

Scully stripes in Araby, Bright and Blue.

SCULLY SCARF

Having seen an exhibition by the artist Sean Scully I was inspired to translate his blocks and stripes into a scarf design. I was interested in exploring the effect of colours butted up against other colours and how they met, and the results were at, times, quite unexpected.

Scully has also influenced my work in that he is constantly exploring pattern and colour in his intricate and complex paintings of stripes. He manages to paint elegant, mysterious pinstripes in two hues of blue. He juxtaposes the horizontal and vertical stripes which swing the colours to left and right, up and down, thus creating movement in the colours over the whole piece. He uses shimmering, soft, reflective colours for subtle stripes and clashes orange with bright blue for an exciting ladder of stripes. Scully also uses unusual colours together: cerise and blue stripes butt up against blocks of dark green and black, and maroon against emerald green, which then all fizz with energy. These works of art are a joy to translate into the knitted stitch and generate a rich design seam to explore and return to for years to come.

The design uses a yarn which will felt, juxtaposed with one which is resistant to felting, to create depth and texture.

Araby is based on the striped awnings of the Marrakesh markets and the clothing worn by the stallholders; rich dark reds and ambers conjure up a thriving, hot and dusty bazaar. Bright uses shocking pink, lime green, purple and any colour which clashes to make a hot vibrant scarf; you can feel the sounds and hustle and bustle of the local market, with shouting, bartering, animals, motor bikes and all the surrounding sounds of people going about their lives. Blue is based on the sea landscape of the Mediterranean.

The scarves are knitted in stripes of 30-, 40- and 50-row blocks and each is divided up into further horizontal stripes using the 1×1, 2×2 or 3×1 card.

The horizontal stripes are made up of six and four rows. To make these even the thicker yarn which felted was six rows and the finer yarn four rows. It may need a little experimenting to work this out depending which yarn you are using, and how much width and depth is lost in the felting. The number in brackets is the number of times the six/four-striped rows are repeated.

Method

E wrap cast on MC, k 2 rows, follow patt sequence. Cast off. Machine wash at 40°, 800 spin speed.

Materials

Finished weight 110g.

Various Cs as shown for each colourway.

Araby colourway

Cs: feltable yarn: A brown, B blue, C cream, D red, E navy, F dark purple, G beige, H pale blue. Felt-resistant yarn: I ochre, J navy, K rusty, L bright blue, M dull pink, N terracotta, O grey.

Bright colourway

Cs: feltable yarn: A bright pink, B lime green, C red, D dark purple, E violet, F black. Felt-resistant yarn: G lilac, H lemon, I bright blue, J purple, K dark green, L white, M olive green, N navy, O amethyst.

Blue colourway

Cs: feltable yarn: A lilac, B mid-blue, C violet, D cream, E purple. Felt-resistant yarn: F dark blue, G blue, H white, I amethyst, J navy, K grey, L pale blue, M bright blue.

Measurements

Width 28cm, length 192cm.

Tension

MT 6• 26 sts – 33 rows = 10cm.

Stitch pattern 1

X0X0X0

Stitch pattern 2

XX00XX00

Stitch pattern 3

XXX0XXX0XXX0

Pattern sequences

Araby colourway

Rows	Pattern Setting	Punchcard	Feeder 1	Feeder 2
30	Fair Isle	2	A	I
6	Knit		B	
4	Knit (stripe × 5)		J	
30	Fair Isle	3	C	K
6	Knit		D	
4	Knit (stripe × 3)		J	
30	Fair Isle	1	E	L
30	Fair Isle	3	F	M
6	Knit		F	
4	Knit (stripe × 5)		I	
6	Knit		G	
4	Knit (stripe × 4)		N	
30	Fair Isle	3	H	O
6	Knit		D	
4	Knit (stripe × 5)		J	
30	Fair Isle	1	E	I
6	Knit		B	
4	Knit (stripe × 3)		K	
30	Fair Isle	2	O	H
30	Fair Isle	1	D	J

Bright colourway

Rows	Pattern Setting	Punchcard	Feeder 1	Feeder 2
30	Fair Isle	2	A	G
6	Knit		B	
4	Knit (stripe × 5)		H	
30	Fair Isle	3	C	I
6	Knit		D	
4	Knit (stripe × 3)		J	
30	Fair Isle	1	B	K
30	Fair Isle	3	A	M
6	Knit		E	
4	Knit(stripe × 5)		L	
6	Knit		C	
4	Knit (stripe × 4)		N	
30	Fair Isle	3	A	N
6	Knit		B	
4	Knit (stripe × 5)		L	
30	Fair Isle	1	C	O
6	Knit		F	
4	Knit (stripe × 3)		I	
30	Fair Isle	2	A	M
30	Fair Isle	1	B	J

Blue colourway

Rows	Pattern Setting	Punchcard	Feeder 1	Feeder 2
30	Fair Isle	2	A	H
6	Knit		B	
4	Knit (stripe × 5)		I	
30	Fair Isle	3	C	H
6	Knit		A	
4	Knit (stripe × 3)		J	
30	Fair Isle	1	D	K
30	Fair Isle	3	B	L
6	Knit		H	
4	Knit (stripe × 5)		C	
6	Knit		K	
4	Knit (stripe × 4)		G	
30	Fair Isle	3	E	M
6	Knit		J	
4	Knit (stripe × 5)		D	
30	Fair Isle	1	C	I
6	Knit		F	
4	Knit (stripe × 3)		K	
30	Fair Isle	2	A	J
30	Fair Isle	1	G	H

Hockney Fields Blossom Scarf, inspiration colours in cashmere and silk.

Hockney Fields Tulip Scarf, inspiration colours in cashmere and silk.

HOCKNEY FIELDS SCARF

This is a variation on the Scully stripes, using a fine 2/34s fine 1-ply yarn. David Hockney uses colour that is bright and exhilarating. Having seen the exhibition of his paintings showing landscapes around Leeds and Bradford and his native Yorkshire, the colours he uses are mesmerizing. Purple, red and bright green stripes are ploughed fields and there are bright yellow trees and tyre tracks on a snowy ground. It was a new way of looking at the landscape and colour.

Hockney Fields Scarves in bright, pale and blue.

Morvah Oak Scarves in Brown and Cream.

Initial sketches for the Morvah Oak design.

MORVAH OAK SCARF

Morvah is a wild and often windy moor, sitting in an area of outstanding natural beauty in West Cornwall near to the Atlantic Ocean. The sparse trees are bent and stoic, and one oak tree, stunted and gnarled, was the inspiration for this scarf design.

Method

E wrap cast on using three ends of different MCs, 80 sts.
K 2 rows RC000.
Start FI patt, work 10 rows MC1 and CA.
10 rows MC1, CB.
10 rows MC2, CB and cont changing Cs every 10 rows alternating C change from MC to C to RC600. Cast off using three ends of MC.
Machine wash at 40°, 800 spin speed.

Materials

Knoll Soft Donegal wool for MC. Cs are in various weights of yarns.

Brown colourway

MCs: MC1 Macean 5510 (brown), MC2 O'Farrell 5549 (chestnut), MC3 Ballycastle 5502 (khaki), MC4 Graney 5525 (green), MC5 Carragh 5513 (dark green), MC6 Boyne 5518 (mid-brown).

Cs: A in rust, B in green, C in mustard, D in brown, E in terracotta, F in moss green.

Cream colourway

MCs: MC1 Greese 5509 (grey), MC2 Duffy 5537 (off-white), MC3 Foyle 5508 (beige), MC4 Swilly 5507 (cream), MC5 Eske 5529 (pale grey), MC6 Boyne 5518 (mid-brown).

Cs: A in mustard, B in orange, C in beige, D in dark brown, E in green.

Measurements

Width 21cm, length 152cm.

Tension

Approx MT 8 40 sts – 30 rows = 10cm after felting.

Machine

Standard gauge electronic or punchcard.

Punchcard stitch pattern

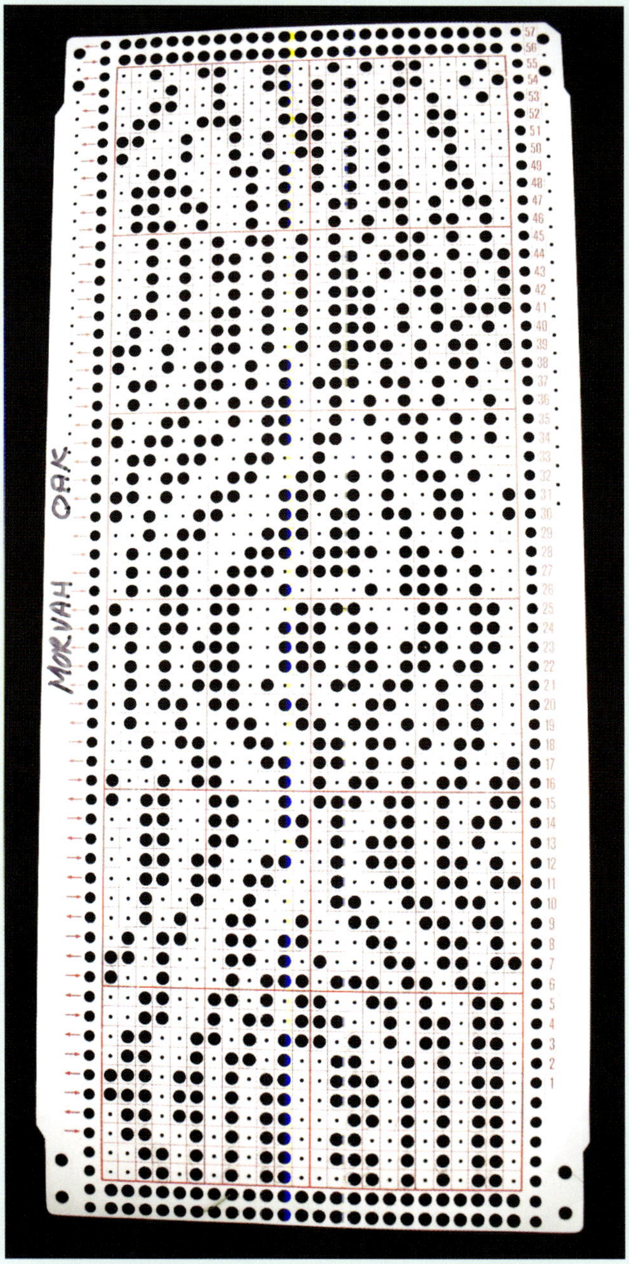

Punchcard stitch pattern for Morvah Oak Scarf.

Tapestry Rose Cardigan, detail.

Tapestry Rose Cardigan.

TAPESTRY ROSE CARDIGAN

This is knitted using antique shades in the Jamiesons of Shetland Spindrift range of yarns. The roses and rosebuds are perfect with the lovely marled colours, the background changes colour and the whole cardigan is worked in pieces and fitted together like a jigsaw. Many different patterns can be used within this format.

Method

Back panel

Cast on 100 sts using WY. RC000.

Using Rosebud punchcard stitch patt, follow patt sequence.

Shape sides by inc 1 st at each end of next row and every foll 10 rows until 120 sts.

Cont to RC190.

Shape shoulder by placing 10 Ns in HP on next 4 rows and 15 Ns on the foll 2 rows. Place markers either side of the centre 50 sts.

Using WY, release from machine.

Right front panel

Cast on 50 sts at R of centre using WY. RC000.

Using Rosebud punchcard stitch patt, follow patt sequence.

Shape side by inc 1 st at RHS on 10th row and foll 10 rows until 60 sts. Cont to RC161.

Shape neck by casting off 5 sts at beg of next row and foll alt row. K 1 row.

Cast off 2 sts on neck edge and foll alt row. K 1 row.

Dec 1 st at neck edge of next row and every foll alt row until 50 sts remain.

Cont to RC190.

Shape shoulder by placing 10 Ns in HP, on next alt four rows, and 15 Ns. K 1 row.

Place back panel shoulder sts onto corresponding Ns. MT+1, k 1 row and latch off.

Left front

Work as for R front panel, reversing cast on and shaping.

Side panels (both alike)

Using Rose 1 punchcard stitch patt, E wrap cast on 90 sts. RC000.

Place marker at centre. Follow patt sequence as shown. At same time, shape sides by inc 1st at each end of next row and every foll 4th row until 50 sts remain. RC86.

Place marker at centre. Cast off.

Materials

Finished weight 520g.

Jamiesons of Shetland Spindrift wool in oil.

MCs: 200g each of Peat 198, Rosewood 236.

Cs: 100g each of Cashew 342, Sunset 186, Bracken 231, Clyde Blue 168, Granite 122, Heron 315, Navy 727, Loganberry 1290, Dogrose 268, Lipstick 575, Madder 587, White 104, Aqua 929, Woodgreen 318, Emerald 792, Splash 757.

6 buttons plus 1 spare.

Punchcard stitch pattern: Rosebuds

Rosebud 1

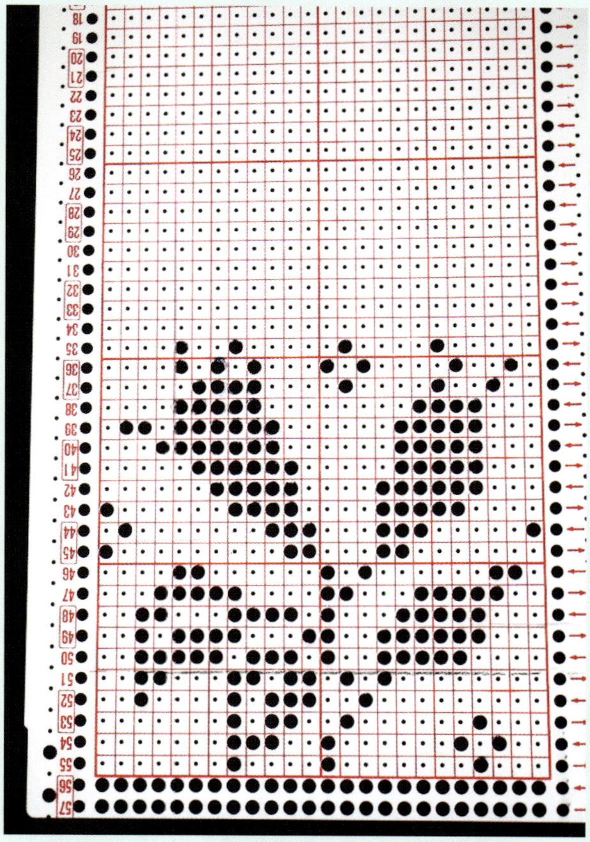

Punchcard stitch pattern for Tapestry Rose Cardigan, Rosebud 1.

Measurements

Finished size: chest 116cm, length to shoulder 56cm, sleeve length 41cm.

Tension

MT 8• 28 sts – 39 rows = 10cm over Fair Isle pattern.

Machine

Standard gauge electronic or punchcard.

Rosebud 2

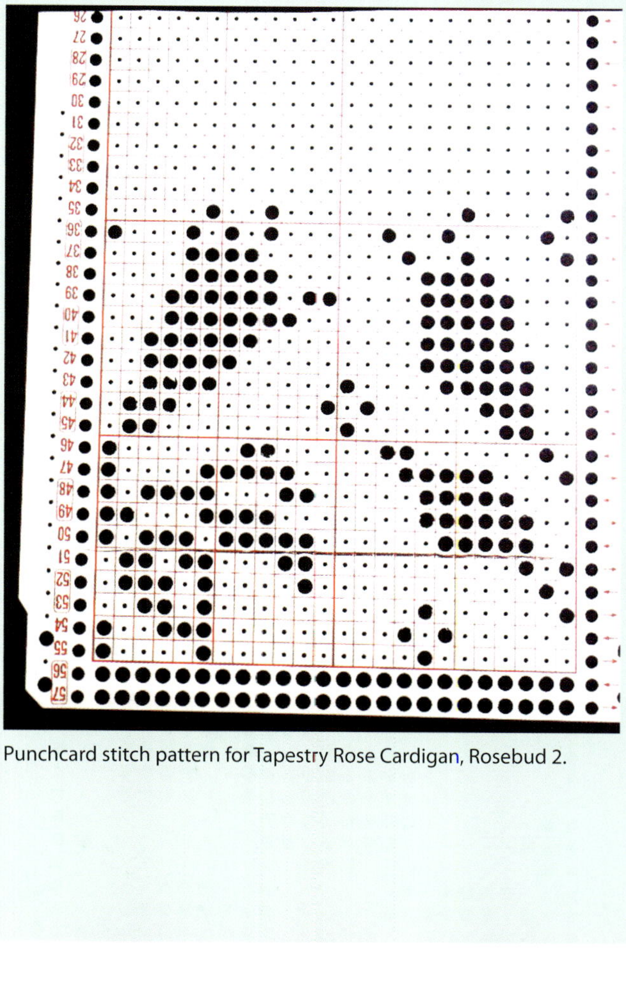

Punchcard stitch pattern for Tapestry Rose Cardigan, Rosebud 2.

Pattern sequence for rosebuds

Rows	Stitch Pattern	Pattern Setting	Feeder 1	Feeder 2
6		Knit	Peat	
10	Rosebud 1	Fair Isle	Peat	Cashew
4	Rosebud 1	Fair Isle	Rosewood	Sunset
7	Rosebud 1	Fair Isle	Rosewood	Dogrose
6		Knit	Rosewood	
10	Rosebud 2	Fair Isle	Rosewood	Bracken
4	Rosebud 2	Fair Isle	Peat	Clyde Blue
7	Rosebud 2	Fair Isle	Peat	Granite

Punchcard stitch pattern: Roses

Rose 1

Note: the Rose 2 pattern is the Rose 1 pattern turned round.

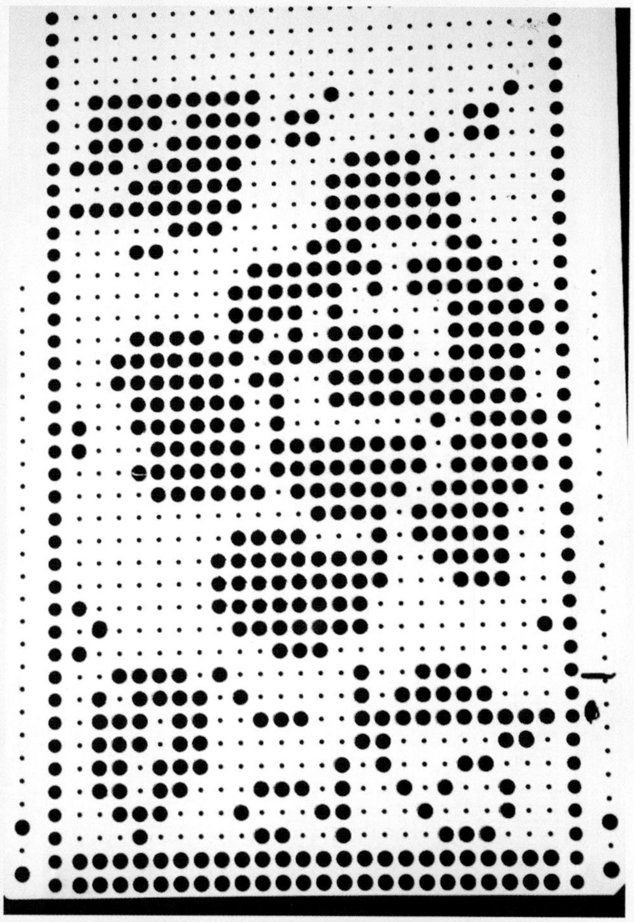

Punchcard stitch pattern for Tapestry Rose Cardigan, Rose 1.

Pattern sequence for roses

Rows	Stitch Pattern	Pattern Setting	Feeder 1	Feeder 2
6		Knit	Peat	
8	Rose 1	Fair Isle	Peat	Woodgreen
6	Rose 1	Fair Isle	Rosewood	Dogrose
4	Rose 1	Fair Isle	Rosewood	Sunset
4	Rose 1	Fair Isle	Rosewood	Lipstick
5	Rose 1	Fair Isle	Rosewood	Madder
7	Rose 1	Fair Isle	Rosewood	Woodgreen
6		knit	Rosewood	
8	Rose 2	Fair Isle	Rosewood	Bracken
6	Rose 2	Fair Isle	Peat	Clyde Blue
4	Rose 2	Fair Isle	Peat	Granite
4	Rose 2	Fair Isle	Peat	White
5	Rose 2	Fair Isle	Peat	Aqua
7	Rose 2	Fair Isle	Peat	Bracken

Punchcard stitch pattern: sleeve top border

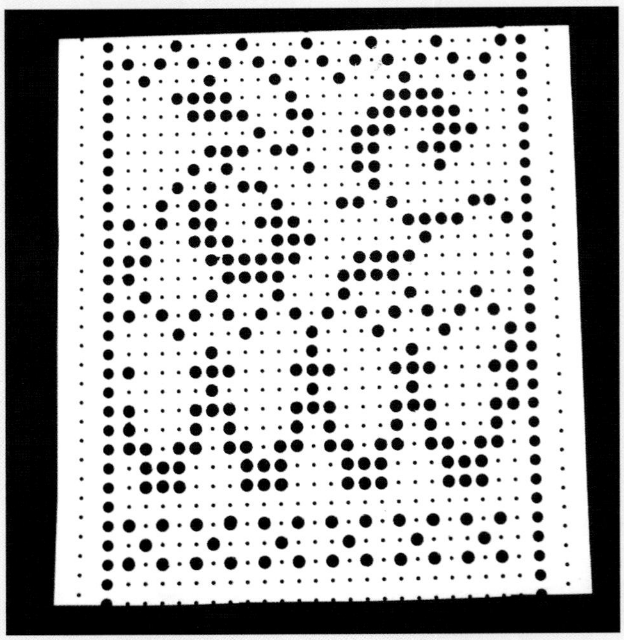

Punchcard stitch pattern for Tapestry Rose Cardigan, sleeve top border.

Pattern sequence for sleeve top border

Rows	Stitch pattern	Pattern Setting	Feeder 1	Feeder 2
3	Top border	Fair Isle	Rosewood	Cashew
1	Top border	Knit	Rosewood	
*3	Top border	Fair Isle	Heron	Woodgreen
2	Top border	Fair Isle	Heron	Bracken
*3	Top border	Fair Isle	Navy	Bracken
*3	Top border	Fair Isle	Heron	Cashew
11	Top border	Fair Isle	Navy	Emerald
3	Top border	Fair Isle	Heron	Granite

Rep * to *.

Punchcard stitch pattern: cuff and bands border

Use the first 12 rows of the sleeve top border punchcard stitch pattern.

Pattern sequence for cuff and bands border

Rows	Stitch Pattern	Pattern Setting	Feeder 1	Feeder 2
1		Knit	Rosewood	
3	Top border	Fair Isle	Rosewood	Cashew
1	Top border	Knit	Rosewood	
3	Top border	Fair Isle	Loganberry	Clyde Blue
2	Top border	Fair Isle	Loganberry	Woodgreen
3	Top border	Fair Isle	Loganberry	Splash
1	Top border	Fair Ilse	Loganberry	

Sleeves

Cast on 80 sts WY. Follow Rose 1, 2, 1 punchcard stitch patt and patt sequence and then sleeve top border.

Shape sides by inc every 3rd row until 130 sts.

Cont without shaping until top sleeve border has been completed, mark centre. Cast off.

Right back border

Pick up 130 sts from centre mark of sleeve and side edge of side panel.

Using first 12 rows of punchcard stitch patt but following C sequence for cuff and border bands, k 12 rows.

Pick up corresponding back panel, k 1 row and latch off.

Rep for all 4 side borders.

Cuffs

Cast on 70 sts using WY. K 12 rows of border patt and k further 12 rows in MC.

Pick up sts between WY to make hem and k 1 row.

Pick up sts from sleeve and place on Ns to dec evenly.

K 1 row MT+1 and cast off.

Rep for second cuff.

Buttonhole band

WY cast on 130 sts. Work 6 rows of punchcard border stitch patt. Make 5 buttonholes everly spaced. Cont to k another 6 rows from border patt. Using MC, k 6 rows, make buttonholes on corresponding Ns, then k 6 rows. Complete band as cuff.

Button band

Rep as buttonhole band but omit buttonholes.

Neckband

WY cast on 140 sts. Follow instructions as for button band, placing a buttonhole at L edge 4 sts from edge. K 1 row.

Pick up sts from back neck and fronts. K 1 row, MT+1 and latch off.

Making up

Neaten ends of neckband and lower ends of front bands. Join border seam at top of shoulder. Sew rows at top of sleeves to top of side panels. Join sleeve side seams and finish buttonholes. Sew on buttons.

Tapestry Rose Cardigan, detail.

A	41cm
B	50.5cm
C	50cm
D	20.5cm
E	25cm
F	10cm
G	3.5cm

H	18cm
I	16cm
J	23cm

K	45.5cm
L	24cm
M	48cm
N	28cm
O	48.5cm

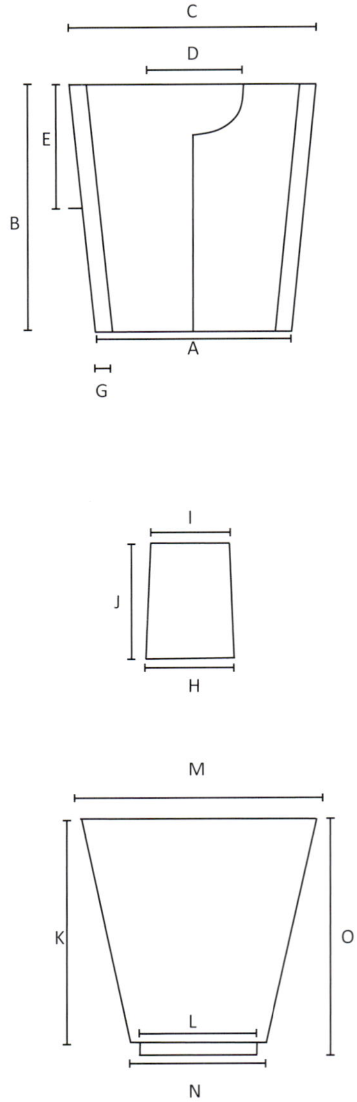

Tapestry Rose Cardigan schematic.

Rowan Berry Cardigan.

Inspiration for Rowan Berry design.

Rowan Berry Cardigan.

ROWAN BERRY CARDIGAN

The colours of the rowan berry or mountain ash tree are most attractive, coming as they do just as winter begins to take hold. The tree itself is surrounded by myth and legend which started as far back as ancient Greece. It was believed that the goddess Hebe carried an ambrosia which she gave to the gods, transporting it in a magical chalice. However, the chalice was lost to demons and the gods sent an eagle to recover it; there was a fierce battle and the eagle lost many of his feathers and was injured. The demons finally lost the battle and fell to earth and were turned into rowan trees. The shape of the rowan's leaves represents the eagle's feathers and the berries the blood that he lost in the battle.

Every part of this amazing tree is useful: the bark can be used in dying, the wood is strong and resilient and the berries are nowadays made into jelly to eat with cold meats. Aesthetically, a rowan tree is beautiful when in full berry surrounded by the feathery leaves. Many designers have used it for inspiration across the ages and its outline is distinctive. One of the relatively few native British trees, it also lives happily throughout Europe and Asia.

Materials

Jamiesons of Shetland Spindrift wool in oil.

300g Birch 252, 100g Grouse 235.

50g each of White 104, Burnt Ochre 423, Woodgreen 318, Autumn 998, Thistledown 237, Sunrise 187, Moorgrass 286, Tan Green 241, Sunset 186.

8 buttons plus 1 spare.

Punchcard stitch pattern: Rowan Leaf and Berry 1

Note: reverse punchcard for Rowan Leaf and Berry 2.

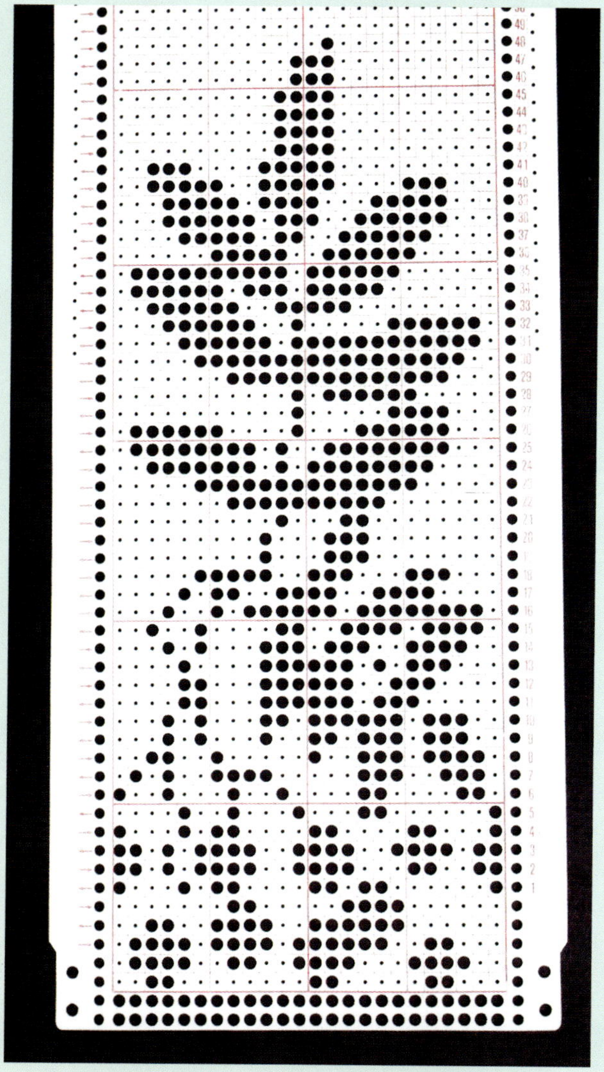

Punchcard stitch pattern for Rowan Leaf and Berry 1.

Measurements

Approx length around chest: small 104cm, medium 110cm, large 116cm.

Length to shoulder: small 61cm, medium 64cm, large 68cm.

Sleeve length to end of cuff: all sizes 49cm.

Tension

MT 8• 29 sts – 48 rows = 10cm.

Machine

Standard gauge electronic or punchcard.

Punchcard stitch pattern: Berry

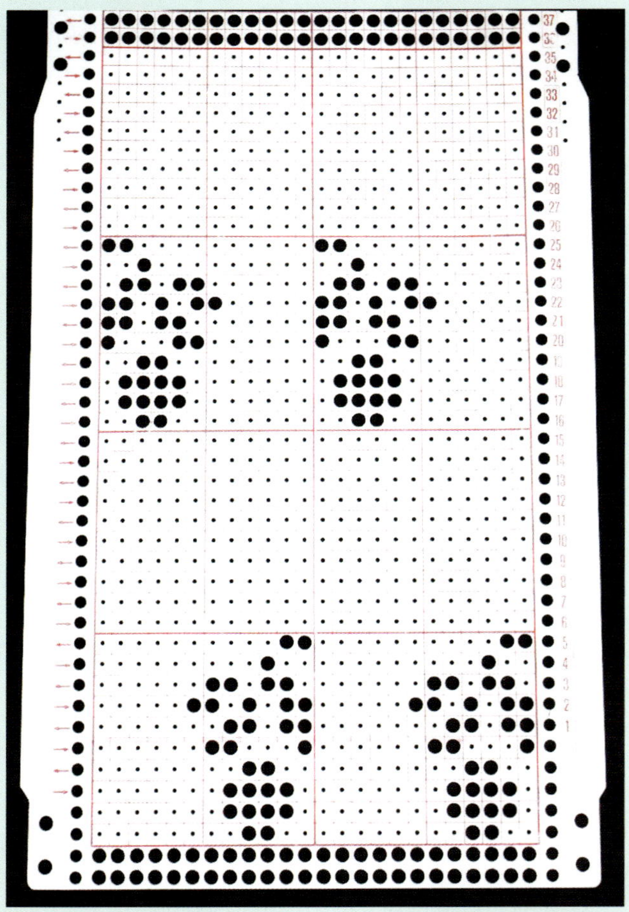

Punchcard stitch pattern for Berry.

Punchcard stitch pattern: Arrow

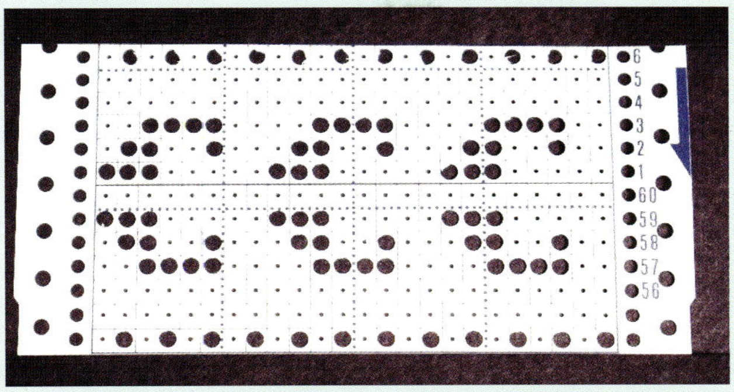

Punchcard stitch pattern for Arrow.

Pattern sequence for Leaf and Berry 1

Rows	Stitch Pattern	Pattern Setting	Feeder 1	Feeder 2
5	1	Fair Isle	Birch	White
4	1	Fair Isle	Birch	Burnt Ochre
17	1	Fair Isle	Birch	Woodgreen
27	1	Fair Isle	Birch	Autumn
1		Knit	Birch	
5	2	Fair Isle	Birch	Thistledown
4	2	Fair Isle	Birch	Sunrise
17	2	Fair Isle	Birch	Moorgrass
27	2	Fair Isle	Birch	Tan Green
1		knit	Birch	

Pattern sequence for Berry

Rows	Stitch Pattern	Pattern Setting	Feeder 1	Feeder 2
10	Berry	Knit	Birch	
4	Berry	Fair Isle	Birch	White
6	Berry	Fair Isle	Birch	Burnt Ochre
10	Berry	Knit	Birch	
4	Berry	Fair Isle	Birch	Sunrise
6	Berry	Fair Isle	Birch	Tan Green

Pattern sequence for Arrow

Rows	Stitch Pattern	Pattern Setting	Feeder 1	Feeder 2
1	Arrow	Fair Isle	Sunset	Grouse
1	Arrow	Knit	Sunset	
1	Arrow	Knit	Grouse	
3	Arrow	Fair Isle	Grouse	Sunset
1	Arrow	Knit	Moorgrass	
3	Arrow	Fair Isle	Grouse	Sunset
1	Arrow	Knit	Grouse	
1	Arrow	Knit	Sunset	
1	Arrow	Fair Isle	Sunset	Grouse

Method

Back

Cast on 160 sts, 170 sts, 180 sts for a 2×1 rib using Burnt Ochre, k 2 rows, change C to Moorgrass, k 1 row, change C to Grouse, k 27 rows.

Transfer sts to single bed machine. RC000.

K 1 row, start to knit Arrow patt and complete I rep. K 1 row Birch.

Follow Berry patt sequence until RC258, 263, 268. Run off on WY.

Right front

Cast on 13 sts to R of centre and 77 sts, 82 sts, 87 sts to L. Cont as for back rib.

Place onto WY 26 sts from centre and remove from machine.

K 1 row, foll Arrow patt (make sure arrow is pointing to front edge), at same time dec 10 sts evenly on L 54 sts, 59 sts, 64 sts remain.

Cont in Berry patt to same length as back.

Mark centre 52 sts, shoulder sts remain 54 sts, 59 sts, 64 sts.

Knit off onto WY.

RC000. Pick up centre 26 sts and follow Rowan Leaf and Berry 1 patts. RC228, 232, 238.

Shape neck. Cast off on alt rows 5 sts once, 4 sts twice, 3 sts and 2 sts then 1 st, cast off.

Rowan Berry Cardigan, back view.

Rowan Berry Cardigan, variation in browns.

Left front

As for R front, reversing all shaping.

Front Arrow border

With right side of central panel facing, pick up 162 sts, 170 sts, 176 sts, making sure arrow is facing towards top of cardigan. K 2 rows Grouse. Complete Arrow patt, at same time dec evenly 10 sts at rib end and inc 10 sts at neck edge. K 2 rows Grouse, pick up front panel of cardigan, k 1 row and cast off.

Sleeve

Cast on using WY, 70 sts, 75 sts, 80 sts. K 2 rows Arrow patt (pointing to L on one sleeve and to R on other). Complete Arrow patt, at same time inc 1 st each end of every 4th row until 160 sts, 170 sts, 180 sts.

K 1 row, follow Rowan Leaf and Berry 1 patt, work 3 patt reps. K 2 rows, cast off.

Cuff

Cast on 70 sts, 75 sts, 80 sts for a 2×1 rib k 28 rows. Attach sleeve by picking up sts from WY and placing them evenly on cuff. K 2 rows and cast off.

Button band

Cast on 144 sts, 154 sts, 164 sts and work a 2×1 rib for 12 rows, at same time dec 3 sts on neck edge to mitre band. Place 7 buttonholes evenly down front, transfer sts and k l row, pick up sts along front edge, k 1 row and cast off.

Rep without buttonholes for L front.

For neckband, cast on 142 sts and work a 2×1 rib for 12 rows inc each end 3 sts to mitre with front bands.

Making up

Join mitres leaving opening for 8th buttonhole. Set in sleeves. Join side seams.

When a pattern is as complicated as this one it becomes much clearer if it is written in diagram form. At a glance you can see where you are and how all the different pieces and patterns fit together.

Rowan Berry Cardigan, detail.

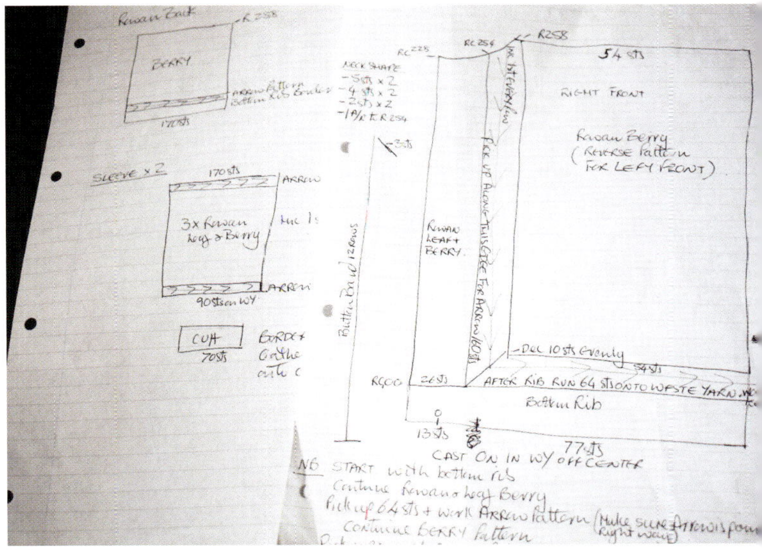

Working diagram for the Rowan pattern.

	Small	Med	Large
A	49cm	52cm	56cm
B	23cm	26.5cm	30cm
C	62cm	64cm	66cm
D	25cm	25cm	27cm
E	51cm	56cm	59cm
F	8cm	8cm	10cm
G	20cm	20cm	25cm

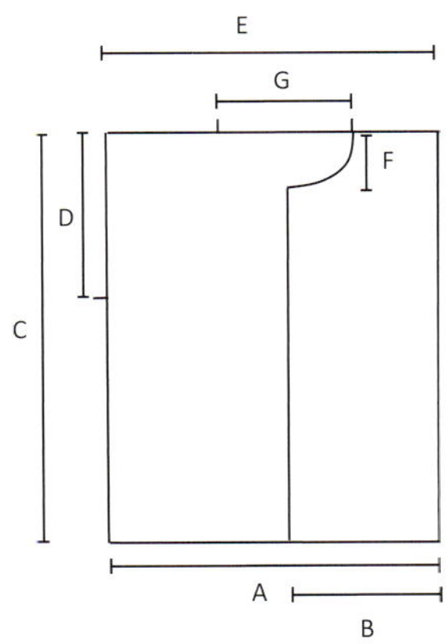

	Small	Med	Large
H	17cm	19cm	23cm
I	43cm	43cm	43cm
J	48cm	50cm	56cm

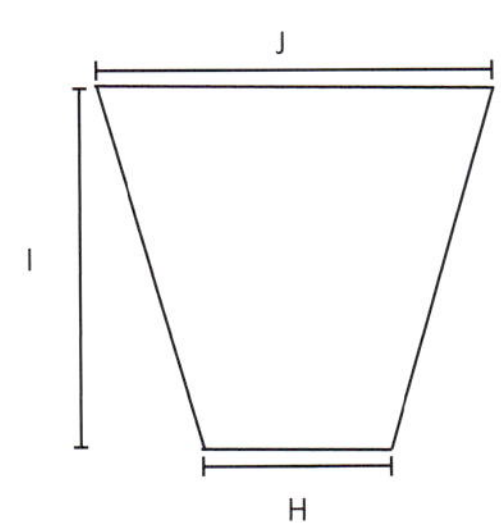

Rowan Berry Cardigan schematic.

Paisley Patch Cardigan.

Paisley Patch inspiration – blacksmith's workshop.

Paisley Patch inspiration – ironwork flower.

PAISLEY PATCH CARDIGAN

Inspiration comes from many surprising sources – the dark strong ironwork in a blacksmith's workshop became the inspiration for the Paisley Patch cardigan. The decorative, writhing, intricate, yet delicate and organic ironwork was twisted and bent like a paisley pattern. Strong colour contrasts were used to enhance the definite pattern. The cardigan was knitted in stripes and these were sewn together and the colours changed after knitting a block of pattern. A Shetland wool was used with bright and dark colours juxtaposed. A later version added Swiss darning as a decorative embellishment.

Paisley Patch inspiration – delicate flowers wrought in iron.

Materials

Finished weight 600g.

Various Cs of Jamiesons of Shetland Spindrift wool in oil.

Small amounts of the following Cs: Loganberry 1290, Madder 587, Rosewood 236, Burnt Ochre 432, Fern 349, Woodgreen 318, Moorgrass 286, Autumn 998, Thyme 226, Blueberry 294, Birch 252, Sunset 186, Granite 122, Thistledown 237.

9 buttons plus 1 spare.

Measurements

The sizing is flexible. Finished measurements: around chest 106cm, length to shoulder 73cm, sleeve length 48cm.

Tension

MT 8 30 sts – 38 rows = 10cm over Fair Isle pattern after washing.

Machine

Standard gauge electronic or punchcard.

Punchcard stitch pattern

Use colours which you like and which work well together; make sure there is a strong contrast between the colours in feeders 1 and 2.

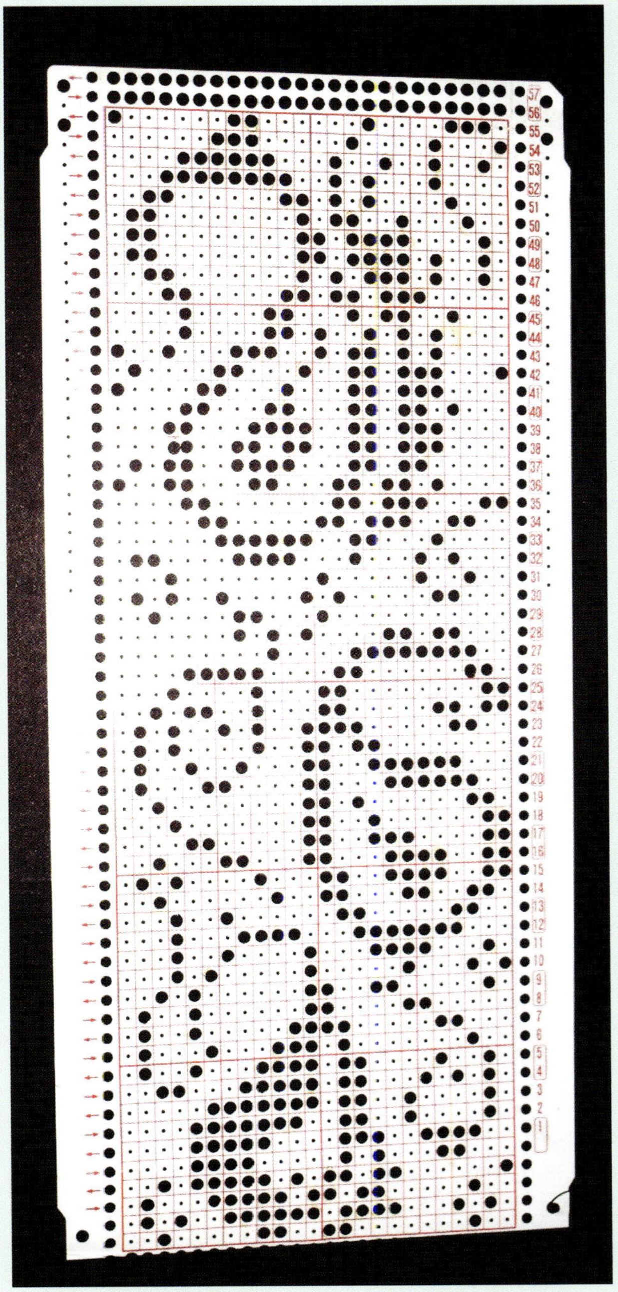

Punchcard stitch pattern for Paisley Patch Cardigan.

Method

Back

Knitted in 4 strips which are sewn together. Make sure that C changes are offset as this gives a more balanced look.

E wrap cast on 40 sts k 2 rows and start to work paisley patt throughout, changing Cs at random. K 250 rows and place on WY.

Rep * to * to make 3 more strips.

Right front

Knitted in 2 strips. Follow instructions * to * for back for 1 strip. Pick up stitches from a back strip, unravel WY, k 1 row MT+1, cast off.

For second strip, rep from * to row 210.

Shape neck

On neck edge cast off 5 sts on next alt 6 rows, 2 sts on next alt 4 rows and dec 1 st on each alt row until 15 sts remain. Cont without shaping to R250.

Pick up sts from back shoulder strip, k 1 row MT+2, cast off.

Left front

Rep as for R front, reversing all shaping.

Sleeves

Knitted in 3 strips.

Outer strip (knit 2): E wrap cast on 20 sts changing Cs at random. At same time inc 1 st at each end of every 3rd row until 50 sts, cont patt to RC160. Cast off. Rep for second outer strip.

Middle strip: E wrap cast on 25 sts changing Cs at random. At same time inc 1 st at each end of every 3rd row until 60 sts remain. Cont to RC160. Cast off.

Rep all 3 strips for second sleeve.

Sew tog all strips for back, and two fronts and the three sleeve strips. Do not sew up final seam as they need to be flat to pick up sts for hems.

Back hem

With RS facing, pick up E wrap sts from all back strips 120 sts. **C1 k 1 row, C2 k1 row, C3 k 12 rows last row MT+2, cast off**.

Right front hem

Pick up 60 sts from the two strips, work hem as for back ** to **, at same time inc evenly 4 sts on LHS to mitre with front band.

Left front hem

Rep as for R front but reversing all shaping.

Front bands

Pick up 150 sts down front of strip and rep ** to **, at same time inc evenly 4 sts at each end of band. Cast off. Place the 8 buttonholes in middle rows of band.

Making up

Sew mitred corners tog, leaving gap for button on button band.

Set in sleeve and sew down side seam and sleeve seams. Sew on buttons.

This design, as with many others, can be decorated by adding various embroidery stitches using Swiss darning, a technique which is ideal for this purpose as it mimics the stitch shape and, used imaginatively, can encourage yet more colour contrast.

Swiss darning is a way of embroidering a stitch that looks like a knit stitch, and so will work well on the Paisley Patch Cardigan design to add an extra embellishment in a third contrasting colour.

The contrasting yarn is taken along the path of the knit stitch that needs to be covered, and can be worked in any direction. You must be careful to choose a yarn of the same thickness as the background yarns, as too thin a yarn will not cover the entire stitch and too thick a yarn will distort the stitch. Also ensure that your Swiss darning is to the same tension as that of the background fabric, as too loose a stitch will show the stitch underneath and too tight a stitch will make the fabric pucker.

Start off by threading a blunt darning needle with a length of yarn in the chosen colour. Secure the end by oversewing two or three times on the back of the fabric, then bring the point of the needle through the fabric to the base of the stitch to be worked on and draw the yarn through. Continue darning until the entire motif is completed. Take the yarn through to the back of the fabric, weave it in and out and cut it off.

Paisley Patch Cardigan, detail.

Paisley Patch Cardigan, detail of Swiss darning embellishment.

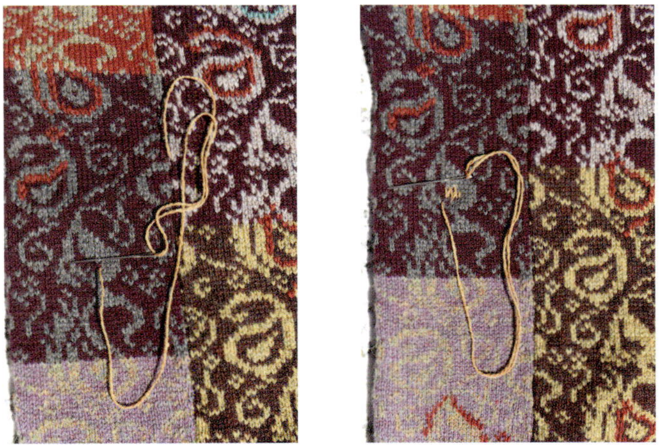

Swiss darning close up.

A	50cm
B	25cm
C	71cm
D	44cm
E	13cm
F	20cm

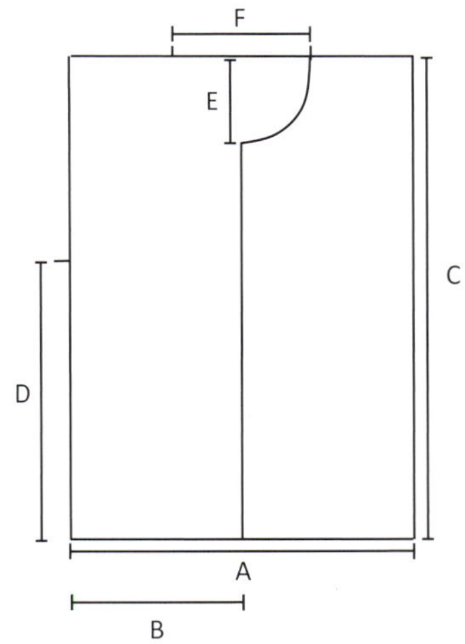

G	22cm
H	47cm
I	49cm

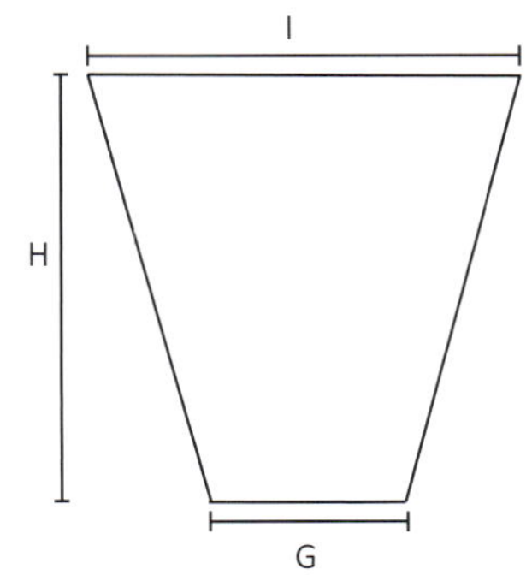

Paisley Patch Cardigan schematic.

CHAPTER 8

LACE AND SCULPTURAL VESSELS

WORCESTER SCARF

The contrast between one side of the scarf and the other is what makes this so fun to make – one side is smooth and the other hairy. The contrast is further enhanced by knitting with a fine yarn and a thicker one which fluffs up when washed at 30°.

The three colourways each have a different character, with bright, dark and pale colours. It would be useful to test out a small swatch and then cut and wash the piece to see how the yarns you have chosen react together.

The samples here are made on a Silver Reed punchcard machine using punch lace. You can also work with other machines using Fair Isle but you will need to use a thicker yarn and not cut the yarn before washing but after. Test out on a small sample first.

Worcester Scarf, detail showing the smooth and hairy sides of the stitch pattern.

Materials
Finished weight 120g.
The smooth yarn should be fine and felting-resistant, while the hairy yarn needs to be thicker and lightly felting when washed at 30°. Use as many Cs as you like within the colour palette you have chosen.

Bright colourway
Background smooth Cs: A turquoise, B red, C purple, D green, E bright pink, F yellow.
Hairy Cs: G green, H purple, I bright blue, J pink, K blue, L coral, M red, N yellow.

Pale colourway
Smooth Cs: A cream, B grey, C lilac, D white, E beige, F pale blue.
Hairy Cs: G pale pink, H grey, I white, J pale blue, K stone, L cream.

Dark colourway
Smooth Cs: A maroon, B rust, C dark green, D brown, E olive green, F navy.
Hairy Cs: G teal, H black, I grey, J navy, K dark brown.

Measurements
Width 36cm, length 90cm.

Tension
TD 8 22 sts – 28 rows = 10cm after washing.

Machine
Punchcard machine with punch lace.

Punchcard stitch pattern
X0000000000XX0000000000X
00000XX0000000000XX00000

Pattern sequence

Rows	Pattern Setting	Feeder 1	Feeder 2
2	Knit	G	
20	Lace	G	A
2	Knit	H	
20	Lace	H	B
2	Knit	I	
20	Lace	I	C
2	Knit	J	
20	Lace	J	D

Method

E wrap cast on with 3 hairy Cs, k 2 rows.
When changing C, wrap 2 yarns around last N.
Follow patt sequence, cont working through Cs and rep until 508 rows or required length reached.
Using 2 hairy Cs, k 2 rows MT last row T10 and latch off.
Carefully cut strands between bars and sew in ends or cut off.
Machine wash at 30° (wool cycle), light spin.

If the threads are left uncut before washing and cut afterwards, the result is that they do not shrink back but act like a cut fringe across the fabric. This is a variation which can be worked on.

Worcester Scarf in Bright, Pale and Dark.

Worcester Scarf, cutting the threads before washing.

Balloon Moon Scarf.

Balloon Moon Scarves in Pale, Blue and Bright.

BALLOON MOON SCARF

This punchcard is about twenty years old and I have struggled to work out what I wanted to do with it: I finally tried punch lace to achieve a see-through, ethereal effect. Having experimented with Fair isle and felting, this pattern was the result which most closely represented what I had seen in my mind's eye all those years ago.

There are three colourways: Pale, Blue and Bright. The Pale colourway represent a pale misty moon in pared-back colours and used every pale shade I had on the shelf in the workroom. The Blue colourway represents the reflection of the moon in the sea, broken up by the waves. And the Bright colourway represents the moon peering through a sunset with lots of festival-bright colours.

Method

When changing C, wrap ends around last N twice so they can then be cut off when work is completed.

Always pull forward first N to be knitted to D position; this will ensure both yarns knit right to end of row, and prevents little gaps.

Using 3 strands of thicker yarn, E wrap cast on 100 sts, with different C of thicker yarn.

K 2 rows.

Start to work through patt sequence using punchcard and machine set to L.

Cont to k for about 500 rows.

Stop card and k 2 rows with 2 threads of thicker yarn, last row MT 10, and latch off.

Carefully cut through threads of circles.

Machine wash at 40° degrees, 800 spin speed, for about an hour to give a firm felt; or 30° degrees, 800 spin for a softer felt.

Materials

Finished weight 150g.

Use a range of Cs in the thicker yarns for feeder 1 and several shades of fine yarn in which the circles are knitted in feeder 2. You can use the same colour of thick and thin yarn as this will show up differently when the piece is cut and felted.

Pale colourway

Cs: cream, grey, lilac, beige, pale blue, vanilla and white.

Blue colourway

Cs: various shades of blue, teal, purple and navy.

Bright colourway

Cs: greens, pinks, blues, reds and yellows; the brighter the better.

Measurements

Width 30cm, length 76cm after felting.

Tension

MT 8 28 sts and 30 rows = 10cm after felting.

Machine

The scarves were knitted with a Silver Reed fine gauge punchcard machine using punch lace.

Punchcard stitch pattern

Pattern sequence

Work through Cs with thicker yarn in feeder 1 and finer in feeder 2 for 10 rows, then change yarn in feeder 2 to another shade of same weight. Work 10 rows. Change C in feeder 1, work 10 rows, then change C in feeder 2. Pattern 10 rows, etc., working through all Cs and repeat, changing sequence of Cs if you like to add further interest.

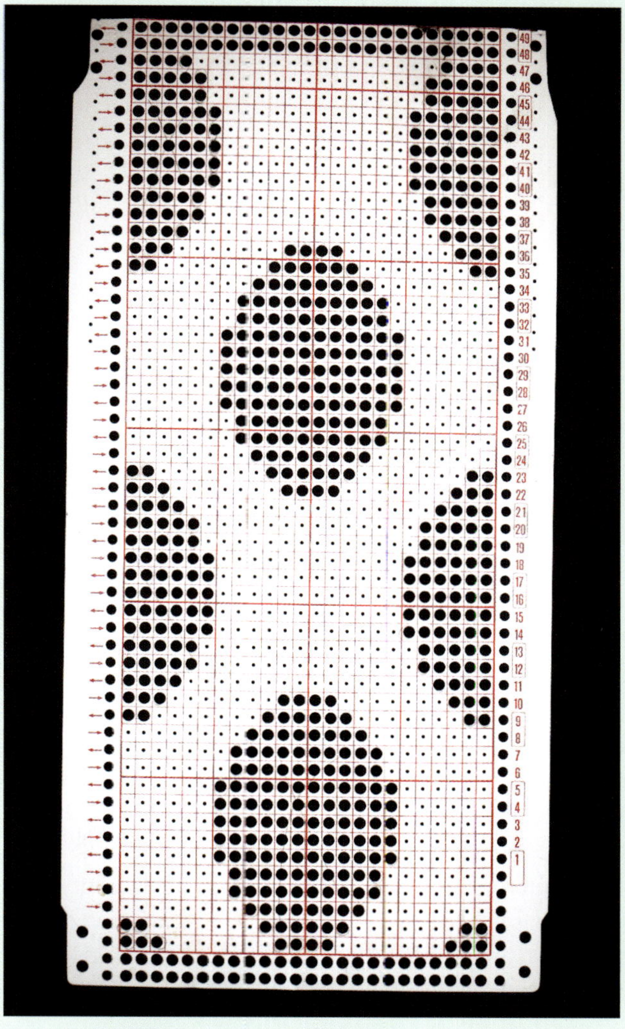

Punchcard stitch pattern for Balloon Moon Scarf.

Slip stitch sample before it became a bowl.

Silk marl pot.

Materials
Milliner's stiffener, cling film, form/mould, oil, jug.

SCULPTURAL VESSELS

A knitted fabric is an extremely versatile medium and the fact that its main characteristic is to be malleable lends itself to this process. The finely knitted fabric can be stabilized using a milliner's stiffener if the floppy fabric is soaked and placed over a form or mould. Fine yarn works well in this process, as does any yarn which is not too hairy as a hairy yarn when dried merely has a matted appearance. Many objects can be used as a form, providing your choice does not have any indents, as even a small one makes it very difficult to release the fabric when dry.

You can experiment with old tension swatches to get the feel for the process.

Method

Wash the knitted fabric in warm soapy water to remove any oil or dressing in the yarn. Rinse well in clean water and dry thoroughly.

Lightly oil the form to aid release. Cover the form with two layers of cling film, and find a base board on which to place it while drying.

Steep fabric in a solution of milliner's stiffener and water mixed to about a ratio of 5 to 1. Make sure that the fabric is evenly coated on both sides and that the liquid has penetrated through to all the fibres.

Lightly squeeze out any excess liquid and place over the form. Gently ease the fabric over the form and make sure it is completely covered – any excess fabric can be tucked under or allowed to lie flat by the side and this can be removed later.

Smooth down and get rid of any puddling liquid. Leave to dry but check frequently and remove any drips and excess liquid and continue to smooth out any drying creases. The drying process can take up to forty-eight hours to dry, depending on the thickness of the yarn and the knitted fabric.

Once dry, either cut off the excess fabric for a raw edge, or cut unevenly to allow for a more organic sculptural style – or having tucked it under, cut around the inside about a centimetre down from the rim.

Fine yarn can be stiffened in this way and the results are can be made quite formal or organic depending which you decide to do.

Fabric placed over a form.

Two 'sea life' vessels.

Vessel removed from the form before trimming.

Completed bowl.

CHAPTER 9

TO BUSINESS

Many designers start off by learning their craft by hands-on experimentation using the knitting machine, then at a later date hand over the making to a factory for mass production. Although the resulting pieces are perfect with not a stitch out of place, what can be lost is the character, depth and originality of the fabric and the product becomes an end in itself. If designers become dissociated from the materials, they can no longer have total control of excellence and standards, or know the versatility of the materials they are using.

There is a great deal of poor-quality knitting for sale; the argument seems to be that the process of designing is the important journey and completing the finished article subsidiary. If you have no control over how an item is made, then standards can deteriorate. This is not Luddite woolly thinking; it is vital to strive to keep both the integrity of the design concept and to also expand the quality and ingenuity of our craft.

It initially takes time to work through and develop an idea, but this process will become quicker with time and experience. Obviously, it is not possible to take three weeks knitting a scarf which is so intricate and then try to sell it to the general public as there are very few customers who would be able to afford such a rare piece. The skill then, is to hone the piece keeping the relevant elements which establish its character and to speed up the making process to keep the price realistic and affordable.

This does not mean that everything has to be totally handmade to achieve integrity. The word 'handmade' is bandied about as if this in itself denotes superior quality as well as being made by the hand of an artisan. It is generally used to allow the general public to distinguish between items that have been individually made by hand and those that have been mass-produced, but can it really be said that machine knitting is handmade as we are using a machine, albeit by hand? Although the knitting machine is operated by hand, we are totally in control of what is being made and how it is being made, from the choice of yarn to the stitch being used and the shape of the garment. The machine is purely an enabler, just like a knitting needle is in hand knitting; it is an extension of our hand, and at any time in the process of making we can change direction, add another colour, change the stitch pattern and constantly reassess how a design is being made and what the aesthetic outcome will be.

Constantly strive for good workmanship, excellence of technique and aesthetic design. To produce a piece of work, it is vital to understand what it is to push to a standard of excellence in the finished item. This can be incorporated into basic actions; for example, how the machine is set up, is it free from clutter, is the yarn flowing freely through the tension brake, are all the tools to hand, is the lighting good and is the chair the right height and comfortable, do you have a clear vision in your mind's eye as to what you want to achieve? Answering positively to all these questions will put you in a frame of mind to start the process of good design and good workmanship, leading to a standard of excellence in the finished item.

JACK OF ALL TRADES

Very often in the design and manufacturing process one person is in charge of one aspect such as design, and another person then takes over for the next stage such as making the swatch pieces, and so on. You are in charge of the whole process, from choosing and purchasing the yarn to designing and making the finished article. You make decisions on a variety of questions, which include choice of colour, surface treatment (which stitch pattern), proportion and size. As the designer and maker you handle the materials, the tools, the yarns; you will know their strengths and drawbacks. You know which technique on the machine is best suited to using the materials to best advantage. And because you are in touch with your customer, you will know very quickly if you need to make changes to an existing design or eliminate a design completely, or ramp up production as it is proving popular.

Your production must be on a scale that is flexible to change, and if a design is unsuccessful, you can be aware and keep an eye on the finances and not take unnecessary risks. Constantly reassess the successful designs, try them out in other materials, in other colourways, and alter the scale and proportion. Can a scarf design be transferred to a jacket or coat, and what are the costing implications of doing this? Knowing and evaluating all of this is the art of the craft. You need to be part mathematician, engineer, accountant, market analyst, production manager, sales manager and, finally, craftsperson and artist. To be a successful designer-craftsperson all these aspects need to fuse together seamlessly as a whole with no one field dominating.

There are knitters making beautiful quality fabrics and they are in direct competition with knitters making ordinary, cheap fabrics. There will always be a rivalry between a piece of work that has been expertly designed and made with time and care, and one that has taken basic elements such as fewer colours, fewer stitch pattern changes and less expensive materials. There will be, or should be, a price differential and there will always be clients who appreciate and are prepared to pay for an item of the best quality. The rule must always be quality and not quantity.

Only a relatively small proportion of designer-makers are full-time. There is often a need for another part-time job, especially in the early days. This does mean that some excellent designers who are realistic about their time and costings are lost to other professions along the way. Others are more determined and through focus and love of their craft they persevere, and to help through financial hardship maybe they work in an unrelated job to pay the bills. Another avenue many designers follow is to run workshops and teach their craft, as this feeds back into their own design process as ideas bounce from teacher to student and back again. There is also a discipline involved when explaining to another exactly what thought processes and techniques you are using, and this is also a generous way to work, to talk about and demonstrate all the developments and the results and pass them on.

BE INSPIRED, BUT DO NOT COPY

The processes of designing and making using machine knitting are not secret and should be made accessible to all. If you are continuing to work in a creative way you will be constantly developing new ideas, and when you create a stunning design you may find that it is copied by less talented makers. Their design will not have gone through the journey which yours has and this will show in their finished results. It is, however, rude and illegal to copy and you can decide to take legal redress if there has been a blatant use of your work and design. You also risk losing your reputation, which is incalculable in business and very difficult to restore once compromised. You may consider joining ACID (Anti Copying In Design), a not-for-profit organization which offers advice and guidance on how to protect your designs and IPP (Intellectual Property Protection). Most designers are happy to talk about their work, but please respect their designs.

To make a business out of designing and making requires constantly seeking out ways to advertise, sell (retail, wholesale or sale or return), teach and publish; in fact any avenue which enables your work to be seen. Focus and motivation are essential: the best motivator is having bills to pay.

Bags, labels and rubber stamps.

Woven labels and 'print your own' labels.

TRADE AND RETAIL SHOWS

There are many shows which enable your work to be seen; however, they are not all of the same standard. Go and see the show before parting with a deposit. Failing this, ask previous exhibitors what their impressions were, and find out the price point selling similar work to yours at the show; you may save yourself a lot of money. Place your work where it will be seen to best advantage; many shows sell space and are not too fussy about what products are put into the space.

If possible, have access to natural lighting, since textiles and their colours will show up better. Attention to display is vital: for example, if selling garments have a hanging rail with all the coat hangers facing the same way; keep the stand neat and tidy with all packaging out of sight. Decide how to group the work – by colour, by yarn, by type of garment, etc.

At a trade show you may be asked if you have a minimum order. Items always sell better with a choice rather than one displayed on its own. Decide how much your minimum order would be in pieces; for example, eight or more would be priced at, say, £250. Bear in mind that for smaller galleries this may be difficult.

Galleries and shops may ask for sale or return: you send them a selection of your work and they pay when a piece is sold. Are you prepared to do this? If so, when you send a sale or return Invoice add at the bottom: 'Title remains with [*your name*] until goods paid in full', as this means that you continue to own the items and if a gallery stops trading then creditors cannot legally seize them.

If an order is placed by an unknown gallery you can use a pro forma invoice, as you then are paid before you send them the goods, so there is no financial risk on your part. When the order has been completed send a pro forma; when this has been paid, send out the work.

You may have a bread-and-butter range which consistently sells well, so don't change it but do update it from time to time to keep it fresh. Running alongside this, have experimental pieces which will be more expensive to the public but which add a depth and weight to your work.

Don't waste money on expensive packaging which will be thrown away and avoid using plastic bags.

Paper bags can be purchased, as can a rubber stamp with your name and logo – so print your own.

When selling to the public have a good-quality label that identifies it as made by you. Woven labels are expensive but look good. Smaller labels for sizing, washing, etc., can be made by using fabric printing paper and buying ribbon to make your own. When preparing the sheet to print, remember to make the writing mirror-image so when printed on the ribbon it will be the right way round.

Always be aware of the competition, and rise up to meet it. While you may not be able to retire early on the financial proceeds of your efforts as a designer-craftsperson, you will have an amazingly fulfilling life which will lead you along unexpected paths. Diversity is the key, always keep an open mind.

COSTINGS

The earning hours are separate from the creative hours. Not every maker is a designer; this process can take time to hone, but it is this element which will give an advantage when competing with industrially manufactured knitting. The risks you are prepared to take will set you apart from the rest.

Calculating the hourly rate

To calculate out your hourly rate of pay be honest with yourself and include everything that you pay to run the business, including heat and light, rent of a workshop, etc. Add this to what you would like to earn (be realistic), divide this figure by how many hours are spent at the machine making. This will give you an hourly rate.

Then add in all the materials to include yarn, haberdashery, wear and tear on machinery, petrol, finishing, washing, pressing, postage, plus outworkers' pay if applicable. Also add the cost of taking part in retail and trade shows.

For example, a scarf takes half an hour to knit and finish. When calculating how long a scarf or garment takes to make, knit a few, time each one and take the average time. The first one will always take much longer and will not give a realistic calculation.

If the hourly rate used is £14, so far it has cost £7. The scarf used 50g of yarn, of which a kilo costs £50, so the yarn costs for a scarf are £2.50. Add this to your £7 and the subtotal is now £9.50. Add 70 per cent to this so that you are making money on items bought as well as made, i.e. £6.65. The total = £16.15.

Adjust the price to cover its perceived value to the general public. For example, if you knitted with cashmere or silk, using a complex design, it could be worth more to a potential customer than the same design knitted in cotton. If at this point the perceived value is less than the calculated cost price, you will lose money if you continue with the design unaltered. You therefore need to consider how you can either adjust the design to increase the perceived value above the cost price, or simplify how it is made so the cost price is less than the perceived value. If neither of these are possible, then it is probably best to not continue with that design.

Wholesale or retail

Wholesale prices are inevitably lower but you will sell more pieces, so there can be advantages. Most galleries will double or triple your price and then have to add VAT to their selling price. Retail sales, direct selling to the public, will mean you receive a higher price per piece but you may not sell as many. For example, if the wholesale price for the scarf is £25, the retail price will be double, £50, or triple, £75.

Working out these calculations is the foundation on which your business is built, they are worth the time and effort spent getting them right. Over the years they will need updating depending on the social, political and economic climate. You also need to be consistent in your pricing, so don't let your retail prices undercut galleries that have invested in your designs, as they will quickly stop stocking your work.

Remember that you do not have to accept every order that you are offered, so be aware of what money will flow out of your business in terms of paying for yarns and outworkers, etc., before you will get paid. Understanding your cash flow is the key to running a financially viable business.

ADDRESS BOOK

MACHINES AND REPAIRS

Andee Knits www.machine-knitting.co.uk

LINKERS AND SPARES

B. Hague and Co. Limited www.haguedirect.co.uk

YARNS

Gaddum Silk www.gaddumandgaddum.co.uk

J. C. Rennie www.knitrennie.com

Jamieson's of Shetland www.jamiesonsofshetland.co.uk

King Cole www.kingcole.com

Knoll Yarns Limited www.knollyarn.com

Pitti Filati Trade Yarn Fair, Florence www.pittiimmagine.com

Robert Todd www.roberttodds.com

Rowan www.knitrowan.com

Yeoman Yarns www.yeoman-yarns.co.uk

Z. Hinchcliffe www.zhinchcliffe.co.uk

HABERDASHERY

Dunelm for cushion pads www.dunelm.com

Frankle Trimmings for ribbon for making labels 281–285 Bethnal Green Road, London, E2 6AH

J. H. Crickmay for buttons 2A Everton Road, Croydon, CR0 6LA

James Grove for buttons www.jamesgroveandsons.co.uk

Karadia for buttons www.karadia-trimmings.co.uk

Morplan for paper bags, labels www.morplan.com

Parkin Fabrics for millinery stiffening www.parkinfabrics.co.uk

Textile Garden for pins and buttons www.textilegarden.co.uk

The Rubber Stamp Company www.therubberstampcompany.com

V. V. Rouleaux for ribbon for making labels www.vvrouleaux.com

Wovina for woven labels www.wovina.com

USEFUL GROUPS AND JOURNALS

Anti Copying in Design (ACID) www.acid.uk.com

Knitting and Crochet Guild www.kcguild.org.uk

Knitting History www.knittinghistory.co.uk

Knitting International www.wtin.com

Knitting Trade Journal www.knittingtradejournal

Machine Knitting Monthly www.machineknittingmonthly.net

Missoni *Newsletter* www.missoni.com

The Worshipful Company of Framework Knitters
www.frameworkknitters.co.uk

Vogue Knitting www.vogueknitting.com

BIBLIOGRAPHY

Here are some books and websites that I found useful when researching this book:

Agee W. C., 1993, *Kenneth Noland: The Circle Paintings, 1956–1963*, extended essay within exh.cat., Museum of Fine Arts, Houston

Albers A., 1961, *On Designing*, Wesley University Press USA

Albers J., 1963, *Interaction of Color*, Yale University Press

Brackenbury T., 1996, *Knitted Clothing Technology*, Blackwell Science UK

Coles D., 2018, *Chromatopia: An Illustrated History of Colour*, Thames and Hudson

Deering C., 1751, *Nottinghamia Vetus Et Nova, or, an Historical Account of the Ancient and Present State of the Town of Nottingham*, available at https://archive.org/details/nottinghamiavet00chicgoog/page/n2

Denver Art Museum, 2016, *Women of Abstract Expressionism*, Denver Art Museum and Yale University Press

Duchting H., 1997, *Paul Klee: Painting Music*, Prestel

Fay C. R., 1955, *Round About Industrial Britain, 1830–1860*, University of Toronto Press

Felkin, W., 1867, A History of the Machine-Wrought Hosiery and Lace Manufactures, Longmans Green and Co

Gage J., 1999, *Colour and Meaning: Art, Science and Symbolism*, Thames and Hudson

Gooding N., 1994, *Patrick Heron*, Phaidon

Grovier K. (ed.), 2015, *Sean Scully: Bricklayer of the Soul*, Hatje Cantz

Henson G., 1831, *The Civil, Political, and Mechanical History of the Framework-Knitters,* Nottingham UK

Jones O., 1868, *The Grammar of Ornament*, Bernard Quaritch

Kemp D., 2010, *Terry Frost Prints*, Lund Humphries

Kinder K., 1979, *A Resource Book for Machine Knitters*, K Kinder UK

Kinder K., 1983, *Techniques in Machine Knitting*, Batsford UK

Knitting Together, *The Heritage of the East Midlands Knitting Industry,* available at www.knittingtogether.org.uk

Lowe, D. E. and Richards J., 1989, *William Lee and Lace,* Nottingham Lace Centre UK

Moorhouse P. (ed.), 2003, *Bridget Riley*, Tate Publications

Mucklestone M. J., 2011, *200 Fair Isle Designs*, Quarto

Musk D., 1989, *The Technique of Slip Stitch,* Batsford UK

Nickas B., 2013, *Painting Abstraction: New Elements in Abstract Painting*, Phaidon

Noble T., 1831, *The History and Gazetteer of the County of Derby*, Steven Glover

Noland K., 1993, *Kenneth Noland: The Circle Paintings, 1956–1963*, exh. cat., Museum of Fine Arts, Houston

Palmer M., 1984, *Framework Knitting,* Shire Publications UK

Pastoureau M., 1991, *The Devil's Cloth: A History of Stripes and Striped Fabric*, Columbia University Press

Royal Academy of Arts, 2012, *David Hockney: A Bigger Picture*, Royal Academy of Arts

Rutt R., 1987, *History of Hand Knitting*, Batsford

Spencer D. J., 2001, *Knitting Technology: A Comprehensive Handbook and Practical Guide*, Woodhead Publishing UK

Stadlem, M. and Aloni, Y. (eds), 2009, *Gunther Stölzl, Bauhaus Master*, Hatje Cantz

Vercelloni I. T. (ed.), 1995, *The World of Missoni*, Electra/Abbeville

Wells F. A., 1972, *The British Hosiery and Knitwear Industry: Its Growth and Organisation*, David and Charles UK

Weltge S. W., 1993, *Bauhaus Textiles: Women Artists and the Weaving Workshop*, Thames and Hudson

Wier C., 2007, *As Poor as a Stockinger: Framework Knitting and the Luddites in Nottinghamshire,* Nottingham County Council UK

INDEX